NEVIN'S HISTORY

NEVIN'S HISTORY

A Novel of Texas

JIM SANDERSON

Texas Tech University Press

This book is typeset in Adobe Garamond. The acid-free paper used in this book meets the minimum requirements of ANSI/NISO Z39.48-1992 (R1997).

Printed in the United States of America

Library of Congress Cataloging-in-Publication Data
Sanderson, Jim, 1953–
Nevin's history : a novel of Texas / Jim Sanderson.
p.   cm.
ISBN 0-89672-518-9 (cloth : alk. paper)
1. Ford, John Salmon—Fiction. 2. Cortina, Juan N. (Juan Nepomuceno), 1824–1894—Fiction. 3. McNelly, Leander H., 1843 or 4–1877—Fiction. 4. Mexican-American Border Region—Fiction. 5. Texas—History—1846–1950—Fiction. 6. Americans—Mexico—Fiction. 7. Cattle stealing—Fiction. 8. Texas Rangers—Fiction. 9. Outlaws—Fiction. 10. Mexico—Fiction. I. Title.
PS3569.A5146N48 2004
813'.54—dc22
2003021006

03 04 05 06 07 08 09 10 11 / 9 8 7 6 5 4 3 2 1

Texas Tech University Press
Box 41037
Lubbock, Texas 79409-1037 USA
800.832.4042
ttup@ttu.edu
www.ttup.ttu.edu

I wish to thank Lamar University and its faculty senate for giving me the release time to research and write this novel.

To my parents, Margie and Sandy,
and to my hometown,
San Antonio

NEVIN'S HISTORY

WHEN the then most recent, one-true-love-of-my-life dumped me, in part because I was not a "cowboy," I decided to let her and the twenty-first century have present-day Texas. I'd take Texas's past. I was just generally dissatisfied with the world I lived in. Maybe that three-headed beast that chased Dante was biting at my ass.

So I went back to my hometown, and on a wet spring day I started walking around downtown San Antonio. My walks through a new sanitized and Yankeeized downtown San Antonio took me to the Texana Collection in the big, new, "enchilada-red" San Antonio Public Library building. This was certainly not the "modern" glass-and-brick building where I went in high school, and definitely not the old, gaudy, concrete building, with its growling lions and Hertzberg circus collection, where I went as a boy. I started reading.

I liked the firsthand, as-told-to accounts. I liked the works by amateur historians published by San Antonio's own Naylor Company. They were prejudiced, usually one-sided, and sometimes wrong, but I liked the idea I got of the writer's relation with *his* or *her* sense of history and place.

You couldn't check out anything in the Texana room, but the director of the Texana section noticed me and helped me. Sarah Hartman, a member of an old San Antonio German family, was the one who went to the special collections of the special Texana collections and let me read through and look at the photos, books, pamphlets, and newspapers that you couldn't get without special permission. A lady in her late fifties or early sixties with glasses resting on the end of her nose and fastened around her neck with a gold chain, Sarah had her own personal history of San Antonio and offered me advice, commentary, and stories.

As I was returning the old books to the desk, Sarah's domain, Sarah said, "You spent a lot of time in here. What are you looking for? Maybe I can help."

I shrugged. "I don't know. Lost youth and a woman who can tolerate me."

Sarah squinted. "You're an odd one. Most men sit in bars to look for those. I've got something for you to look at."

Sarah went into the room behind the desk and came out with a wrinkled, dirty, cardboard box. She pulled out an old, typed manuscript that an elderly lady had donated to the library some years back. She had not read it; she had not cataloged it. It waited on a stack to be dealt with. She asked if I would like to read it for her.

Thus, I sat for two days, and as if touching holy writ, turned the yellowed pages of Andrew Nevin's attempt, in the last year of his life, to account for history. He had hurried. Words were misspelled. Certain fingers must have been weak or arthritic, because certain letters or punctuation signs were consistently barely visible or just missing, particularly those pounded onto the page by the keys worked with the little fingers. How unfair that Andrew Nevin, in the last year of his life, could not have seen and used the wonder of a word-processing program.

Some of the pages had water stains and smudges. Whoever owned the manuscript must have let it get wet or damp. Some pages were so brittle that they didn't rip but cracked when I turned them. Some pages were just missing.

I recalled the psychology, philosophy, and theology I had read. I also thought about certain novels, poems, plays, movies, and stories. I recalled my indoctrination in Lutheran catechism. I had read that there is very little in the world that we can control, even with a trained mind, certainly not our own minds. But sometimes luck or accident or insight will just happen. I wanted to call this luck "grace." I didn't read far enough in theology to decide where this grace comes from or what it really is. Paradoxically, you can't work to achieve this grace, you can't prepare for it, but unless you prepare for it, unless you work for it, you won't recognize it when it occurs. You have to be ready for accidents. I think that the philosophers call this mind-tangler "serendipity." Thus I found Andrew Nevin's manuscript.

I knew of all those Texas heroes that Nevin claims to have known. But in his manipulation of them to suit his own history, in order to prepare for his grace, he made them finally heroic to me. I *liked* Rip

Ford, Lee H. McNelly, Juan Cortina, Jack Harris, Richard King, and Ben Thompson more after I read Nevin's sometimes caustic comments than before.

And in Andrew Nevin, who couldn't control a horse, who detested firearms, who didn't like cowboys or Texas heroes, I saw the kind of cowboy I was. I imagined myself as that nancy, spurned lover, pimp, whoremonger, adulterer, spy, liar, pervert, coward, rogue, drunk, and movie and theater critic, Andrew Nevin. What was wrong with Andrew one hundred and twenty-five years before was what was wrong with me—and some like me.

Andrew prepared himself for grace in his observation, his thinking, and his writing. So operating out of faith that might never be rewarded, waiting for an insight that might never occur, Andrew tried to be a writer. Writers have to give up something for the writing, for the chance, and worse, writers *know* that they must give up something and thus *know* that they risk failing as fathers, mothers, husbands, wives, or lovers. Even with a wife, husband, lover, or children, we are often excruciatingly alone with that blank page or screen, with both our best and worst selves. What we write is never as good as one delicious moment from reality, yet we sacrifice those moments from reality to fail at reproducing those moments through words. Success is never what we thought it would be, and it is never enough. So we always fail. We always know our limitations. But we can't quit. Even if we don't sit in front of a page or a screen, we can't quit writing—even with lovers or our children. Andrew must have known, as I now know, why writers drink too much. But sometimes we find what we aren't looking for.

In the atmosphere of that ersatz cowboy Andrew Nevin's San Antonio and Brownsville, I could feel a little of Andrew's San Antonio seeping through the present-day streets. Besides the billboards, the chrome, the newly developed, ever-growing north side, besides the residual inferiority complex and the yearning to be more like Houston or Dallas, besides the political squabbles, the identity debates, the ethnic claims and counter claims, San Antonio was still Nevin's city, too.

When I thanked her for allowing me to see Nevin's words, Sarah Hartman said, "I thought you looked desperate. And I saw what you were reading. I thought Nevin might help."

"You told me you hadn't read it."

She winked at me. "I went to school with Rip's granddaughter. Of course I read it."

"Thank you, thank you," I said.

"Thank me by seeing something done with this." Her face grew serious, but then her wink covered her whole face, and for all the elderly ladies who for generations kept family genealogies, for all the amateur historians, for all our embarrassing relatives, for all those forgotten by history and those of us who are and will be forgotten, for the sake of San Antonio, she said, "Thank me by remembering."

I asked Sarah Hartman where she got the manuscript. Sarah *harrumphed* and returned with an index card with a name printed on it. In her own librarian manner, Sarah was preparing for grace. On the back was an address and a phone number.

Elvia Gomez lived on the roughest part of the west side, the "Mexican" side of town. Her house was just a cottage, but it was well kept, the grass mowed and trimmed, and on a slight rise, it had an impressive view of downtown San Antonio. A petite woman, remarkably well preserved for her age, answered the door. Her hair was gray but not permed. Rather, it was long with an attractive, backward roll over one side of her forehead. She wore jeans and a silk blouse. Her smile was infectious. She had that patrician look of the old Spaniards. She spoke impeccable English. It was a nice spring day, the kind that made you want to drive south or east of town to have a picnic in a field of Indian paintbrushes or bluebonnets, so she invited me to a seat, not in her house, but on her front porch swing.

Because she was short, she could barely reach far enough to get the swing going. So I got the swing swaying with my feet. She took a long time to tell her story. She was objective, factual, like a reporter. Elvia's mother, Carmen, had found Nevin's body, and because she worried about the scandalous things the old man had written in the book and because he had made her promise to rescue the manuscript, she carried the book away with her and then phoned the police. Later, she found that he had left everything he had to her—not much, other than his old house, but a fortune to a graduating high school senior.

According to Carmen, Andrew, with no one to talk to, would spend his mornings writing himself to exhaustion. Then, after school, Carmen would come by and clean the place up and maybe prepare a supper for him. After Carmen cleaned and cooked, the old man would dictate, and she would type for him. Sometimes she would proofread what he had written. Elvia couldn't look at me as she told me that sometimes after their "writing" together, Carmen would take her clothes off in front of Andrew. Sometimes, Elvia told me, Carmen would cry. Sometimes, during that last year of Andrew's life, Carmen left him crying.

When she got married to a carpenter, Carmen moved into Nevin's small house on Flores Street. Carmen filled the old bachelor's house with her children. I asked Elvia what Carmen thought of the book. "She helped write it," Elvia reminded me.

Elvia recalled that, when she was a teenager, her mother took her three daughters aside and told them about the book. Carmen said it was all about some wicked people. Then, because the book, to Carmen, explained some Texas history that she felt wasn't being taught in her children's schools, she gave the book to her daughters to share. Elvia was the oldest, so she got to read it first. When she married, Elvia got the book as a dowry, though she'd let the other sisters borrow it from time to time. And eventually she let her husband read it, and then she let her own two daughters and one son read it. And so her sisters let all of their children read it. Elvia's grandchildren, living professional lives in San Antonio suburbs, weren't interested in the book.

I asked her what she thought of the book. A smile just barely made the corners of her mouth turn up. "I didn't like it much—when I first read it. On the second reading, I felt sorry for Juan Cortina. Then I began rereading to think of my dead mother."

I asked why she gave it to the library. She answered that her children were now married with their own families and that her husband had died. But the book was something that all her family had read, so it was theirs. But she reasoned that if other people could read it, then they might share something with her family. "And besides," she said. "My grandchildren aren't interested in 'olden times.' They're not even Mexicans anymore but rich, yuppie Americans. But for some very old people around this very old neighborhood, the only pleasure is a trip to the library."

"But Elvia, suppose I can get this book published. Would you like that?" Elvia tilted her head back to look at me. "What could you fill in between the end of Nevin's book and now?"

"I think that we need a couple of beers."

"I could use a beer." Elvia hustled into her house and was quickly beside me with one bottle of beer for her and one for me. It was the first beer of the day for both of us. That is always the best beer, and it was a warm morning, almost lunchtime, on a sunny spring day, reminding us of the oppressively hot summer ahead, but still comfortable. Elvia closed her eyes and smiled. She went backwards. "My daughter, Dolores, was the 'different' girl, the 'bad' girl. She had her grandmother Carmen's genes. When Dolores was a little girl, Carmen would tell her these crazy stories about outlaws and lovers." Elvia opened her eyes and pointed at me. "Carmen would get real close to telling my little girl about the nasty things she did in front of Nevin. Dolores was still too young to hear those things." Elvia smiled as though asking me if I understood. "And then when Dolores was an impatient teenager, Grandma Carmen would give her advice about watching out for herself, about choosing for herself, about knowing what she wanted."

Elvia leaned back against the swing and turned her head toward me. Our eyes locked. We sipped our beers. She shrugged and smiled. "I told her not to listen to her grandmother." Elvia shook her head. "Grandma Carmen had tried to tell my wild little girl that, with old man Nevin's help, she, Carmen, had yearned to be a bad girl. And here I was trying to raise Dolores to be a nice Mexicana. Carmen told Dolores that, curse or not, a little badness in your blood was good for you." Elvia lifted her hand, like a tiny paw, and patted my shoulder. "I tried to protect Dolores from her grandma's curse, the badness in her blood, and of course failed. Mamma, Grandma Carmen, was right." Elvia left her hand on my shoulder and tilted forward to look at my face. "Dolores is about your age. Getting old, but not that old yet. She teaches junior high, but she paints things. I don't understand her paintings, but they're big, bright, and full of things. She's lost four husbands because they didn't understand that Dolores had her grand-mother's wildness. You should go see her. Her name is Dolores Jones. Look at her paintings. See if you understand them." At that moment I wanted nothing more than to find Dolores Jones.

Instead, I went to see Sarah Hartman. In the time I had off, Sarah Hartman and I, with some advice from paper experts, carefully made copies of Andrew's book. And then I took one copy with me back to my dank East Texas home. I began to retype his words onto my computer. I corrected some of his grammar and punctuation. I changed some of his words that had become archaic. Where there were parts that I just couldn't read or that had been destroyed by time, I tried as best I could to imitate Andrew's style. I typed in excerpts from Andrew's own articles from the *Brownsville Sentinel* and the *San Antonio Express* and from Rip Ford's memoirs. Probably trying harder to write well than I ever had before, I tried to fill in the gaps for Andrew.

Then, during my next time off, in early August, I returned to San Antonio; but now, Andrew's Brownsville and San Antonio had worked their way into my consciousness—I was no longer plagued by an ex-one-true-love-of-my-life's Texas. I spent whole days downtown, sweating in the San Antonio heat, just as all those friends of Nevin must have done. And I wished for a clean, cool river like Andrew Nevin had had. And after several days, in amongst the glass, chrome, sculptures, billboards, buses, and tourists, I began to feel the presence of Rip, Addie, and Andrew. I could feel their city around me. My San Antonio heat must have been a little like theirs.

I stood in front of San Fernando Cathedral and stared down at the street, hoping to see through asphalt, pipes, and dirt to get a glimpse of the manuscript Andrew Nevin had buried there. I walked the ten blocks in the heat that bounced in wavy beams between the buildings to Alamo Plaza. In front of the Alamo, I sat on a bench and looked across Alamo Street at the new Hyatt Hotel entrance. The tourists crisscrossed my line of sight and moved in groups around me. But then, on either side of me sat Andrew Nevin and Rip Ford. Confederates, Rangers, and cowboys filled the plaza, and Addie Ford walked across the plaza calling for Andrew and Rip.

I found Rip's tombstone in the city's old, weed-grown Confederate cemetery. And next to his tombstone, in high grass, was a cracked tombstone lying face-down. Putting my whole body behind it, I straightened the tombstone and saw that it was Lula Maddox's, Rip's daughter. I had hoped that I might have found Nevin mistaken, that I might have found Addie's tombstone next to Rip's. But I didn't. And several calls and genealogical searches later, I still couldn't find Addie's plot. As Andrew Nevin said, history, for better or worse, simply forgot her. Andrew, of course, has no tombstone. In August, in the evaporative afternoon heat, I volunteered to help mow and clean up the old Confederate cemetery.

And then I remembered what San Antonio was like when I was a boy, and I began to feel it. The south side when I was a kid was a working-class area. It was big news when franchises first hit the south side. Instead, we had mom-and-pop convenience stores, restaurants, garages, "filling stations," and insurance agencies. Nothing was very fancy, sophisticated, or appreciated. My mother would all but prohibit us from the house during the summers. So my sister and I would spend our summers outside. When we came home, our mother would make us wash our dirty feet with the garden hose before we came into her house.

I went to the mobile library, a trailer pulled to different areas of the city so kids far away from the downtown public library could check out books. When I was old enough, I put down the books that I got from the mobile library and took the bus to downtown San Antonio, mostly alone, to go to the Texas, Aztec, or Empire Theaters. The best, though, the finest, was the Majestic Theater, the same one that Andrew Nevin frequented. Who knows, I may have sat in the same chair as Andrew.

In high school, during the summers, I worked at a bank in downtown San Antonio. In one of the hottest cities in America, I walked through the downtown streets on my lunch hours and before and after work. I remember the clean, morning smell of sidewalks being washed off with a hose. I imagined the evils that caused the filth that accumulated on the sidewalks. I made up stories about the downtowners I saw from my bus's window: the panhandlers and pimps evading the police; the airmen riding the buses in from Lackland where they had just finished basic training, their buzzed heads looking strangely ill-suited for the dark-blue uniforms, their giggles and whoops as prostitutes solicited them; the conglomeration of types—construction workers, lawyers, the city's elite on their way to a steam at the YMCA, bums, winos. And I realized that my San Antonio was now as much condemned to history as Andrew Nevin's San Antonio. But Sarah Hartman and Elvia Gomez also owned part of my San Antonio. So, I reasoned, must Dolores Jones, who was my age and raised in an older, sloppier San Antonio.

So I went to the Blue Star Gallery, an old warehouse turned into a rather chic artists' gallery. I found Dolores Jones's studio space and looked at the splashy, bright, busy paintings. They were collages of out-of-proportion historical figures mixed with newer modern figures, usually tattooed and pierced young people. I didn't understand the paintings. "I'll hope that you want to buy something," a voice said from behind me.

"I'd like to buy you a cool beer, so I can listen to you tell me about your grandmother and Andrew Nevin."

The petite woman folded her arms and leaned against the wall. Her sleeveless tank-top exposed a shoulder with a orchid tattoo. "How many beers? It's a long story." Over lots of beers and a couple of plates of red enchiladas, I watched her fingers dance in front of her face and listened as she smiled and told her version of her wicked grandmother's wayward genes—just as Andrew must have watched that wicked young grandmother shrug her clothes off in front of him as he listened to the long-dead voices in his head. Dolores and I perhaps should have become lovers, but instead we became compatriots, confidants, compadres (or comadres), and that was maybe better because we both had a strong dose of what had infected Andrew, Carmen, and later in her life, Elvia. And then, too, Carmen and Nevin, finally, were friends.

In the last year of his life, Andrew Nevin tried, as best he could with gnarled fingers, to pound out the story of his grace. The facts don't matter. His effort and his record do. What he tried to say does matter. That he saw grace in the flickering images projected on the screen of the wonderful, ancient old Majestic Theater, where I went as a boy to watch my own flickering images, does matter. That he wrote and perhaps shortened his life in order to turn what he saw on that screen into his world does matter. That he saw his personal story intertwined with history also matters. In our wish to tell, though we may get history wrong, we show ourselves, and we ourselves with our own private histories are history too. So I think that Andrew got himself right. And beyond himself, I want to believe him about Rip, Cortina, McNelly, Addie, and Catalina. Reading from my twenty-first-century vantage point, I'm not sure that we deserve Andrew's nineteenth-century friends, heroes, and foes. I think they would be satisfied with us, but I think they deserve better.

With Nevin as an example, with all my ex-one-true-loves and other failures turned to simple but pure loss and sadness, with youth behind me, I wait and prepare and hope for my own grace, wherever it may come from. And I pray that I have worked hard enough to recognize it and be ready for it. After a loss or despair, we shouldn't seek "closure." Move on, but tow the past behind you. Drag it if you have to. Because somebody has to remember. Because our histories are all knit together, yet are unraveling so fast. Because if we don't remember, we lose a little decency, a little humanity, and our chances at grace. As Andrew tells us, write it down—*write it down.*

PART ONE

*Spy and Coward and
Civilized Man*

CHAPTER 1

Brownsville, Texas, May 1875

If Brownsville is ever to truly become a civilized, peaceful American community, then the barbarity in this region must stop. And behind this barbarity is this awful banditry that ignores all laws. So this newspaper applauds this great state's formation of the Special Force, commanded by that hero who fought valiantly in our Civil War, L. H. McNelly. Citizens of Brownsville should look forward to the arrival of this small but intrepid band and to the cessation of lawlessness in our tropical valley.

ANDREW NEVIN
Brownsville Sentinel, *May 1875*

I N the stultifying, late afternoon Brownsville heat, which made even the flies fat and lazy and promised an even hotter, marrow-shriveling summer, I waited in my favorite whorehouse, the Bivouac, to buy a goat for my nephew. This hot, late spring afternoon in May of 1875 was to begin the greatest adventure of my life, the one that would confirm Texans' long-held suspicions that I was cowardly and unmanly. I had suspicions myself, which had been growing since that detestable late war between sour-faced abolitionists in the North and misplaced, misguided would-be cavaliers in the South.

The Bivouac probably had the most eclectic mixture of clientele of any whorehouse in the legal limits of the United States. Negro soldiers from Fort Brown bumped elbows with their white officers, and naval men from the gunboat *Rio Bravo* drank with vaqueros from both sides of the border. The genteel merchants who ran the town would stay with their good wives, but they might buy a lady for a visiting Anglo cattleman or steamboat customer. And the Bivouac's ladies were olive-skinned young girls from across the river in Matamoros.

As soon as I walked in from that mean-spirited heat, Rose Montero, the owner, poured me a cool beer. The blessings of civilization had given Brownsville a new ice factory, and so we had cold draught beer year-round. "Why you want a goat? Has your old uncle Rip got a taste for cabrito?" Rose asked, then added, "That goat you buying is too old for cabrito."

"John William is afraid of horses," I said.

Chita, my favorite young lady from across the border, had heard me discussing my nephew, really my cousin, John William's fear of horses, so she suggested a wagon pulled by a goat. John William could get used to the smaller animal until he was ready for a horse. I agreed. Chita just happened to know where she could get a goat and a wagon. So I was to meet and pick up my goat and wagon.

I had finished my stories for the *Brownsville Sentinel*, and like everyone else in the lower Rio Grande Valley, I was waiting for the worst part of a hot spring day to be cooled by the evening breeze following the Rio Grande up from Brazos Island and the Gulf of Mexico.

My pleasant conversation with Rose was interrupted by U.S. Navy Lieutenant Commander Dewitt Kells, who pushed his way beside me. Kells slammed his fist down on the bar and ordered straight-up Scotch (yes, Scotch; Brownsville, a river town near several sea ports, now with the Rio Grande Railroad to Point Isabel, always had a choice of liquor, and wasn't limited to rotgut as in those hard Texas cattle towns). Kells's beaming smile, red hair, and beard shone even in the dark bar. "So I hear you're going to join the Texas Rangers and kill some bandits," Kells said.

Dewitt Kells commanded the gunboat *Rio Bravo*, which when repaired, could steam as far upriver as Rio Grande City. I didn't answer him, so he started again. "Going to join up with that Confederate fire-breather, that state policeman who worked for the Reconstructionist, nigger-loving Republicans and kill some Mexicans? Leander H. McNelly his own self."

Rose clucked her tongue, then said, "We don't like politics in here." She moved away from us. She knew better than to listen to gossip. Someone might be willing to beat a whore to hear certain gossip.

"This is theory, not politics," Kells said to Rose's back, then to me. "Have you met McNelly?"

"I'm going to talk to the man. I've never met him," I said.

"You're going to join him."

"Not necessarily." At this point, like Rose, I didn't want to say or hear too much.

"But if ol' Rip Ford says you're a fire-eating, Mexican-shooting, fil-ibustering son of a bitch, who's to say no?"

"I'm a reporter, not a Ranger."

"Nevin, look, you tell this McNelly to see me."

Another man appeared at the bar on the other side of me.

"I hear you're going shoot the Meskins?" Sergeant Ezekiel Johnson said, reaching for his beer. He smelled like dust, dried sweat, and horse manure. "I hear you gonna do what the U.S. army can't do." He pulled his flat palm over his dark face, spreading sweat and grime down to his neck. "All this fussing over cows."

"Ezekiel, get yourself out of here while I talk to the gentleman. This doesn't concern the coloreds," Kells said.

"It concern this colored if he get shot at," Ezekiel said. "I don't want to get shot because of no cow."

When Ezekiel left, Kells shook his head. "Some of the coloreds need to remember their place, from whence they've come." Two years before, the colored soldiers had introduced some more tension in this border town. One morning, I had seen the mutilated body of a col-ored soldier left in Washington Square. The other blacks blamed the *charamusqueros*, candy vendors, most of them children. The next night the colored soldiers attacked the *charamusqueros* in several alleys around Washington Square. This time, in the pale dawn, I saw the bleeding, bruised children lying in the square. One *charamusquero* died several days later.

Kells watched Ezekiel walk back to a far table, then leaned his elbows on the bar and edged closer to me. "Tell McNelly that once I get my little gunboat in working order, I can point my cannon toward the Mexican side, and if anyone fires at me, I can fire back. Hell, I can point my guns toward Matamoros and bombard ol' Juan Cortina himself. All I need is an excuse to let go on the Mexicans. And tell him not trust those nigger troops. Hell, they'll run."

"Governor Coke ordered McNelly to stop the rustling. That doesn't mean an invasion of Mexico."

"That's the shame. It's the perfect opportunity." Kells pushed his naval cap back onto his forehead and his red hair tumbled out from underneath it. "How else are you going to stop the thieving unless you deal a quick, decisive blow?"

I sipped my beer and looked at Kells. "If McNelly takes me on, I'm not about to invade Mexico with your gunboat and some East Texas farm boys," I said.

Kells moved down the bar to put a proper distance between us. He shook his head and said, loud enough for others to hear: "You've gotten weak and insipid, writing for that Democrat tool. A good Republican newspaper would see to it we were liberating Mexico."

"I ain't invading no Mexico," Ezekiel said. He had come back to the bar for another beer.

Kells shook his head, "Ain't that gratitude? After the Grand Army of the Potomac set you free."

"Didn't set me free to invade no Mexico," Ezekiel said, as he walked away from the bar.

Kells looked around, moved closer to me once again, leaned on his elbows, and stroked his beard. Our conversation, again private. "Can't you see the sense of it? If Walker would have had any sort of troops behind him in Nicaragua, we'd have territories and states as far down as the equator. You Democrats think only about a border and a few cattle. Why, with land stretching south, we'd dominate all of Europe! Don't you see, here it is. This is our chance!"

"I never knew that Lincoln's party had worldwide ambitions. I thought that the Democrats of Andy Jackson and Sam Houston were the ones who wanted to snatch Mexico away from the Mexicans."

Kells sipped at his scotch, then grunted, "Small-mindedness."

"My small mind keeps me out of harm's way."

"So to keep out of harm's way, you're going to join McNelly and crush that cattle-thieving villain, ol' Juan Neptemo Cortina?"

"Yeah, I don't pay attention too well. But that villain, ol' Juan *Nepomuceno* Cortina, used to steal cattle from the Mexican side and bring them to this side. For Charles Stillman, Mifflin Kenedy, and Captain King."

"Are you a history teacher, too? I guess you don't remember last month when Cortina hung the alcalde and his American friend not but maybe half a mile from here. Right on the edge of the river, right in sight of Fort Brown, where those lily-livered nigger troops just watched." I had seen the two bodies dangling from the ropes and couldn't help feeling disgusted and estranged from the man who had helped me survive the war.

Chita saved me from the conversation by leading the goat into the bar. We heard the tapping of his hooves on the board floor, the tinkling of a bell around the goat's neck, and then we heard a bleat when he stopped. Chita pulled him by the reins attached to his bridle. Behind the goat, attached to a harness around his neck, was a tiny, bright red and green wagon. Chita was no longer a youngster, a little wear and wisdom to her, golden brown skin with just a tint of Mediterranean yellow. She was glorious.

Rose looked at Chita and said, "Get it out of here. Wait outside."

Kells said the obvious, "It's a goat."

"Cabrito," Sergeant Ezekiel Johnson said, and his men laughed.

"That stringy ol' goat wouldn't be much more nourishing than the cheap beef you soldiers eat," Kells said toward Ezekiel.

"It's a good goat," Chita said to all of them. "This goat is trained better than a horse. It's smarter than a horse." I took the reins from Chita and pulled several new Yankee dollars out of my wallet to give to her.

She looked up at me and said in a whisper, "Why don't you stay, Andrew?"

I shook my head and smiled back her. "Not today." I pulled the goat and wagon toward the door of the bar.

"Vámanos. Get!" Rose yelled.

"Remember, Nevin," Kells shouted after me, and I waved to him from the door.

Outside, in the sunshine, I pulled at my bow tie until it came undone and then unfastened my collar and stuffed it in my pocket. The nearly tropical heat made Brownsville a casual town; like any tropical town, Brownsville was full of goats, but not ones with a bell and a wagon being dragged down the main street, so shopkeepers and ladies found an excuse to laugh. I kept off the sidewalks, and he proved himself to be a well-trained goat. He obeyed my tugs and kept pace with me, his bell tinkling, the bright red and green wagon trailing behind him. Vaqueros rode by me and laughed; I smiled and tipped my hat. I didn't own a horse, preferring not to go any farther than my own feet or a rented buggy could take me. It is no small understatement to say that I, as well as everyone who knew me or even saw me, was certain that I was better suited for the East, but the East soured for me when it started choosing up sides for the War Between the States.

I was in a hurry, but my feet could not pull me past the Gem. The goat balked when I tried to pull him down 13th Street, but I tugged until he followed me. I tied his bridle next to the hitching post, alongside the horses that eyed him nervously. He pulled his head against the bridle and gnawed at it. He shook his head to ring his bell and demand that we move on, but he would have to wait for me to have a beer.

I walked through the tall French doors, following the tinkling of piano keys. A breeze coming through the open doors and door-length windows on the southeast side of the building cooled my face. I turned toward the bar, walked past the gaming tables, and squeezed in between French and German conversations.

The Gem was the finest bar in town. It was built in 1848, with the second floor serving as the home of Brownsville's first mayor. It was a grand, opulent, even decadent old building. Like most of the better buildings in town, it was coastal Southern: tall windows and doors, pale sky-blue paint, an iron-railed balcony—pleasant, like all of Brownsville. Unlike the dark Bivouac, which hid its wares and customers from polite society, the Gem left its doors and windows open to the spring's gentle breezes and bright light. Years before, the Gem had installed a hydraulic pump to bring water to a cistern on the roof. So the Gem had a water closet for ladies and another for gentlemen—no privy in the alley.

My cold beer was spoiled by a goat bleat that sounded like a child strangling and the faint tinkling of a little bell. The conversations stopped, and those gentlemen businessmen stared in the direction of the bleat. A few figured out that the complaining goat was my responsibility, so they stared at me.

I was already known somewhat as a Brownsville eccentric. I was suspected of several vices and sins, some of which could only be whispered and then not in mixed company. But I had been useful to four armies during the war. And my uncle, Rip, while not rich nor a merchant, was a hero for the Texas cause in the Civil War, the Mexican War, the Comanche Wars, and the Cortina Wars. Because he was honored, Brownsville accepted me and my eccentricities. So I was just the sort of fellow to parade a goat and its gaudy wagon down Elizabeth Street, named for Charles Stillman's beautiful wife who couldn't stand to live in the town. The French and German conversations started again, the bartender smoothed his whiskers, and I smoothed my moustache and sipped my beer.

My drinking pleasures were again interrupted. Sheriff James Browne waddled up to me. Though the style at the time was for the middle part of the coat to remain unbuttoned, thus allowing a man's stomach to protrude, Browne's stomach took far too much advantage of style. Browne, a poor merchant, wasn't sheriff material. A member of "the Blues"—as opposed to the wealthy "Reds," the prominent triumvirate of Mifflin Kenedy, Richard King, and Charles Stillman—Browne had just found himself elected sheriff. I turned my back to him, hoping that he would not be rude enough to disturb me, but he put his hat on the bar and scratched at his whiskers. His loud voice, still faintly Irish, thus disrupted the European conversations around me. "Tell your uncle, Mr. Rip by-god Ford, to get his Austin friends to pull this McNelly out of here. We've got a fort of U.S. soldiers here, and the last thing we need is that hair-trigger, ex-Confederate soldier to come here shooting people up. This is not a military problem. This is a local problem." Browne blew between his lips to get some of his moustache hairs out of his mouth.

"Sounds like 'problem' understates the severity. What about that teacher from north of here? I reported on that story." A teacher, working at a rural school, would ride out to some of the ranches to instruct children. When he happened upon some bandits, they cut him apart, first his digits, toes and fingers, then limbs, arms and legs. A rancher, known as Old Rock, who mostly just roamed over the area, had found the torso. I went with Sheriff Browne's search party, guided by Old Rock, to retrieve what was left of the teacher.

Browne shook his head like an angry bull. "That was the actions of trash or thugs. But we can work things out with Cortina. Or he'll get run out again. Same as always. Trust the local ways. Mark my words. This McNelly will do nothing but stir up trouble."

"You mean he might stir up what should remain secret."

"Good thing you have an important uncle."

"Good thing you won another election."

Browne harrumphed and scratched at his moustache and beard. "I'll not play favorites."

When I turned back to my beer, I heard another voice from behind me. "As long as it's not a city problem." City Marshal Mike O'Shaughnessey stood next to Browne. Small-statured, well-dressed, O'Shaughnessey pushed his derby farther back on his head and let a polite smile, almost a smirk, creep into one corner of his mouth. With his ornate vest, he looked like a gambler.

"What could possibly happen to the city? What can I possibly do?" I asked.

"Keep me informed," he said.

"For as many people as I'm keeping informed, I'll just put what I know in the *Sentinel*," I said, and sipped my beer. O'Shaughnessey chuckled. He always had a sense of humor, unlike Browne, so I could tolerate him. But my mood had grown darker. "Mike, do you ever go anywhere without Browne? Do you ever do anything without asking him first?"

His smile dropped. "I have my own opinions."

"If Browne tells you what they are."

"Just as Rip Ford informs you of yours," O'Shaughnessey said. He smiled.

I added, "I'm sure that old Blues provide just as sound advice as Rip Ford."

"I recall, all on my own, a city ordinance banning goats from being tied up outside of businesses."

James Browne grimaced at Mike O'Shaughnessey. I started an apology. "I'm sorry, Mike. You caught me at the wrong time. I'll try to find out what I can. I'll try to tell you and Jimmy." Mike smiled at this. "And the goat will be gone as soon as I finish my beer." We had no more that either of us could think of to talk about, so O'Shaughnessey tipped his hat and left me to my beverage.

The breezes that came off the coast, the small Sabal palms, and the fierce loyalty to profit made for an easy, tropical corruption, which in turn allowed gentle debaucheries mixed with the finer liquors and coastal Southern architecture to suit a civilized nature like mine. But cattle and the land that they needed were also a part of the snobberies, profits, and tropical life of Brownsville. Juan Cortina, the mayor of Matamoros and the general of the army garrisoned there, allowed cattle thievery to continue, and Lee H. McNelly meant to put a stop to it. The pleasures of Brownsville, my pleasures, were in danger. I finished my drink, stepped outside, and dragged my goat to the house that Richard King gave to my uncle Rip Ford rent-free simply because he was an ailing hero.

CHAPTER 2

The Fords

Mexican affairs are unsettled and will no doubt remain so. The revolutions have paralyzed business and impeded industrial pursuits. The elements of reform, if there, can be made available with difficulty. A protectorate will become indispensable in my opinion.

RIP FORD TO O. M. ROBERTS
[future governor of Texas and law professor at the University of Texas],
February 1877

I WALKED past Market Square, a block over from Elizabeth, to the very end of the street and turned toward Levee Street. My goat and I stopped at the last frame house before we came to some of the jacales of the poor Mexicans. Rip might be a mayor, editor, senator, and hero, but he spent a good portion of his life after the war worrying about having to move into a jacal.

I stopped my goat at the gate to Rip Ford's small house. Addie and Lula jumped off the porch and ran toward the gate. No doubt they had started the morning with ribbons in their pigtails and with their flowered dresses clean, but in the course of a hard day of play they had lost their ribbons, shredded their pigtails, and dirtied their cotton dresses. Lula, the elder, at twelve, was just starting to wonder about boys, and her father told me that he worried that he'd have to shoot one. Addie, at ten, would be more interested in the goat than in any boy. "Let's see," they both yelled. As Lula held the gate, Addie ran outside and tried to pet the goat.

"Give us some room," I said as I led the goat through the gate. "Close that gate now," I added.

Addie yanked a remaining ribbon out of her hair and began to tie it around the goat's neck. Lula ran to her sister and said, "No, let me do it," but she straightened and said, "He stinks."

"Goats do stink," I said.

Their mother stepped from the front door to the porch: the refined Addie Ford, daughter of the Brownsville merchant Elihu Smith, twenty-three years younger than her husband. Addie bore no trace of the lonely nights she spent with her infant children while her husband chased Yankees or Mexicans, or of the sparse times after the war when old Rip had no money and borrowed from his friends. I also, at that time, was short of funds, and because I shared meals with the colonel and his family, I contributed much of my earnings to the family.

Addie's face always lit up when she saw me. She clasped her hands to her cheek, only this time she said, "A goat." Addie was Rip's prize instead of money.

Then peeking around from behind her print dress, eight-year-old John William, named for Rip and Rip's father, stepped boldly out to the edge of the porch. "He's got a goat, Mamma."

"*Your* goat, John William," I said.

"What about me?" little Addie said.

"I got you ribbons last time," I said.

"I don't want ribbons. I want a goat!" Addie said.

Lula, growing old enough to pretend to be above all of this, snorted. "Who wants a stinky goat?"

John William, followed by his mother, edged toward the goat and stuck out his hand. I tugged on the rope and brought the goat up. "Just pet him," Addie said. But the goat lowered his head, shook it, and rang his bell.

John William stepped back from the goat and backed into his mother, who put her palms on his shoulders.

"This is a special goat, John William. I got him from a special lady friend of mine. He belonged to this crippled man over in Matamoros who didn't have any legs. He got them blown off by an Imperialista's cannonball."

"Andrew," Addie admonished.

"Uncle Andrew, come on," Lula said.

"No, no, it's true, this goat used to pull him around in that cart." I scooped up John William (who pushed against me), put him in the cart, and handed him the goat's reins. "That fellow died. This lady friend got the goat and sold him to me." John William's hands shook as he picked up the reins. He gave me and his mother a scared look. "Go on, John William," I said.

"Go on," added his mother.

Lula and Addie began taunting, "Go on, John William."

John William said, "Giddy up," and the goat walked slowly toward the porch then gained speed. John William yelled again, and the goat started to trot.

Little Addie trotted with it and yelled, "Let me try, let me try!"

I walked to Addie Ford, and she smiled and leaned her head to her right. I could see worry lines. "That goat will probably end up on our table."

"No, he'd be too stringy. Old Rip wouldn't roast him."

I patted her back and heard, "It's a goat wagon," from the porch. We both squinted our eyes against the sun sinking behind the house to see arrow-straight, white-bearded, beak-nosed, sixty-year-old Rip Ford. He stepped down. He looked across his street, then to each side, then deliberately, one step at a time, met us in his front yard. It seemed he kept himself from shrinking, from curling just the least bit, as aging men are prone to do, by force of will. In spite of malaria, battle wounds, rheumatism, and general aging, he just wasn't going to give in to age. He had the state of Texas to defend. He had a much younger wife and three young children to provide for. "What's John William doing in a goat wagon?" he asked.

"I thought, maybe, since he got so scared of that horse you got for him, he ought to start off a little smaller." Rip was trying to teach his son how to sit a horse and ride. Little John William was terrified of the horse, but he kept a stiff upper lip and didn't cry until Rip slapped the horse's flank and sent the horse running with John William holding on for dear life. Once, Rip encouraged John William to take the mare out on his own. The boy came back on foot, leading the horse, crying, and not wanting to talk.

"A goat." Rip shook his head, but smiled, then added, "How about the supper we've all been waiting for?" he asked and looked at me in that way that meant he wanted to talk privately. Addie gathered her children and herded them before her toward the porch, and we all followed Rip into his house.

After supper, Rip and I sat on the front porch and smoked Cuban cigars. The cigar smoke tasted good, but the smell was affected somewhat by the smudge pots in the corners of the porch. After a bright sunset, it had just rained, and the evening breeze had died down, so the mosquitos were out. "You give a couple of those cigars to McNelly," Rip said and exhaled a billow of smoke. "I hear he likes cigars."

"Even smuggled ones?"

"You don't need to tell him," Rip said.

"I'm teasing."

"Stop your teasing and listen. I hear he's a stern man. He wants only his special men. Don't beg him, but respect him." I nodded. "And don't forget to show him my letter." I nodded.

"Rip, I consider myself a pretty good salesman, especially when what I am selling is myself."

Rip waved his hand in front of his face at some buzzing that escaped the smudge pots and the cigar smoke. "Don't insult the man. Don't throw any of your smart-mouthed obfuscation at him."

The mosquito must have left Rip, for he quit waving, and I heard buzzing over my ear. I slapped and got nothing. "Sure could use a drink, now," I said and smiled over at Rip.

"You always want a drink." Rip held his cigar between two fingers. He twisted in his rocker, looked at me, and pointed with the fingers that held his cigar. "You let me know what kind of man he is, how tough he is, whether he can handle the job. He's got to be a good man. First goddamn Ranger force called in fifteen years. Damn." Rip banged his flat palm against the arm of his rocker.

"He was one of the few honest State Police. He was even wounded." I leaned back in my chair, let smoke though my lips, and said, "Rip, Governor Coke was not going to let you command McNelly's Special Force or the Frontier Battalion."

Rip scratched his head. "Addie wouldn't let me even request the position."

"Rip, Rangers aren't sixty years old."

Rip settled back into his chair and let his eyes close. He must have seen something. He seemed to talk to himself. "You can beat the natural, human instinct of fear. You keep the abstraction in mind, in this case the order. You forget about yourself and think of you only as the company, the regiment, the tribe, the posse. And if you're giving the orders, you have to think a step ahead to the next order, so you set yourself busy and think and forget about your own welfare." Then he stopped talking to himself and turned to me, "You listening?"

I faced him. "How do you go about surrendering?"

Rip shook his head, then smiled. "Don't know. I never surrendered."

"Well, I haven't exactly surrendered," I said. "But I've compromised a bit."

"For that reason, Andrew, I won't worry about your safety. You may not be good at fighting," he hesitated, "but you are good at protecting your own hide."

CHAPTER 3

Juan Nepomuceno Cortina

It is true that Mrs. Kenedy [former Petra Vela de Vidal, wife of Captain Mifflin Kenedy] did not meet any of the bandits, but she could reach them through others. In this manner her influence was exerted and bore good fruit. She did many charitable acts and had many warm friends who loved her. She was clear-headed and liberal in her views. She possessed none of the bigotry which causes many to persecute their neighbors and become firebrands in the community in which they live. Although a Catholic herself, she possessed much good sense and too much kindness of heart to persecute those of a different opinion.

RIP FORD
Rip Ford's Texas, *ed. Stephen B. Oates, 1963*

THE next morning, pebbles bouncing against my window woke me. Stepping around the bullet hole in the floor, I opened my shutters and looked at Rip Ford sitting in a rented buggy. He got out of the buggy. The sun was barely up, and he cast a long shadow up the side of my wall. "We ought to get a start," he yelled up to me.

My room rested above a saloon. One night, a rowdy vaquero fired above his head, startled me from my sleep, and added the bullet hole in my floor. The bartender beaned the vaquero with a shovel for putting a hole through the saloon's ceiling and my floor.

I leased the dangerous place because Mr. McGuffey's saloon had a variety of comforts, all stemming from the fact that he had a share in a well. A pipe from McGuffey's well led to a cistern, and another pipe led to a smaller cistern inside the house and then to a boiler and a kitchen sink. A hand pump brought hot and cool water into the first floor, and I had access to both.

As a hydropath, I felt the curative powers of water, whether steam, cold, or hot. I bought a hip bath, small and portable, and tried to sprinkle water on me at least twice a day. Sometimes I'd walk to the river, strip, and plunge in. Some people in Brownsville still felt that water was best avoided. Too much water, they reasoned, invited colds and kept the body's natural lotions from their jobs. I continued to bathe.

Along with my belief in water, I had a belief in hygiene and hygienic modesty. My large room—just a dressing curtain, my chest and boudoir, table, two chairs, a brazier for the winter, and a bed—had a small closet for privacy. I had other comforts. Rows of windows lined two walls. I could walk out my large French door to an iron balcony.

I dressed but left off a tie and came down to meet Rip. He smiled at me, "You sleep late. Here, you drive." He held the reins out for me. He wore an old slouch campaign hat, his boots, and a pistol on his hip.

"Are we planning on a fight?" I asked.

"Mainly for show."

He didn't say much other than where to turn as we bounced and rocked out of town in the rented buggy. We took the road toward Boca Chica beach. On the way, the land flattened out and turned marshy. When we got to long stretches of sand and could smell the Gulf, we stopped. Rip pulled out a handkerchief and wiped the sweat off his face. Already, the heat was starting to suck the moisture out of us. As we neared the old Palmito battlefield, I knew that Rip's intentions for this trip had surrendered to his memories.

"No. Pull over and find some shade," Rip said. "We'll have an early lunch."

I steered the horse toward a small oak. Rip stepped out of the buggy, stretched himself, and looked around, again wiping the sweat off his face with his now drenched handkerchief. I sweated too, but not as much as Rip, and I hoped that he was not sweating from one of his malarial fevers. "We didn't come out here to relive Palmito again, did we?" I asked.

He shot me a stern look. "That was a long time ago," he said. "Today, we've got business." On this spot, in May of 1865, Rip Ford won the last battle of the War Between the States. This needless fight over who was to confiscate some bales of cotton was perhaps his greatest victory. "But this country changes. It's, it's, well, overgrown looking."

We sat on a blanket and ate Addie's sandwiches and sipped cool tea from a jug. Another buggy came bouncing down the road toward us. Rip's eyes focused on the buggy. He pulled himself up, bone by bone, like an old hound dog does, never taking his eyes off the buggy. Then, as it got close enough to make out who was in it, he smiled. In the buggy sat a driver and the mayor of Matamoros, General Juan Cortina.

Cortina, still spry at fifty-one, but showing his weariness in his face, stepped out almost before the buggy stopped. Cortina wore his navy blue general's uniform with its gold braid and commander's cap. Rip said, "Compadre, huh?" Cortina nodded. "I see you still sleep late, amigo."

"And stay up later," Cortina said in Spanish and chortled. "I have things to do in the dark. Not like you, you old gringo."

"Nothing productive or moral comes about at night," Rip said.

"Strange for a man with children to say that," Cortina said.

Cortina gave Rip the traditional Mexican abrazo. Though they had shot and betrayed each other, one a former Know-Nothing party member and nondrinker and the other a womanizing and drinking opportunist, the two were compadres, in the old Spanish sense of the word.

All of this was over cattle. Rip leased a little land and ran a few cows. He paid the rancher part of the profits from the cows for their upkeep. Cortina *supposedly* supported himself by shipping stolen Texas cows out of Bagdad, on the mouth of the Rio Grande, to Cuba. With state and national writs, with American customs inspectors recording brands at Bagdad, Cortina, as mayor, had turned back only two herds of cattle, and these he had personally seen driven back across the river to their owners: Rip Ford and Sheriff James Browne.

Cortina and Ford turned their backs to the driver and me and walked away from us, toward the coast. I let our horse go and joined them. They stopped, and Rip looked at me and said, "Wait with the driver."

"What?"

"Give us a second," Rip said. Cortina looked at me and shrugged.

I walked back, another hired hand, another peasant, and waited with the grinning peón. "You work for Cortina?" He nodded. "Is he good to work for?" He grinned and nodded. "Have you seen any cattle at Bagdad?" Another nod. "Any with a running W?" I traced King's brand in the air with my finger. He shrugged. "Are you going to talk to me?"

He dropped his grin and looked at me. "No."

"Orders?" Another nod.

I watched the two men walking away from me, one stiff, rigid, and purposeful, the other animated. The old Ranger was about six inches taller than the general. After a few more steps, they stopped. Cortina reached up and waved a finger in front of Rip's face. Rip looked in my direction, then back at Cortina. He shouted, but I couldn't make out what he said. My companion, as ordered, looked as uninterested in them as he was in me.

In September of 1859, newly married Juan Cortina saw the Brownsville city marshal, a social inferior, a member of the lesser rich, arrest and beat one of his vaqueros. Cheno, as his loyal vaqueros called him, shot the marshal, pulled his vaquero up on his horse, and galloped away to form a wild, untrained cavalry. He returned to shoot up Brownsville. His first attack was on the home of woefully unfortunate William Neale, one of the leaders of the Blue party and the then mayor. One of the wild shots killed the Neales' oldest son.

In November of 1859, the United States Army sent Major Samuel Heintzelman to chase Cortina into Mexico. The great state of Texas sent the fabled Texas Ranger John S. "Rip" Ford. John Salmon Ford had become "Rip" during the Mexican War. A grieving widower, having lost his second wife to death instead of a mysterious divorce, as he had his first, Ford joined Captain Jack Hays's Texas Rangers in their march from Vera Cruz to Mexico City and became Hays's adjutant. In this capacity, he wrote home about Rangers' deaths, closing his letters by writing "Rest In Peace" above his signature. In 1851, he entered a plot with his old friend José Carbajal to invade Mexico and was wounded in the head. In 1858, Rip chased the Comanche chief Iron Jacket and his band out of Texas.

In December of 1859, Rip Ford led the charge that chased Cortina into Mexico. From Mexico, Cortina began his guerrilla war that lasted until April of 1860. Rip fought him the whole time. But Sabas Cavazos, Cortina's half-brother, introduced Rip to Cortina's mother; Rip guaranteed to her that he would see to her safety and to the protection of her property. And because Cortina had deserted his new wife, Estéfana Goseaschochea disowned her wild son.

The two old men in front of me argued with words and fingers. Then, as though on cue, they stopped. They walked back over the rough ground toward me and the other peón. Cortina hurried to me, leaving Rip behind him, and held out his hands. He hugged me and apologized for being rude. "Andrew, we shouldn't be such strangers after all that we have done for each other." If it had been safe and possible, I might have switched my lineage and loyalty from Rip Ford to Juan Cortina. He was more fun than old Rip, and we did share many things, including a mistress.

Cortina's green eyes sparkled over his ruddy cheeks, none of Rip's stoic, secular Puritanism in this man full of appetites. But I noticed splotches of gray in his trim red beard. "Your pronunciamientos are still my favorites. If you ever want to leave the newspaper business, come see me."

He pulled me to one side to wait for Rip to come up to us. Rip said, "Andrew, Juan thinks maybe you shouldn't join up with McNelly."

"I'm not afraid."

"The hell you're not," Rip said.

Juan laughed and slapped my back. He shrugged his shoulders. "I'm not afraid for you, Andrew. You always turn out well. You dodge bullets better than anyone I've ever seen. I just don't see why you should waste your time with him. You and I have survived Unionists, Confederates, Juaristas, Imperialists, and now this, this little pissant Lerdo, who thinks he is an equal president to the great Benito Juárez." Cortina, who remained illiterate because he preferred whoring, drinking, and fighting with his vaqueros over school, had grown more articulate in his speech—with some of my help. "What I am worried about is that you will just embarrass yourself with him. You can be of more use to your uncle and me by staying here."

"Juan, some of the Confederates, Imperialists, and Union officers, not to mention myself, have chased you out of Texas and Matamoros more than a couple of times," Rip said.

Juan smiled. "But we have both survived and watched out for each other, so I want to watch out for Andrew." Before I could say anything, Cortina shouted to the man left with both buggies and horses. The mestizo ran to us carrying a wine bottle and four glasses. Juan poured all of us a glass of wine, even the peón, who knew his place and took his glass of wine back to the buggies.

Cortina and I sipped, but the old temperance man, Rip, sniffed his wine before he sipped. "Not bad," Rip said. "Leftover French contraband?"

Cortina smiled. "When have I ever discussed business without some refreshments for my associates?"

Before I could answer in Spanish, Rip said in English, "Juan, this McNelly is different. He's a Ranger. He's not bound by agreements. He'll chase you all the way to Mexico City if need be."

Cortina feigned hurt surprise. "Me? Why me? I'm not stealing Mamma's cows."

"In fact, you aren't stealing your mamma's cows or Sheriff J. G.

Browne's cows. Probably, Juan Flores organizes most of these raids from Las Cuevas. But, as mayor, you can make a tidy profit for his army by shipping smuggled cows from Bagdad to Cuba," I said.

Cortina frowned. "These suppositions, Andrew, where do you get them?" I liked him, but if he had to, he would kill me, or rather, see me killed.

"Juan, all I'm saying is—" Rip breathed in, then switched to Spanish. "Texas wants the cattle thieving stopped. If this state is to progress, and this area is to become a vital part of the state, then the thievery must stop."

"How am I to stop it?"

"You remember Santos Benavides?" Juan Cortina nodded. Santos was a one-time enemy of Rip's, but became his ally during the War Between the States by leading Mexican troops for the Confederacy. "We testified to the legislature about the problem and demanded that it stop. This is a new government. No more Reconstruction governors. No more E. J. Davis. We're writing a new constitution in September. I'll be there. And one way or another, this new constitution, this new government, or Governor Coke will stop this." Cortina sipped his wine as Rip talked. "Last year, I was mayor of Brownsville. . . ."

"And I am mayor of Matamoros," Cortina chuckled. "Compadre," he said and held out his hands toward Rip. Rip's forehead turned red, and some of his white hair even seemed to turn red.

He threw his wine glass into the brush, wasting Cortina's good European wine. He was silent for a moment after we heard the glass shatter. "As mayor of Brownsville, I know that some of the moneyed interests are turning against you. Brownsville wants to be a part of Texas. And Captain King . . ."

Cortina interrupted. "Captain King moved to his ranch. What? Seven years ago?"

"But it is his cattle that are missing," I added.

Rip saluted me with a nod. "And McNelly is headed to King's ranch. That's where Andrew will meet him. Captain King's wealthy. He wants it stopped."

"And he pays your rent," Cortina said, then gulped down his wine and threw the empty glass into the brush. Rip held his face still, his eyes focused on Cortina. He stepped back. I stepped back. Cortina looked at Rip's pistol. "You going to shoot me?" he chuckled. "After all these years?"

"Let's just say King can and will do something."

Cortina stared at Rip awhile, then shifted his attention to me. I took a sip of wine. I felt my stomach push a gush of hot air up my throat. I felt as I had so many times when I had to conveniently lie to protect myself. In this instance, at this time, I owed my allegiance and comments to Rip. I reared back and threw my wine glass farther then any of them.

"General Cortina, I know about your petition to Governor Coke to regain your American citizenship. I helped write it, if you recall. But U.S. consul Thomas Wilson is set against you, and he has recommended against you. Whether you are guilty or not, the United States blames you for the thievery. You won't have a chance of renewed citizenship as long as the thievery continues."

"Where do you find all this?" Cortina said. "You are so good at finding facts, but you should see if they are correct."

"You've had several profitable years. I would advise that you stop what you can and deal with Lerdo and Mexico. In return, Rip and I will help you renew your American citizenship."

"Well put," Rip said.

Cortina cocked his head. "Thank you. So now you change my mind. Maybe you better go join this Texas Ranger." He didn't laugh. Cortina smiled at Rip and then looked back at me with smiling eyes that were as scary as Rip's cold stares. "And perhaps you can let me know what he is doing. As you have explained to me, I need all the help I can get."

I wanted to curse them both. I knew why they had left me with the horses. Besides spying for my uncle, for Captain King and the rich merchants of Brownsville, for Captain Kells, I was to spy for Cortina. My uncle had protected me from the war, but he had made me a spy. A spy during the Civil War was beneath a soldier, not really a man. Spies were drunks, traitors, nancies, prostitutes, actors, or thieves. A spy stayed in darkness, took bribes, wasn't acknowledged by decent people. But in learning how to survive as a spy, how to avoid a real fight, and how to find the facts, I had become very useful. "Why, you conniving old men," I said and exchanged stares with both. Then we all forced ourselves to smile, then to laugh.

CHAPTER 4

Catalina Taracón

FTER my meeting with Rip and Cortina, I said a few more good-byes. I walked down the levee along the bend of the river, next to Fort Brown, and crossed, with several bales of cotton, to the Matamoros side. A hack was waiting for me, so I took it rather than the slower, mule-drawn streetcars, and it took me past the square to a small frame house. In the twilight, I walked toward the door. Catalina stepped into the frame of the door lit in gold and yellow. Her white gown was scooped low in front, and thin lace covered her chest. Her hair was swept up on top of her head.

I pulled off my hat, got across the porch in a step, and kissed her. As I pulled away from her, she held my hands in hers, and I looked at the colors dancing on her olive-tinted face. She shook her head, "Poor Andrew. You are losing some more of your hair." I looked up as though trying to see my forehead. "I don't like bald men. I like full, thick hair."

"I'm the one who is here now."

"So you have been. Always here. Always consistent."

I stepped into her small cottage, stuffed and decorated with the mementos of her life as a courtesan.

With a deliberate and courteous manner that showed European training and refinement, she moved to a small table with a bottle of champagne chilling in some chipped ice. Not just anyone could afford ice. Next to the champagne was caviar and little triangles of bread. She pulled the chair out for me. She turned out all the kerosene lanterns to let the candles on the table light her house, and she rubbed my shoulders, then poured me the champagne. Not until after I had eaten some of the caviar did she join me: an aristocrat's treatment, from Catalina.

We finished our glasses of wine. She took my hand and led me to the only other room in the cottage, the bedroom. She slowly made her way through her layers of clothes. I watched as her olive skin caught lost pieces of light coming from the window. Her skin was still smooth, only her face had wrinkles; the sparse light showed the dark hollows, angles, and sags of her face and the one silver streak in her hair. She was a very small woman, not voluptuous as were the women of the time, but small-breasted, buttocks no wider or fuller than a large man's hand. The sprite in her physicality mixed with her deliberate moves made her seem other worldly and exotic. But sometimes she seemed to have a sad, wise knowledge of her fate and mine that scared me.

She had Spanish Creole blood in her, but when the family wealth no longer matched her upbringing and training, she turned her avocation into her vocation. She came to Matamoros probably because of the volatility; one wealthy man was always replacing another. She acquired what she could from the wealthy men. But now, because of her age, she had dropped a level or two in society.

We both played out our fantasy and listened to the forlorn, lonely voices of the night: watchmen, drunks, a few birds. I looked at her face and saw beyond the wrinkles to the lovely young woman I had first met years before in the company of Juan Cortina. I wished I could lavish money and gifts on her. She, as I did, fully appreciated the pleasures of Brownsville and Matamoros. I wasn't sure that I loved her, but I was with her for love. She was with me for something other than love, but something like it, maybe comfort, serenity . . . advice.

She drew circles in my chest with her forefinger, as she did when the pleasure was over, but intimacy and appreciation were left. "So are you going to go through with this silly plan, Andrew?"

"I am. I've decided."

"No, you haven't decided anything. It's been decided for you."

Though she couldn't see my face very well, I smiled to try to show her how much I appreciated the fact that she was concerned for me. "If I can get this McNelly story, be the one to tell it, then I will have achieved some notoriety as a writer. And with notoriety comes some money."

"Andrew, don't be foolish. Stick with what you are good at."

"Evidently, I am."

"Not that. You silly," she said.

"I'm doing what I've always done. I'm spying on everyone for everyone else."

"Who will you be loyal to?"

"You." I kissed her.

She returned the kiss but rolled on her back, not pulling a sheet over her, not at all worried about her nakedness. "What you do is dangerous, so we should watch out for each other." She giggled. "In a way, poor dear Andrew, we have the same profession. We are courtesans. We both earn our way by endearing ourselves to influential men."

I didn't find her comment very funny. "That's not exactly correct. I don't . . ."

"You don't what?"

I didn't answer. I dared not. She scared me. "So what is to become of us?"

We both waited while she decided whether to be angry with me or not. She rolled her head to face me and said with full sincerity. "I can guess what will become of me, but I'm not sure about you."

WHAT indeed was to become of me? It was a question I had pondered. I should have left Brownsville right after the war and followed my few ambitions that survived the war. I should have tried to retrieve my fancied destiny that I had before the war: a safe, civilized, Eastern gentleman. But Addie and John William kept me close to Rip. I would desert armies and causes, but not them. I grew fonder of Rip, and his enemies became mine. I tried to compromise my way to victory, but Rip grabbed the opposition by the ears.

Several years after the war, in 1868, Rip and Jesse Dougherty took over the editorship of the *Brownsville Sentinel*. Then Rip hired me as a reporter. Addie was glad and begged me to watch over Rip. In his own bombastic editorial style, Rip attacked the Reconstruction Republicans so much that the Reconstruction government temporarily suspended his right to vote, then tried to kill him.

We had met one evening in the Miller Hotel, where Rip was to instruct me in the manly game of billiards. In the midst of our game, Sheriff Rudolf Krause and his deputy Cruise Carson came into the billiards room. Rip didn't lift his head from the table, and Krause starting cursing: "You goddamn unreconstructed rebels! The war is over. And you lost. You got to pay for it." As he finished his shot, Rip caught my eye. He never acknowledged Krause. "Just because you own your own goddamn miserable lying newspaper gives you no right to spread your viciousness." I had a hard time keeping my eyes off Krause and Carson and missed most of my shots, but Rip played well and beat me. Krause was a bit smaller than Rip but younger, and as

Rip was hanging his cue, Krause came up behind me, preparing for another verbal lashing. Rip spun around and grabbed Krause's ears. Krause tried to wriggle away from him, but Rip held tight and pulled. Krause let out a yelp, probably feeling his ears tearing from his head. Whether he meant to or reacted out of instinct, Krause slid his hand inside of his coat and pulled out a pistol.

Carson made a step toward the two of them, and I put the handle end of my cue across the front of his face. He fell to his knees. Rip let go of one ear and made a slap at the pistol. The bullet went through the meaty part of Rip's left hand, and Rip let go of Krause to grab his wounded hand. Krause squealed, grabbed both ears, pressed his back against the wall, and slid down it. Rip held up his hand and, uncharacteristically, smiled. He knew it was not a serious wound.

I stood over Carson, who cupped his hands over his bleeding crushed nose and stared up at me with a certain incredulity; then people rushed in and started grabbing and pushing us out. Out in the street, looking at the glare of the kerosene lamp, I noticed Rip. He was actually smiling and holding his bloody hand. "Sometimes, it's almost fun," Rip said. Addie bandaged his hand and blamed me as well as her husband. No one got arrested.

Several months later, Rip got just too sick and worn from another bout with his malaria, and I took over his duties at the *Sentinel.* My job, again, was to know people and find out what I could from them. In short, I excelled, I found my calling. In many ways, a reporter is much like a spy. Perhaps, my reports would become my destiny. I wished that Catalina were a part of my destiny.

CHAPTER 5

Addie

I TOOK one more day of shopping and preparing myself. Rip had volunteered to outfit me for the trip and promised to deliver my essential supplies to me at breakfast. So the morning I left, I bathed in fresh water and lined up my clothes on my bed: tan canvas pants, two white shirts, a string tie, a black wool vest, and a canvas riding jacket. I folded them and put them into a gunnysack. Next, I put in several pencils and a tablet. I laced my ankle-high shoes and wrapped and buttoned leggings around my calves. I wrapped a scarf around my waist, vaquero style, and tied a cotton kerchief around my neck. I left my derby on the cabinet and pulled my new, wide-brimmed, rabbit-fur hat onto my head. I looked, I hope, like a cultured man, even if I was about to start a career shooting Mexicans.

I heard Rip shout my name. I saw him mounted on a small mare, silhouetted in the soft morning light, beard trimmed. He looked reinvigorated, like he was at the head of cavalry, instead of alone on the street in front of my apartment.

Gunnysack at my side, I stepped out onto the wooden sidewalk under the saloon's awning. Rip guided the mare to the sidewalk. He eyed me. "Well, nobody would mistake you for a vaquero. You look, like, like you're an earl out for a hunting trip."

"Thank you. That was the intent. I don't want to be mistaken for a vaquero."

Rip dipped his chin toward the horse. "Now a Comanche boy wouldn't be caught dead on a gentle little mare like this, beneath his dignity. But this creature ought to suit you since you don't particularly like horses."

"She doesn't look very big," I said.

"These don't get too big."

"Is she strong enough?" I stepped closer to the horse. "Wasn't this John William's mare?"

"Yeah, but she's also a Comanche mustang. She can eat anything, survive anywhere, and outrun a bigger, stronger horse. Hell, Iron Jacket outran us Rangers and the U.S. Army on one of these little mares." Rip swung down from the horse. I stepped up to her.

"I'd prefer a more independent horse of my own choosing."

"An independent horse of your own choosing might independence right out from under you." I slipped my foot into the stirrup.

I pulled myself aboard, tied the gunnysack to the horn, and shifted my weight in the crowded saddle. "Up under your leg in a scabbard is a Winchester. Take good care of it. That gun belt on the horn has an 1851 model Navy Colt converted to cartridge in the holster. On the other side, I just looped some string around the trigger guard of one my converted old .44 Dragoon Colts. It's a hell of thing to heft. Be careful with both. There's hardtack, bacon, coffee, and jerky in the saddlebags. A slicker and a blanket are rolled up behind the saddle. You're outfitted like a true diablo Tejano. Short like you are, up on a horse, you look a little like Captain Jack Hays." Somewhere in there, I think he paid me a compliment.

I swung myself out of the saddle and faced Rip. I was short, like Cortina and Jack Hays, and Rip towered over me. He should have been riding to Richard King's ranch to take command of McNelly's troops. "Let's get some breakfast," Rip said.

Rip got up early every morning before his family, dressed in a suit, and took a walk. Then he'd stop for coffee or breakfast with some of the important people of the town, usually right across the street from Public Market Square. We didn't have to tell each other where we'd go.

We walked down Elizabeth, leading the mare behind us, turned over a block to Washington, and got to the square as the peddlers were spreading out their wares on the covered first floor of the market. City workers emptied buckets of water and mopped some of the previous day's stink away. Butchers chopped up slabs of beef. The smell of cilantro mixed with the salty Gulf morning air. I hitched the horse, and we sat at a table outside. A waiter brought us coffee, then eggs with frijoles, peppers, and fresh tortillas. Like Rip, I liked the early mornings in a city. Things were washed down and shutters opened and coffee sipped; the world seemed fresher, held some promise. I should have enjoyed less of the late evening so I could enjoy the mornings more.

I left Rip to himself to enjoy the market and untied and mounted the mare. Rip dipped his head, looked at me with those fierce eyes, and said, "Now Andrew, I know your abilities, so I shouldn't worry about you. I don't need to tell you to be careful. But carry yourself with some dignity. Don't disgrace yourself. And with a company of men, you must be obedient to the man in charge."

"I'll try not to embarrass us."

"Damn it! Sometimes just keep your mouth shut. Think. Don't connive."

He handed me a sealed letter. "I stayed up late last night thinking about that letter. It's a letter of introduction. Show it to McNelly."

"I guess I should say thank you for getting me this chance."

"Don't get lost."

I steered the mare away. She wanted to trot, as though in a hurry, so I let her, and I felt the gunnysack bounce against my leg. Even though I was not used to being on horse, I felt the small of my back catch some of her gait, and my body followed her motion.

I was headed north, but I turned southwest and led the horse to Rip's house. Cleaned for the day, his hair slicked back, John William was already outside pulling on his goat's bridle. "That was supposed to be my horse. Daddy gave him to me," John William said. "But I didn't like him."

I tied the horse up to Rip's fence, opened the gate, and walked in. "John William, I just want to borrow him awhile. And besides, that horse isn't a 'he.' It's a 'her.'"

"Keep her. I like the goat better." He tugged on the goat's bridle, but the goat tugged against him.

"John William, come here for a moment."

The obedient son of Rip Ford let the bridle of his pet go and walked to me. I dropped to a knee so that I was looking up into his face. I took his two shoulders in my hands. "I'm going away, John William. So you won't see me for a while."

"Daddy said that you were going to shoot some villains."

"John, really, really truthfully, I'd rather not shoot anybody. Really, really truthfully, I'd rather be riding your goat than your horse. But I'm doing this for . . . for my job . . . and for your father."

"So don't go. Stay here, then."

"Would you want me to stay?"

"Yes."

"I'm sorry, but I have to go, but I wanted to tell you 'bye." He was too big a boy for hugs and kisses, but I pulled him to me and held him tightly for awhile. As I held him in my arms, I opened my eyes and saw his mother standing on the porch of the house. I kissed him on the side of the cheek.

He wiped at the kiss, "Goodbye, Uncle Andrew."

I let him go back to his goat and walked slowly to Addie. As I got up the steps, she held out her hands, and I took them in mine. Her light brown hair was pulled into a twist at her neck. Her work dress had lace at the collar. Several small veins showed on her neck. "I guess you saw your whore," she said.

"Addie!" I scolded her, and I squeezed her hands, making her squeeze back. She looked quickly about, then wrapped her arms around me to squeeze me some more. The only acknowledgments of our little endearments were John William's quick glance and the creaking wooden slats of the porch.

Addie stepped back from me but still held my hands. She dropped her head to stare at her shoes. "You have this woman, this whore. At least people say that she is a whore."

"Let's just say that I have a friend who in some people's opinion is a whore. In my opinion, she is a very wise lady."

She pulled her head back up to look at my face then stepped back, still holding my hands, and ran her eyes the length of my body. "You look dashing in your costume."

"It's not a costume, Addie."

She patted my cheek. "It is *you*, though, Andrew, so much like you. What have you let them push you into?"

"This is my choice."

"I know that Rip has given you all sorts of advice."

"His voice buzzes around in my head. 'Dignity. Obedience. Don't embarrass the name.'"

"My advice is to use all your cunning, all your devious ways to survive. Don't let them kill you, Andrew. I should never be able to look at Rip if his ways got you killed."

"But would you miss *me*? Pine for *me*?"

She kissed me on the cheek. We looked at each other a moment longer, and I rubbed my cheek as though to push the feel of her lips into my skin.

As I rode away, I looked over my shoulder and saw Addie still standing on the porch and John William riding around the house in his goat wagon.

CHAPTER 6

Brownsville, 1861–1863

They [Captains Richard King and Mifflin Kenedy] attempted to perform services for themselves that should have been performed by the United States government. The citizens of south and west Texas would not have been subjected to such outrages and indignities had the government claiming their allegiance taken measures of redress and retaliation. It might have been that the powers of government remembered the course of Texas during the Civil War and left her to take care of herself in the emergency brought about by the Mexican raiders.

RIP FORD
Rip Ford's Texas, *ed. Stephen B. Oates, 1963*

WHEN the proud Confederacy started that great uncivil war, I was a Southerner stuck at Kenyon College: a northern, Episcopal bastion of a school, where faculty and students professed allegiance to Unitarianism, Abolitionism, or Transcendentalism. I remained in-different to South or North, Democrat or Republican, war or moderation, slavery or abolition. All I wanted to do was finally to pass my Greek and Latin studies and to continue to excel in rhetoric.

My mother, Elizabeth Ford, received correspondence from her brother, the famous Texas hero Rip Ford, that he would keep me as safe from the war as he could if I came to Brownsville, Texas. So I ran from pressured enlistment in the North and the draft in the South, and started my career as a coward.

At the start of the Civil War, Brownsville, at the very southern tip of the Confederacy, right upriver from the mouth of the Rio Grande, seemed far away from the war. Northeastern American or European merchants, Charles Stillman and William Neale most prominently, had settled in Matamoros when Texas was still a Republic because of the easy European trade. They believed in trade, not political causes. In 1861, Brownsville had no more than ten or fifteen slaves, but for Brownsville, not just states' rights but also regional rights and international rights were good for trade, so Brownsville sided with the South.

I'm not sure why Rip, the old lion of the South, had agreed to sponsor me. Maybe he wanted to make up for his sister's disapproval of his divorce from his first wife and subsequent desertion of that family. That disgrace brought him to Texas back in 1835. Maybe helping a fellow deserter, a relative, too, evened the score. Maybe deep down, Rip wanted to spare as many children as he could from the bloodbath that was to become the country's greatest nightmare.

So late in 1861, Rip met me at the Brownsville levee as I stepped off one of Captain King's steamboats. Rip's hair had not yet turned white. His eyes had already assumed his penetrating stare, as though looking through trees or across a great distance for Comanches, Mexicans, bandits, or, now, Yankees. I stuck out my hand, thinking, because of that stare, that he might pull out a tomahawk and hack me into little pieces. But he smiled, showing some warmth from inside of him, and shook my hand.

Following him along the borders of the newly evacuated Fort Brown, down Elizabeth Street past the Gem saloon, I saw the steamboats' smokestacks rising up over the second floors of the buildings; off in the distance I saw the spires from some of the churches and mansions in Matamoros; I heard the chiming of Incarnate Word Cathedral's bell; I walked past the clean, modest home of Charles Stillman, the richest and most powerful citizen; I continued on past the flies and carcasses and vegetables at Market Square and came finally to the western end of town, and beautiful Addie, Rip's new twenty-three-year-old bride.

Addie opened the door of the house that Captain King provided for her husband. Her light brown hair, braided and looped with some attached ribbons, shone like a halo. She held a hand out to me. I took her hand in both of mine and then kissed it. Rip looked surprised, she looked at her husband, then returned her gaze to me. "It will be nice to have a well-mannered, Southern gentleman to entertain."

"Thank you, Mrs. Ford."

"Addie," Rip corrected me.

I looked to her, "And what would you prefer that I call you, Mrs. Ford?"

"Call me Addie, Mr. Nevin."

"Call me Andrew," I said.

With Colonel Ford's help, I became a customs inspector for the Confederacy, meaning that I worked for Captains King and Kenedy and Charles Stillman, the shipping magnates who made Brownsville. I quickly learned that Charles Stillman's and Captain King's boats were not full of *Confederate* cotton bales but *Mexican* cotton bales because their boats flew Mexican flags, not Confederate ones, so that they wouldn't be stopped by the Union blockade out on the Gulf. I learned passable Spanish when the Matamoros customs inspectors explained to me that the Confederacy should not demand such high tariffs on its much-needed supplies from Mexico. I learned more Spanish when Matamoros merchants (many of them Americans and now Confederate sympathizers) explained to me when I shouldn't look while goods crossed the river farther downstream. I learned the exchange rate for dollars and reales, and I learned what my favors should cost in both dollars and reales. I became indispensable.

In the spring of 1862, the Texas Confederacy recalled Rip to San Antonio because he wouldn't turn over his old friend José Carbajal, who was hiding out in Brownsville, to the Matamoros citizens who wanted to hang him. On a day full of drizzle and fog, before Rip stiffly stepped into the mud wagon that would take him to San Antonio, Rip Ford pulled his wide-brimmed hat off his head and let the rainwater run out of its brim, then turned to kiss his pregnant wife good-bye. She offered him her cheek. I knew they had said their real good-bye and had had their real argument the night before.

A pregnant woman was in no condition to be bounced nearly three hundred miles in a stagecoach. She was better off staying with friends and family in her hometown. The mud wagon pulled out and splattered mud on me and Addie. Rip stuck his hatless head out of the window cut into the canvas of the mud wagon and waved. Addie held her head up and chin out, and I held an umbrella above her head. I held my arm out for Addie. She lay her hand on my arm, and I kept the umbrella above her as we made our way through the mud and around the deeper puddles.

Later that day, a messenger knocked on my door (I lived at the time in a small cottage next to a livery stable) and gave me a note from Elihu Smith. With an ornate, looping hand, he scrawled a thank you for helping his daughter in her husband's absence.

Later that year, on an August night thick with humidity and the threat of a rainstorm, I waited with Elihu Smith and his wife in Rip Ford's small parlor while Addie went into labor. In the bedroom with her were two nuns from Incarnate Word. At her first scream, I jumped up from my chair and ran to the door. Elihu was up, too, and took me by both shoulders. "No son, that is nothing to worry about. It's just 'loosening up.'" I looked at Addie's mother, and she smiled. After several more screams, a baby cried, and a nun opened the door. The Smiths and I stepped into the bedroom and saw Addie still sweating, smiling against a pain that only I could see, and holding a cleaned, bundled, wriggling Lula. Both Elihu and I wrote letters to Rip that night. Mrs. Smith slept in the bedroom on the opposite side of the house, and I slept in the parlor that night in case Addie or the child needed help.

Eventually, Uncle Rip, without any rank in the Confederate army and denied a commission by Jefferson Davis himself, became the director of conscription for the state of Texas with his headquarters in San Antonio. One of Rip's first edicts was that those who functioned vitally for the manufacturing and trading in the state be excused from conscription. My uncle's edict made me safe from the Southern draft.

About a month after the birth of his first child and after his edict that made me safe, I walked Addie to a waiting wagon. Rip had hired an old friend to transport his young wife and infant daughter to San Antonio. I held my cheek still while Addie kissed it, then stepped back for her to kiss her mother and father. Her mother could not fight against tears, and so she held her face in her hands as the mud wagon churned up dust; it pulled Addie Ford and her infant daughter to her husband in faraway San Antonio.

MY SPANISH, my abilities, and my finances all improved in Rip's absence. I knew a lot of men and learned a lot of secrets. Before the War was over, with Confederates and Unionists occupying and retreating from Brownsville and with Juaristas and Imperialistas occupying and retreating from Matamoros, with refugees from all the armies crossing and re-crossing the river, I got paid for many secrets.

Late in 1863, General Banks and his Union troops had landed at Brazos Santiago and were advancing toward the town. We looked to General Hamilton Bee to protect us. But first we heard gunshots in Matamoros.

For several years, in the traditional form, General José Cobos hid from political rivals and a firing squad in Brownsville. But with the French now advancing on Matamoros, he recruited a Brownsville army, raided a Brownsville armory, held the town hostage while the

Union troops advanced, and then crossed into Mexico—where he was met by Colonel Juan Cortina. Together, they took Matamoros for the Imperialistas. As the two warriors gathered Juaristas to shoot, Cortina looked at his ally and co-commander and said, "You first," then had him shot. With Cobos dead, Cortina was in charge of Matamoros and Tamaulipas, and he declared himself a Juarista.

As we listened to the shots across the border, General Hamilton Bee, the Confederate defender of Brownsville, got drunk with Henry Miller in Miller's Hotel while his troops loaded a wagon with his personal effects. Then he ordered the burning of Fort Brown, and in his wagon, with his troops behind him, he left us to the Union.

As the Union forces entered town, the out-of-control fire from Fort Brown ignited the cotton bales next to the levee. I was at my station on the levee and tried to organize a bucket brigade. Most of the panicked Brownsville citizens raced west, while the more rational boarded the ferry. But there was gunpowder at the ferry and in Fort Brown. Before it blew up, sending bodies into the river, I too abandoned the bucket brigade and was on the last load of Confederate refugees to cross into Matamoros.

Several days later, a messenger brought me a note from Juan N. Cortina. I walked from a cottage I had found near the river to the town square and then went to City Hall, where Cortina had made his headquarters. A soldier led me to a big door and knocked. We heard a voice from inside, and the door opened. In front of us was a large desk; in front of it was a high-backed, padded chair. The chair swivelled around, and a tall, hawk-nosed American stood up. A smaller man, really a man of about my stature, emerged from behind the desk. Juan Cortina's green eyes immediately smiled when he saw me.

I let my eyes go to the long painting behind him. It was an oil painting of Don Mariano Matamoros, the namesake of Matamoros and one of the heroes of the Mexican War of Independence. The hero's eyes gave a stern command to uphold the Republican ideals responsible for the break from Spain. The painting was a part of the city's pride. Cortina had moved it to his office. Now Don Mariano Matamoros, Juan Cortina, and the representative of the country I had betrayed commanded me with their eyes.

"Andrew, Andrew, Andrew," Cortina said. His green eyes sparkled over his rough and ruddy cheeks. He didn't have on a uniform, but a very expensive and well-tailored suit with an embroidered vest. "Not Mr. Nevin. No. Because I know you already. You are like family. For Rip Ford's family is like my family." I wondered what sort of heroism, what sort of ferocity and cruelty was in this man who had declared war on the United States and who had just put his partner in front of a firing squad.

I tried to say something, but he interrupted. "And this gentleman is Leonard Pierce, U.S. consul here in Matamoros. We've been having a discussion."

The formal Pierce, who reminded me of those fierce-looking, transcendental professors at Kenyon, stuck out his hand, and I shook it and thought that I had perhaps implicated myself into some sort of bargain.

"Please sit," Cortina said. He looked around and, seeing there was no chair for me, brought another high-backed office chair to the front of his desk. Pierce sat, then I sat in the empty chair. I placed my hat in my lap and noticed that the brim was cracked and charred in several places. I needed a new hat.

"Now, now, Andrew, Mr. Pierce and I were discussing the possibilities of cooperation between the Union and the Juárez government." He smiled and tapped his chest with both hands, "Which I represent here in Matamoros. And we choose you to represent the Confederacy." I looked over at Pierce, who kept his head turned away from me. He seemed to be snickering.

"But . . . ," I said, and Cortina held up his hand.

"Your uncle suggested that you might be able to help me."

"Rip?"

His eyes smiled. Pierce cleared his throat as though pushing his snicker into his chest. He said, "Of course on this side of the border, the *United* States of America cannot detain you or prosecute you as a spy or traitor."

"What? Spy? I look at cotton."

"Please, please, Consul. Harsh words. Please," Cortina said.

I glared at the consul until he turned his head away from me. Cortina talked. "Rip Ford has suggested that, like Santos Benavides, his old friend from Laredo, I might cooperate with the *Confederate* States of America, who are opposed to the Imperialistas. He is also willing to ask the Confederacy to make me a citizen in return for my efforts. But Consul Pierce has suggested that the *United* States of America, who are also opposed to the Imperialistas, might be willing to give me a commission in their army and later reinstate my citizenship in this great country."

I looked at Pierce, at Cortina. "Has Rip heard about the second option?"

"No, but now you have. What do you think?"

"I think that I don't want to get shot as a spy." I took a chance and muttered, "or as Cobos got shot."

Cortina cringed, "Oh, Andrew, Andrew. That incident is behind us. Maybe you read my pronunciamiento explaining all that." I looked at Pierce. He cringed. "Consul Pierce helped me with that. I have a little problem with writing." He was, as he remained all his life, illiterate. "Rip tells me that you are a very good writer."

"I am content. I don't think that I need to be involved. . . ."

"I need another pronunciamiento. I need to explain to the people about difficulties I am having with a few jealous rivals."

"I write in English, not Spanish."

"My brother Sabas can translate."

Before I could get another word out, he pulled me out of my chair. "Excuse us," he said to me, not so much to Pierce. With his arm around me, he led me to the door. I glanced over my shoulder at Pierce, who stared after us. Cortina opened the door and led me down the hall. By the stairwell, he checked over both shoulders and abruptly stopped. Head to head, eye to eye, both of us about the same height, we stared. I broke the gaze from his smiling eyes, fearful that he was about to hypnotize me. He spoke again, "I want you to help with my writing, but I want some more help. Private help." He checked over his shoulder. "So of course I should go with the Union. But I can't just walk into Brownsville. People have long memories. I need an envoy. Someone smart, who knows how to, to bargain. Someone to talk to this General Banks."

"Did Rip suggest me? He wouldn't want to see me shot. I'm not so sure about Pierce or you."

"When he was chasing me out of Texas, for protecting my own property . . ."

I dared interrupting him. "You shot up Brownsville. You started a guerrilla war."

He didn't drop his smile. "When your uncle was fighting me, my half-brother, Sabas Cavazos, introduced him to my mother. Rip guaranteed my mother's safety. And promised that she would lose none of her land or her property. I have yet to repay him. Now I can repay him, some. A partial payment. I can protect you."

"Protecting me is sending me to the Union Army?"

"You have my guarantee." He held out his hand, and I shook it. "Rip was right. You are a good one. You are the man I need." Down the hall, Pierce stuck his head out of the door. Cortina gently flexed his fingers to shoo Consul Pierce back inside. Cortina waited, then said, "Now please excuse me. I must get back to my meeting with the United States." He gave me an abrazo, then left me in the hall.

Fearing for my safety no matter what I did, I made it through the Union sentries to meet gruff General Nathaniel Banks. He adamantly refused to give a "bandit greaser" a command in his army, but he promised to send the note on up the ranks. To his credit, he recognized me as a man with valuable insights. He gave me Yankee dollars to send him information about Cortina's forces. In turn, I sent a letter to Rip Ford on a mud wagon headed to Camargo, just up river, then to Laredo, then to San Antonio. In it, I told him what I had observed of the number of Union troops, their supplies, and their positions. I gave the same information to Cortina. The Confederacy couldn't pay anything, but Cortina did.

Throughout the winter and early spring, I hunched down in the streets of Matamoros and avoided bullets and detection. All of this would come to an end. For up in San Antonio, with a special commission from the state, after studying my notes, Rip Ford was organizing and training the Rio Grande Expeditionary Force. Rip and his band of former Unionists, boys, and graybeards were going to rescue Brownsville from the Yankees and again make it safe for decent merchants and their profits.

CHAPTER 7

Addie Ford, 1864–1866

I have delayed addressing you officially, as the military representative of the Confederate States upon the lower Rio Grande, until I could announce that the forces of Mr. Lincoln's government had retired from the mainland. They are confined to Brazos Island. . . .

I have to thank you and your government for many acts of kindness to our citizens while enjoying the security and protection of your flag, and your laws. Those generous acts will not be forgotten by us, and should turn of events cause any of your countrymen to visit our shores we should be ungrateful not to reciprocate the kindly acts of our hospitable neighbors.

Letter from **COLONEL RIP FORD CSA,** *to*
GENERAL JUAN N. CORTINA,
August 1864

ADDIE had grown lonely being away from her family, and so in March of 1864, just as Rip gathered his Rio Grande Expeditionary Force and left San Antonio, Addie and baby Lula joined Manuel Treviño and his wife in a slow ambulance journey from San Antonio to Eagle Pass. They crossed the border, and several armed men met them and escorted them to Matamoros. Juan Cortina had sent the escort.

Sabas Cavazos, Cortina's ever-attendant half-brother, saw to finding Addie a house. When I went to visit, Addie's back was to me as she hung clothes out to dry. She turned to see me, her hair in braided loops. She wore a homespun blouse and skirt and looked somehow larger. Her ready smile and the knit of her brows greeted me as though she only dimly remembered me, but then she ran toward me and wrapped her arms around me. She stepped away from me while I drank her in with my gaze.

"Andrew! You're my second visitor. Juan Cortina himself has come by, and he has offered me every assistance."

"I guess he is a gentleman after all. And I guess he has repaid his debt."

"Oh, he's a perfect gentleman. What debt?"

"Rip helped his mother. Now Cortina has helped you." I looked over her shoulder to see Lula toddle on the house's porch. "She's just beginning to walk." Lula fell to her behind, and our greeting was interrupted as Addie raced to her crying daughter. I followed her to the porch, and as she scooped up her daughter, she looked at me, "Andrew, I'm with my second child."

"I guess old Rip is ecstatic." Addie just hung her head.

So, along with Manuel Treviño and his family and Sabas Cavazos, I was a frequent visitor. Once, as I walked to her porch, the door opened and Sabas left. I saw Addie's face over his shoulder. He then patted my shoulder. "It's been taken care of," he said.

"What has?"

"She will see her mother in Brownsville."

He left me, and Addie approached me, took both my hands in her own, and then kissed my cheek, "Juan Cortina has fixed it. When I first got here, my sister Lu said that Union men were asking about me. And she was sure that they planned to make me a prisoner. So I dared not cross to see my mother."

"And you didn't tell me? I could have done something. I could have spoken to someone."

"Juan Cortina has interceded for me, a perfect gentleman. He has persuaded the Yankee commander to allow me a visit. Mr. Cortina will even accompany me if need be."

Cortina did accompany Addie. That perfect gentleman prepared everything: rented a carriage, secured a pass from the Union troops, and found a woman to tend to Lula. When Cortina's dark green and gold gilded carriage pulled up to Addie's Matamoros house, Cortina was out of the carriage and hugging Addie and me. He helped Addie, who was just beginning to show from her new child, into the carriage. Then, as I boarded, I saw for the first time the beautifully sculpted face, the shining black hair, and the pleasing olive skin of Catalina Taracón, Cortina's newest mistress.

Addie and I were on the border between two countries and two wars, and our guests were an outlaw general and a courtesan, but the company and conversation of the two refined people with lineage back to European gentility made the delicious afternoon all the more pleasant. We drove through Brownsville in Cortina's carriage and dropped Addie off at Elihu Smith's house. Then, Catalina, Cortina, and I drove to the square for coffee and liquor, and in mid-afternoon we retrieved Addie.

On our trip back to Matamoros, Cortina had his driver take us down a deserted road that ran east, along the river. At a certain point, under cottonwoods and oaks, Cortina's driver spread out several blankets and set up two folding cavalry officer's chairs. Catalina and Addie were able to fit their bustles, petticoats, and skirts over the chairs, and Juan and I sat at their feet while the driver brought wine, fruit, and pan de dulce.

The shade, mixed with the salt-filled Gulf breeze, cooled then slightly chilled us. The same breeze rustled the tree limbs above us. Several feet away, the river lapped at stones and brush. Frogs croaked. The two wars going on around us seemed far away and long ago. On either side of me was an example of feminine beauty. Catalina was dark, petite, olive-skinned. Her conversations showed an intellect and intelligence approaching wisdom. Addie was light, crystalline almost. Her smile, the flutter of her eyes, her politeness showed loyalty, care, and deep humanity. Juan, like me, must have felt the world stand still while we absorbed the afternoon. And Juan, like me, must have thought that he would have given up all that he had for a woman with just some of the beauty of one of these two. Had either Juan or I been poets, the world would have had more poems in praise of women.

After Cortina left Addie and me at her house to return to a night with his mistress, I walked Addie to her door, and she invited me inside. "Maybe, I shouldn't," I said. "Without Rip around, suspicions, you know."

"Damn suspicions. This is Mexico." She stepped to one side and held the door open for me. After I came in, she checked on the sleeping Lula and dismissed Cortina's maid. While I sat at her table, in the light of a single lamp, Addie removed her light jacket and unpinned her hat. Then she went into her kitchen and motioned for me to follow. She reached into a cabinet and pulled out a bottle of whiskey. She sat two small glasses at either side of the kitchen table. Then she filled each glass with whiskey.

"I feel cramps from my baby. My mother told me that a sip of whiskey is good for the cramps and for the child." We sat behind the drinks, and we sipped the whiskey. The light from the one kerosene lamp danced on Addie's pretty face, but her eyes were sad. "They are such charming people. I am nearly jealous. But a gentleman does not give in to infidelity or debauchery with prostitutes."

"This is a wild land and violent times," I said in defense of Cortina. "And Mrs. Taracón seems every bit the lady."

"Outwardly, yes."

"I meant inwardly."

"Rip, though, Rip is a good man. A good man, a hero. As far as I know, no, since I know him, I am sure that he has risen above any temptation."

I felt as though she intended to compare me to Rip and had found me wanting, so I said, "Rip has no money because he's spent all his time being a hero. And so he doesn't treat you as you deserve." I saw a tear splatter on the table between us.

"He was a hero. A girl my age could do much worse."

"Or much better."

"I'm a lucky woman." Her hand trembled slightly, and I felt like reaching for it. "He's a good man and a gentleman." She couldn't get out the words. I found my hand resting on the table and scooting toward hers. "But first he left for San Antonio, and I had my child alone. Now I will have my next child alone." By the lamplight, I saw more splatters of tears on the table.

"I'll be here," I said without looking at her.

"As you were with Lula."

I scooted my hand toward her, and she took my hand. "I'm just so lonely, and this war and his absence."

"I know what you mean."

She lifted her eyes to stare at me. "A woman can never say what she means." Her grip tightened on my hand. I didn't dare to ask what she meant. "I feel deserted. I feel. . . . "

I comforted her that night. In all my years of seeking comfort from olive-skinned women, I found far more comfort from comforting Addie Ford.

AFTER several battles across the southern tip of Texas, a malaria-stricken, weary Rip Ford led the young boys and old men of the Rio Grande Expeditionary Force to Brownsville on July 30, 1864, and the Union troops retreated back to Brazos Island. In a hard campaign that became a game of cat and mouse, Ford kept his untrained irregulars together and kept himself on his horse through his reputation and his will. He shivered and grew so weak that, if he could lift a pen to write Addie, he couldn't keep it from shaking. Once in Brownsville, having achieved his aim, the liberation of the dying South's backdoor to the world, Ford fell off his horse in front of his men.

Word reached Addie even before we knew that the Union forces had left. Round and clumsy from her unborn child, Addie found me and told me that with or without me she was going to her sick husband. I escorted her across the ferry, then over to Fort Brown. I shouted at Confederate troops trying to detain us, asked them if they knew who this poor woman was. Until finally, I got her to Rip's cot in a patched officer's quarters in the charred fort.

Rip could barely lift his head, but he pushed himself up on an elbow and fixed us with that stern, commanding stare. Then he smiled at his wife and his next child. Addie ran to him and wrapped her arms around him and kissed him all over. I walked back to the ferry, then crossed back to Matamoros and waited for the conquering heroes to put things in order before I went back to Brownsville.

When Addie gave birth to a daughter, named for her, she did so in her father's Brownsville house. Elihu, his wife, Lu, Lula, and I waited while a nun from Incarnate Word ministered to her. Rip was still sick, and everyone thought it safer to keep him separated from the new child.

By May of 1865, everyone knew that the war was over; there were rumors, but not confirmation of Appomattox. Yet Union Commander Colonel Theodore H. Barrett, out on Brazos Island, wanted to fight. If Barrett could take Brownsville, the confiscated cotton bales would be *his*. So Barrett sent his colored infantry upriver. Rip Ford mustered his army. Glad at one more chance to shoot Unionists, and this time Negroes, and essentially defending the cotton bales and profits of Kenedy, King, and Stillman, Rip's forces surprised the Yankees at Palmito Ranch. It was Rip's greatest victory, the last battle of the Civil War, taking place three weeks after the war ended. And the cotton was safe.

The war was over, and Addie thought that she would finally have a family. But Rip grew restless. Then that nefarious old friend of his, José Carbajal, showed up and started whispering in Rip's ear about another filibuster. Something in their nature or blood or in the soil and water of Texas made those old Texians covet Mexico. Rip just couldn't resist some intrigue to become the next Cortéz and conquer at least a piece of Mexico. With the American states reunited but distrustful, and with shots still being fired between Juaristas and Imperialistas right across the river, Rip, Carbajal, General Lew Wallace, and several other prominent Americans and Mexicans found another opportunity to grab Mexican soil. Mexico itself, with its Catholicism and easy morals, may have appealed to the likes of old Rip. Maybe what made Texans covet Mexico was the same thing that attracted me to—no, made me love—Catalina Taracón. I can't fully explain it.

In September of 1866, while Rip was in the midst of his last campaign, on a night full of thunder and lightning—hurricane weather—Addie knocked on the door of my apartment. I opened the door to see that the wind had gotten into Addie's light-brown hair and had pulled it from the rolled buns she wore on the sides of her head. She had on a plain skirt, a Mexican blouse, and no jacket—inappropriate dress for the first lady of Brownsville. As I held the door open, we looked down the street in both directions. I let her in, embarrassed by the stable smells that seeped into my apartment. "Has anyone seen you?" I asked as she stepped in.

"No, no. No one knows. No one is on the streets."

I lit two lamps, and we sat, once again, at opposite ends of a table while we stared at each other in the lamp and lightning light. Addie had not known a permanent home in her five years of marriage. She had seen more of me than her husband. She had had no time to make lady friends. I asked, "Where are the girls?"

"They are with their grandparents. They will spend the night."

The thunder became an offbeat metronome. "Addie," I finally said. "You've come to tell me something."

"Oh Andrew, Andrew, after the battle at Palmito, I thought that it would all be over. And then finally, finally we would come back to our place, our home, to Brownsville, and now this damned scheme." Lightning lit up her face, showing wrinkles that should not be under her eyes and across her brows. "Damn, damn them all. Sabas, Cortina, Wallace, King. And whoever else." She hung her head. "No, no, I don't mean that. I want no one hurt or damned."

This time with no hesitation, I reached across the table to take her hand. "If he can survive this . . ." A crash of thunder and her look stopped me. "This will be it for him. I'm sure," I said.

"No, he'll never quit. Maybe he'll stop fighting, but he'll always have some mission. He will always owe the state of Texas something." The smile in the corner of her mouth gave her a wise look that I'd not yet seen on her face. I had to lean forward to get a better view of her face. Her eyes blinked, and then in a flash of lightning my eyes caught hers. As though it was too much effort to keep smiling, the corner of her mouth dropped. And then her eyes dropped from mine. I squeezed her hand. Then she said what was really on her mind. "Oh

Andrew, I don't want to be with him. I want to leave him, but I don't know how."

My hand started to shake and thus shook her hand. We both looked at our trembling hands, and I swallowed my fear and my shame. Through will and want, I stood and pulled her to me and wrapped my arms around her and finally felt her body pressed into mine. "Oh, Andrew," Addie said, now through a sob. "What am I saying? What am I feeling?"

I wiped at her cheek with my hand and felt her tears. With the same hand, wet with her tears, I wiped tears from my cheek. "I ran away from this war and wound up in the midst of it. I survived. I can run away again, and I will survive again. Come with me. Get your children and come with me." She lifted her head to look up at me. "We will go East. New York or Philadelphia, away from the South and from Texas."

Lightning lit her face fully for me, showing the stark, panicked look in her eyes, then the soft light of the candles erased the panic. "You would do that for me? You would take my children?"

"Yes, yes. You are the only cause I've had during this silly damned war."

"But my children?"

"Our children."

"I'll pack them. I'll go."

The force of the moment and our conviction pulled our faces close, and then we kissed.

I took her hand. She stood back from me. Another flash of lightning let us look at each other for just a moment. In that flash we made the decision. I led her by the hand to my bed.

She left my apartment shortly before daybreak. I told her to get what she could in order and to bring the girls to my house that afternoon. And even though we had made promises throughout the night, both of us checked down the still dark streets to see if anyone saw. Addie hurried home so that the sun wouldn't catch her in the streets, and I spent the morning making arrangements for a discreet acquaintance to sneak us on to a steamship that would take us to a Mexican ship anchored off Bagdad. I waited well into the night for my new family to come to me. The next morning, a messenger brought me a note. "Please, forgive me. I can't. Daylight has changed my mind." Addie wrote and signed her name.

On a November evening in 1866, with Addie craddling little Addie and Rip calming Lula, we listened to the fighting in Matamoros. We all knew that the old warrior had retired from his dreams of conquering Mexico for the glory of Texas, of the Confederacy, or of the United States. In the dark, with a few surviving mosquitos buzzing around us, balancing her child in one arm, Addie reached out for Rip with the other. She told him that she felt that she was again carrying a child.

Rip Ford wasn't present at either of his daughters' births, but he was present at my son's birth. The good nuns from Incarnate Word brought the newborn to him instead of me. I was in the newly redesigned Gem, a glorious bar, serving the society of Reconstruction Brownsville.

I should have left the area that evening, eight and a half years before my journey to document the exploits of L. H. McNelly. Addie, Catalina, and I had helped each other suffer through history. So far, John William had remained free of history. I hoped to see that he remained so. So I stayed, and now, I was on my way to join another firebrand.

PART TWO

Ranger and Traitor

CHAPTER 8

The King Ranch, May 1875

I RODE north from Brownsville, on the old Taylor road, to intercept McNelly at the King Ranch. A horse is a dumb creature. Like a dog, he will come up to you and sniff at you, but unlike a dog, or even a goat, he will show no pleasure in your company. I had no patience for them; I didn't care if the nervous, distrustful things gained confidence in me or not. A buggy ride was far more enjoyable than a trot on a horse. The rhythm of riding while a horse lopes is not natural for the human body. We aren't meant to bounce in a saddle and make waves in our spines from shoulder to rump. No matter how skilled, a horseman still must ache. So my body was tortured by my two full days of riding.

I congratulated myself on having the good sense to wear shoes and leggings instead the more fashionable boots. Boots' main purpose is to keep a rider's foot planted securely in a stirrup. But everyone has to dismount sometime, and then the problem with boots becomes obvious. Besides the high, sloping heels, boots have this steel shank embedded in the sole and running the length of the instep. So, as you stand, you rock from side to side. I liked to stay planted firmly on the ground, so I wore my English lace-up shoes. If bootmakers could devise a wider shank for just a little security, I might try a pair of boots.

I rode through the birthplace of the American cattle industry. Here, the wild cattle were used as barter, stock, and investments. Everyone owned cattle. Banks gave loans based on cattle and land. So Juan Cortina was endangering the economy of an entire industry. As I headed north, I could see the sandy stretches of marsh grass to my right; to my left, the sand gave way to firmer clay and higher, richer grass, the reason for this being cattle country. Legend has it that, when

Texas cattle on the trail north got separated from the herd, if they survived, they would return to this grassland, the memory of the taste of this sweet, lush grass pushing them on and guiding them.

In places, the grassland became marshes. In spots, thick motts of oak, brush, mesquite, and prickly pear became islands of tangled thorns and limbs. This time of year, I could feel summer coming. The grass was no longer green. Pale, golden stalks circled in the breeze, looking like wheels rolling across the prairie.

But the breeze that blew the grass also brought rain, just to make me more miserable. In the blowing spray of rain, I was afraid that I would fall out of the saddle, so I dismounted and led my horse. I put on my waxed slicker, and I put my blanket over my head. My mare pushed me with her nose as though she wanted the blanket or wanted me to hurry and find her a dry spot. I sloshed until the sunset, and then I pulled my mare up under the limbs of an oak.

My horse and I both bolted as cows, trying to stay dry, came running out of the brush. I caught some breath and pulled off my saddle and unrolled my blanket. As I got on my knees, I heard a rattle. Very slowly, I turned to my left and reached for the Navy Colt with my right hand. Surprisingly, I actually shot the rattler, and then another one, and then an armadillo that ran out of the brush toward me. All these creatures had gathered under these trees, along with my horse and me, to escape the rain. They had felt themselves safe and a little dry, and here I was blasting them with my revolver.

With my mare haltered and hobbled, I sat down, slowly, feeling the ground for more burrowing or crawling creatures, to a dinner of hardtack and cold bacon. Wet, aching, first hot, now cold, I knew that this sort of life was partially why I had run away from the Civil War. Part of being a civilized man was being a man accustomed to comfort and to walking, not riding and sleeping in the field.

After a cold, miserable night, with little sleep for me or my mare, I woke in a fog that softened the rough edges of the oaks, mesquite, chaparral, and cacti that surrounded me. After a breakfast of strong coffee and hardtack, I tried to make up for lost time as I gingerly pressed my crotch into the saddle. I somehow rode for eight hours.

Along the way, I passed a Mexican hanging in a tree. Buzzards had already gotten to his eyes and genitals. Whoever had hanged him meant for him to dangle as warning. The *Brownsville Sentinel* and the *Galveston News* carried a story a week about hanged bandits found in this strip of prairie between the Nueces and Rio Grande. And since the Nuecestown raid, in which some bandits killed a store owner and his wife, roving posses of thugs were shooting and hanging Mexicans and burning their houses.

I had seen the mutilated torso of the young schoolteacher that bandits had hacked up. I had seen the two Americans that Cortina had caught spying and hanged across the river in full view of Brownsville. I had seen enough bodies, so I pushed my mare past the corpse without cutting it down. Let the buzzards have him, I reasoned. Besides, I didn't think that I could have tolerated the stench.

Several hours after passing the hanging corpse, I began looking for the tall tower that Captain King had built as a lookout for bandits. From this flat prairie, a rider could see that tower miles before he got to it. And King's men could see the approach of bandits or Indians well before they got close to the ranch house.

Anyone of any importance who was headed south to Brownsville or north to Corpus Christi stopped at Captain Richard King's Santa Gertrudis Ranch. It wasn't so much a ranch but a fortress and town of about a hundred people. Captain King had been hit hardest by the bandits, many of whom blamed him for stealing their lands. What he actually did was buy the land. He kept a team of lawyers busy and wealthy settling claims. Rumor had it that he bought several tracts three and four times. He had bought so much land that he didn't really know how many cows he had. So lately, he was determined to stretch fences around all his property and make sure that the cows on it remained his.

Soon, I spotted Captain King's watchtower, which looked, to me, like a church steeple. As I rode into Captain King's compound, Kineños, as King's vaqueros were starting to call themselves, turned from their duties to eye me. I nodded and got closer to the great ranch house that looked like a lost, eccentric, Southern plantation house. It was surrounded by barns, stables, and vaqueros' houses. And like a park, King's compound was surrounded by a tamed grass and the shade from dozens of oak, mesquite, huisache, and hackberry trees.

As I rode up to the house, Captain King himself, one pant leg stuffed into a boot, one pant leg over the shank of the boot, came out of the house and down the steps. I recognized the squat, limping figure with the mop of unruly black hair from the times when he'd walk down Elizabeth Street. Rumors also circulated about his limp: caught his leg in an anchor chain during his steamboating days or caught a bullet in it trying to outrun bandits.

I don't know why he bothered with a tie, for his thick, black chin-beard covered it, and as rich as he was, he ought to have gotten a better wardrobe. His trousers didn't match his frayed jacket. His face was almost a square, and as he had gotten older and broader, his face had flattened out. Short, muscular, strong, he could still whip a man with his fists. The man loved fights. "How do you do, Captain King?" I said.

He tilted his head. His bulk and his flat face gave him the features of an overgrown dwarf. "You look familiar," he said.

"Andrew Nevin." He tilted his head. I swung off my horse, and I saw his fists double up. "Colonel Ford's nephew. Reporter for the *Sentinel.*" He nodded approval and unclenched his fists. "During the war, you sent me a letter through my Uncle . . . ," I began. He looked at me for a moment. "In all modesty . . ."

"Modesty takes up too much time. As it has done already. What was in the letter I wrote you? Did I cuss you?"

"You thanked me." He motioned with his hand for me to continue and said, "For what?"

"For watching your property in Matamoros when the Union took Brownsville."

"Well, thank you again, Mr. Nevin." Captain King himself reached for my mare's reins. He called, and from out of nowhere a servant or stableboy ran up and led my mare away.

"Your horse will need some feed," Captain King said as Henrietta King emerged from the house. She too had grown larger, and as she walked to her husband, I could see the seams of her gown fighting against her growing bulk. To the prim, Presbyterian, still faintly Puritan Mrs. King, buying new clothes was vanity. "Why Mrs. King," I said. "How are you and the girls doing?"

"You remember this man?" King asked.

Henrietta walked to her husband and stood beside him. "Why, Andrew Nevin, I remember you. How is your uncle?"

"Grateful," I said.

Henrietta smiled at me. "Very good answer."

"This state owes that man," King said.

"Do you think that my husband and the state have compensated Mr. Ford well enough?" Henrietta asked.

"Your husband certainly has."

"My, my, Andrew. Tomorrow you will join us for dinner. We will be entertaining Captain L. H. McNelly." With her command and her invitation given, Henrietta turned her back to us, lifted her chin, and swayed back into her house, her old, unfashionable, tight dress threatening to explode off her.

When she got out of earshot, King turned to me, "Goddamn women. I'm surrounded by goddamn women. My daughters are home from that overpriced finishing school, college, high school, whatever it is. It's like being in a henhouse."

"It must be nice to have the family in."

"It's truly fun to buy the play-pretties for girls," he said. "Even though Etta objects, my girls will want for nothing. My boys are gonna learn to be tough with the times, gonna learn to run this place and make it profit, but my girls are never going to know tough times."

Thus I had gained the approval of the Kings. But I was not yet at the same social level as Rip Ford or Juan Cortina or Lee H. McNelly, for I didn't sleep in the huge ranch house, but in a bunkhouse. For dinner, I wasn't invited into the ranch house, but dined with King's vaqueros, the Kineños. They stomped into the bunkhouse with their big Spanish spurs jingling. They smelled of cattle and sweat, just as I smelled of the road. In amongst us, regulated to their own lower social levels, were Hiram Jr., Bland, and Willie Chamberlain, Henrietta's younger half-brothers.

I sat with the Chamberlain boys and talked about Brownsville, which they vaguely remembered, and Philadelphia, which they missed. When Hiram Chamberlain died, his widow took her youngest two children back with her to the proper Presbyterian East. By that time, Henrietta had married Captain King and grown wealthy. But the older boys had no work back in their prosperous, refined East, so Captain King hired them on too.

Henrietta, the daughter of Brownsville Presbyterian minister Hiram Chamberlain, had turned the Santa Gertrudis Ranch into a resort, a haven from all the thievery and killing going on in the area. It was sparse but civil. Captain King liked to spend his money, but Henrietta's Presbyterian ban on vanity and foolish expenses kept the decorations and extravagance to a minimum. After King gave her diamond earrings, she painted over the diamonds with black enamel so as not to be ostentatious. But like her Puritan forebears, she had good business sense. For as she would prove when Captain King died, she was as adept at management and investing as he was. She and Captain King's lawyer, Richard Kleberg, would see the ranch prosper even more after Captain King died.

* * *

MCNELLY arrived riding in front of about forty boys. Some rode plow-horses, others small mustangs, and some rode creatures that seemed barely able to bear the weight of their riders. As they dismounted, stretched, and tried to walk, I noticed that they, too, were unaccustomed to being in the saddle. A few squinted at everything with shifting eyes, as though wary of an adventure on this side of the law. Most had mud splattered all over them. One rather tall, muscular one had a patch sewn into the back of his britches, and he wore a hat with a brim that had lost all its rigidity and just drooped all around his head. When he shoved his hat to the back of his head, I saw that he was just a large boy.

I spotted a figure who I assumed must have been McNelly. He was tall and thin. Either the wind or his own deliberate folding and pushing had pressed the brim of his hat up to the crown. He had a large, silk bandana around his neck. He carried himself with confidence and authority and had a dashing, heroic look. So I moved toward him. But a small man, dressed like me in canvas pants, jacket, and leggings, stepped from the crowd and gave an order to the man I had assumed was McNelly. The slight man, who barely seemed able to cast a shadow, stepped up to the porch and offered his hand to Captain King.

King enthusiastically shook the little man's hand and waved at the other Rangers. The tall man stepped up on the porch and shouted some orders. The Rangers looked around, country boys in the city, trying to figure out where they were to go and what they were to do. A while later, an ambulance, driven by a middle-aged man, pulled by four mules, pulled into the compound.

That night, while the Rangers ate in the mess hall, McNelly and I were to eat at the Kings' table and then attend a piano recital. I had found a tub and a pump, so I had a bath and tried my best to dress for dinner. Plain black will give most outfits some elegance. So I put on my black vest over my white shirt after I had smoothed a few of the wrinkles out.

Henrietta King met me at the front door, her blackened diamond earrings adding to her dull but tough Presbyterian demeanor. She smiled and turned her back to me to guide me to the kitchen. "Mrs. King, pardon me," I said. "But I'm a reporter. I'd love to see what you've done with your mansion." She smiled and raised her hand to a her throat. "Please return to your guests. I'll show myself around, and I'll find your dining room."

She looked around for Captain King's approval, as though his spirit would be there in the room. Then she said, "Well, I'm sure that will be fine, but please, dinner is about to be served."

I showed myself around the great room, filled with the stuffed heads of wolves, panthers, bulls, deer, and bobcats. All, no doubt, Captain King's own kills. And because of the rumors south of the border, I half suspected to see the mounted head of a Mexican, maybe with a rope still around his neck.

The furniture was utilitarian and reflected the self-sufficiency of the rancho. Most all was tanned leather from King's own beeves. The candles, too, were probably made from beef tallow. And the stuffing of the sofas and divans looked like untreated wool from King's stock.

I wandered into his armory room, not quite as big as his great room, but lined with racks of vertically stacked rifles. I saw rows of Winchesters, boxes stacked on boxes of cartridges. More prominently displayed were old Sharps, Springfield muskets, and shotguns, King's collectibles. I couldn't even begin to count the revolvers.

I found myself in a library. But rather than books, I was surrounded by ledgers, charts, maps, statements, deeds, and timetables. King could trace everything on his ranch. He was meticulous with his numbers. The only real book was an almanac. As I turned my back to the accounting room and headed back through his trophy room, I happened upon a man traipsing proudly through the great room.

"And who might you be?" he asked. His mouth seemed full and his jaws tight from his thick Irish brogue.

"A dinner guest," I said.

"That way," he pointed.

"And who might you be?" I asked.

The man smiled and held his chin up. "I steamboated with the Captain. Been his mate since the old days. And now he keeps me around to cuff me onst in awhile."

"Cuff?"

"Captain likes his playful little fisticuffs. And I'm old enough so as to not do him much harm, and he can't do me much harm. So when he's upset and bothered, me and him have a go at each other."

"He pays you for this?"

"Right handsomely," he said. "You better find your place at the table. The Captain, he don't like stragglers."

Dinner was a quiet, orderly affair, with our attention turned to praying (Mrs. King did the praying) and then eating. After dinner, we adjourned to a parlor, and I sat in a proper but under-stuffed chair while the older daughter, Nettie, played the piano, and when either of the younger daughters, Ella and Alice, heard a song either knew, they would both try to sing along. As the evening wore on, we tired of "I Dream of Jeanie" and "My Old Kentucky Home" and were glad that Nettie had turned her attention to waltzes. Ella scowled at her sister for not being able to display her passable vocal talents. All three girls tried to display their finishing school skills, hoping to attract a suitable husband. As far as I could tell, there were no suitable husbands nearby. Within this outpost of civilization, with daughters wanting to entertain, the closest Mrs. King could find to refined men were McNelly and me.

Certainly, neither girl could have been interested in Captain McNelly. He was the smallest man in the room, not just short, but slight and skinny. Like me, he wore a black vest, and had correctly made the knot in his tie and fluffed out the bows. He in no way looked sophisticated. His mouth, or what you could see of it when he brushed his beard to the side, seemed to pucker as though he had just sucked a lemon. His curly dark hair was brushed off his forehead in waves; his thick goatee was fluffed. I could see his thin lips and saw him try to smile, not because he enjoyed anything, but because he wanted to be polite. His dark eyes, unlike his mouth, played no games; they showed his boredom. He would not look away; he would not avert his gaze when Netta stumbled over a melody. Though Captain King had served all of us bourbon and offered cool well water and a slice of lemon to go with our liquor, McNelly held a glass of buttermilk. This timid man, whom everyone said looked like a quiet Methodist minister, not a Baptist pounding on his pulpit and scaring us with damnation, was going to confront the thousands of Mexican raiders and shut them down.

Richard King's thick chest and biceps bulged against the cloth of his badly tailored jacket. Trying to be polite, but having no idea how to act at his daughters' recital, he nodded his head in time with their music. The dignified Mrs. King tapped her folded fan on her knee in time with her husband's nodding head.

After a bit more music, the plump but comely Caroline came into the room. Captain King's daughters did well with what natural beauty they had, but couldn't hide their plainness, and their growing mother revealed their physical fates to them. I myself was more accustomed to women with more and a different beauty. An alcalde's or caudillo's daughter, a Frenchman's mistress, or even the discriminating whore made their appearance their business. Most of the rough Anglos who marched out of the woods of Tennessee and Kentucky to come to Texas had no time for beauty; they wanted breeding women, not passionate women. Their wives reflected their attitudes. But this young Caroline, a niece of Mrs. King, whose father had seen to her better breeding, whisked into the room in her kitchen skirt and low-cut blouse and shamed the King girls in their white formals with pink and blue ribbons. She had just gotten through serving McNelly's men a dinner of beef stew in one of the bunkhouse kitchens.

I did what a courteous, educated, "finished" man should do. I rose, I bowed, and then, as a European man would do, I placed my arm around her, without asking, and waltzed inside the circle created by the chairs surrounding the piano. We whirled, constantly circling, as was the fashion then, not the stiff, squared movements in back-woods dances. Caroline, delighted, giggled. "Why, thank you, Mr. Nevin."

"No 'Mister,' just Andrew," I said, and she curtsied. I dropped my head in half of a bow, and when I raised my head, I saw two faces with their noses touching the glass of Captain King's window. One head, then the other, dropped, as I smiled. One had on a hat with a drooping brim that hid his face.

"Andrew, Andrew, Andrew," Mrs. King said as she clapped. "Your abilities amaze me. Just what can't you do?"

"Ah, Etta," Captain King said. "Why don't you show him what you can do? I remember when you could twist around in your dancing gowns like a whirlwind in an empty sack."

Henrietta lifted her eyebrows to command her husband to be still. I looked at her daughters, "I'll try to do anything that a pretty young lady requests. Perhaps one of you would like a short waltz."

The sisters giggled and dropped their eyes and then their heads, as they had been trained to do, then I heard a chair and a voice squeak. "Excuse me, Mr. and Mrs. King. I do appreciate your cordiality, but I hope for an early start," McNelly said, and without waiting, stepped across the room.

"But Captain McNelly, please, let me have someone show you to your room," Captain King said as he got up from his chair.

McNelly pulled at his goatee and said, "I'll sleep with my men."

"But Captain . . ."

But before he could finish, McNelly said, "They're a new bunch. I want them to think I'm around."

He said it like he meant it, like it was a command. But Captain King was just as used to giving orders. "Please, please, we have a room. I find that men respect a leader who represents their interests to other leaders. I think that your men would have more confidence in you if you were sleeping in my house."

McNelly dropped his eyes, but immediately raised them and nodded, "Tonight."

"Dear," Captain King said and motioned toward his wife. "Show Captain McNelly to his room."

She rose amidst a flurry of ruffling and waving bows and ribbons. "Oh, Mr. McNelly, I just can't say how proud we are."

I glanced at King, who jerked his head toward McNelly, then I bowed to the girls and said quickly, "Excuse me, ladies." They looked genuinely disappointed.

I followed Mrs. King and McNelly out the door of the parlor and down a long hall. McNelly noticed me, but let Mrs. King tell him how proud she was to have the savior of Texas in her own home.

"Excuse me, just a word, Captain McNelly," I said, and stepped up with my hand extended. McNelly reluctantly shook my hand. There was nothing to the hand but bone.

"Oh, men's business bores me," Mrs. King said and backed away from us, patting me on the back. As she walked away from us, down the hall, she nodded at me to wish me good luck.

"My uncle says that you have a taste for cigars," I said. I reached into my vest pocket and pulled out both a cigar and my folded introduction from old Rip.

McNelly stroked at his bushy goatee, reached for my introduction with one hand and the cigar with the other. He looked as though he were about to smell first one then the other. I let him unfold and read the letter. "I've met Colonel Ford." He deliberately folded the letter and handed it back to me, but he stared at the cigar.

He turned away from me to pull at his door, but I put my hand against the door as he turned the knob. I said, "I don't want to be just 'another man.'"

"The letter says nothing about your military experience. I know my officers personally."

"I'm a reporter, the *Brownsville Sentinel*, a good Democratic newspaper."

"The newspaper your uncle started," McNelly said, and the sides of his goatee raised in a genuine smile. Then the smile dropped. "I lived through this state's Reconstruction by working for a Republican governor—from your area, E. J. Davis, not one of our more popular governors."

"No one blames you for participating with Davis's State Police. Your comments to the *Galveston News*, your wound suffered in Walker County, completely exonerate your honor from the high-handed methods of your fellow policemen."

"Did you later read my comment that I was 'misquoted'?"

"I never believed the later quote."

McNelly pulled a match from his pocket and lit his cigar. I did not tell him that it was a fine Cuban cigar with no customs paid on it when it entered either Mexico or Texas. "You should have had me to edit your comments. I've written speeches for Juan N. Cortina. The petition to the State of Texas for his pardon was mine."

"You seem to switch sides easily," McNelly said. He did not change expression.

"When my Uncle Rip Ford was chasing Cortina across the Rio Grande, Juan Cortina reined his horse and fired two revolvers at the charging Rangers. A Ranger bullet snipped a lock of Cheno's hair, another bit his bridle in two, another hit his belt buckle, and another nicked his horse's ear before he wheeled his horse around, outran the Rangers, and swam with his horse across to Mexico. Captain, Juan Cortina has survived by outfighting and outwitting Yankee generals, Confederates, Juaristas, and Imperialistas. I am familiar with Cortina. You want to know who to see, how to get something done, who's related to whom, I can help. You'll need a translator. I know Spanish."

"What you aren't, Mr. Nevin, is modest."

"Neither of us has time for modesty."

"And what if I give the order to shoot and Juan himself is in front of your barrel?"

"If you find Juan in front of your barrel, I'll be the one who got him there."

He leaned against his door and inhaled the smoke from his cigar. With his cigar between his fingers, he pointed toward me as though he were going to say something, but quickly doubled over, pulled a handkerchief out of his pocket, put it to his mouth, and turned away from me. A growl started from somewhere in his little body and shook him as it worked its way up his throat and then exploded out his mouth. He then spat into the handkerchief. He straightened himself, stuck the handkerchief into his pocket, looked at the smoldering end of his cigar, then turned his attention to me as though nothing at all had happened. "Is Juan Cortina behind this smuggling?"

I had to force my thoughts away from his strange cough and back to the matter at hand, "Legally, no."

"But surely, a bandit like Cortina, who once waged war on this state, is capable of stealing Texas cattle."

"He doesn't *stop* stealing. And every cow that passes from Bagdad to Cuba gives him some customs money. He's above the thievery; he's more concerned about the fate of Mexico."

"You sound as though you are a Cortinista."

"He's always considered them his 'Mamma's cows.' She's a gentle woman. Men along the river, the haciendados, like Juan Flores in Las Cuevas, they're the ones doing the actual stealing. And they're heroes to some people."

"So Mexicans mistake thieves for heroes?"

"They consider them to be like you, sir. They're trying to right what was made wrong."

McNelly again looked at the lit cigar, puffed, but did not inhale. A stream of smoke curled around his face, and he again reached for his doorknob. "It was a pleasure," he said.

"Sir, how old a man are you?" I asked as he opened his door.

He seemed to be taken back. He kept the door slightly ajar in case he had to dash inside to escape me. "I'm thirty-one."

"A man with your exploits during the great war, a man with your reputation . . ." McNelly held up his hand to stop me.

"A man as tired as I am and man with so little time is not fond of false sentiments."

"I am three years your senior. I thought you might like the company of someone who is your contemporary."

Holding his lit cigar that was forming ash to one side, he turned to face me. He got a stern look on his face. "I've got men over forty and under twenty. When I'm on patrol or a mission, I don't want company. Now you tell me why you want to go with me."

"Captain, shooting is going to follow you. I want to witness it and write about it. How many generals in the recent war had their biographer with them?" McNelly looked at the ash forming on his cigar and held his other palm underneath it. I began again. "You will have to admit to yourself, right now, that I have the ability to record your adventures. As to any of my other abilities, just ask Captain King or Rip Ford or Juan Cortina." McNelly looked again at the ash forming on his cigar. He leaned back against the wall. I said, again, "I can speak Spanish. I can serve as an interpreter."

"Ranger McGovern is my interpreter."

"Why not have two?"

"How good a spy are you?"

The words stopped in my throat. I hesitated, and when I tried to speak, I had to force the words out. "I was a spy in the war, for both the Confederacy and the Juaristas. I'm very good at it."

"This operation will depend upon inside information. I've got a good man in Bagdad and Matamoros. But I'd like a good man in Brownsville."

"But I just came from Brownsville. What about a record of your exploits?"

"We'll see how you work out as a soldier, then if I can use you as a spy, we'll see."

"A soldier? Is this a military operation?"

McNelly looked at the ashes in his hand then at me. "The pay is thirty dollars a month. Supply your own horse and pistols. I prefer you have a Colt .45, and I have some extra Sharps rifles. Be ready at dawn. And when I give an order, you jump."

I stuck out my hand, and he looked around for a place to empty the ashes in his palm. Seeing none myself, I dropped my hand and said, "Thank you."

To celebrate my acceptance into the Rangers, I went out to the porch to smoke a cigar and take a sip from the flask that I had taken from my gunnysack and put into my inside vest pocket. The wooden boards creaked as I stepped on to the porch. The lights from the parlor were turned off, but a lantern was hung on the porch. With the bandits roaming about, no one slept in complete darkness at Santa Gertrudis Ranch. I struck a match on a pole, lit and inhaled on the cigar, and heard creaking on the wooden slats. I saw two shadowy figures trying to sneak across the porch. "Whoa," I said, and walked toward the figures. "Instead of my walking into the dark, why don't you step into the light here?"

A large fellow stepped gingerly into the light and took off his hat, and I saw that he was a youngster. A smaller, younger youth stepped up behind him. The larger one tilted his head as though to size me up. His mouth hung open. The smaller one grabbed his hat off his head and held it in his hand. Neither one looked like a Ranger. Neither had on boots. The larger one wore brogans with a split toe, while the younger one had on ankle-high, laced shoes. Their shirts were frayed, their pants patched. As the larger one twisted, I noticed that he was the Ranger I had seen in the morning with the floppy brimmed hat and the pants with the patched seat. I blew smoke from my cigar, "What are you two doing sneaking around in the dark?"

The older one looked at the younger one. "We're not sneaking," the older one said. "We're looking."

The younger one stepped forward. "We saw you dancing with that girl. I never seen that, the way you just scooted her around the floor like that. I mean I've been to dances, but none like that, where you just moved like that."

I sucked in on my cigar and blew out more smoke. "Well, sir," I said, "a gentleman should study some of the feminine refinements if he intends to seek female company."

The larger one stepped forward. His mouth gaped open, his head was cocked as though he were trying to piece together what I had said. "So you're a gentleman?" the smaller one said.

"Andrew Nevin," I said and extended my hand. They both looked at my hand and then at each other.

The larger one extended his hand first. It was a rough palm with scarred knuckles, and as I shook his hand, he said, "George Durham."

The other boy rapidly pumped my hand and said, "Berry Smith."

"You two aren't vaqueros, I take it."

"No sir, no sir," Berry said. "We're Texas Rangers with Captain McNelly."

George looked at Berry. "We ain't either Texas Rangers. Not really. I told you that. We're McNelly's Special Forces. We're McNelly's boys is all."

I looked at them again, up and down, and wondered whether they, or I, would survive an attack on or from Cortina's bandits. "Well gentleman, we are comrades."

"We're what?" the larger one, George, asked.

"He's saying, he's a Ranger too," Berry Smith said. "Or he's a Special Force or McNelly boy or whatever it was you said we was."

George looked from his friend to me. "You an officer? Another lieutenant?"

"Just a private." They looked at me. "But one who can record your expedition."

I stepped forward and sat on the steps leading to the front porch. The two boys sat on either side of me. "What do you mean, 'record'?" George asked.

"I'm a writer, a reporter," I said.

"Damn, we got a reporter with us. Damn," George said.

"Where did you learn to dance?" Berry asked.

"In college," I said.

"College?" George said. "What are you doing here if you are a college man?"

I looked at the tip of my lit cigar. "I'm not sure. What are you doing here?"

George looked at his brogans, then at me. "I come down from Georgia. My daddy served with Cap'n McNelly during the war. Since times are bad in Georgia and Daddy has enough mouths to feed, I come looking for Cap'n McNelly and found out he's got a expedition. So same as my daddy, I'm following McNelly."

"You're father served with McNelly in the war?"

"Yes sir, with him and Colonel Tom Green over in Louisiana. And they shot, fooled, chased, and ran from Yankees. And my daddy said L. H. McNelly was the smartest man he'd ever worked for."

"Well, McNelly couldn't have been much over twenty."

"He was invading New Mexico to take it away from the Yankees when he was seventeen," George said.

"That little man in there?" I jerked my cigar toward the King ranch house.

"My daddy says that little man's a hellion when he gets fire under him," Berry said.

"So who's your daddy?"

George answered for him, "He's the man driving the ambulance. Figured he could keep an eye on his boy if he drove the wagon."

"I signed up before my daddy did," Berry said.

"Were you the two heads I saw bobbing up and down outside the parlor window?"

George hung his head and said to Berry, "See, I told you he saw us."

"We just wanted to look," Berry said.

George hung his head. "That woman, that Caroline. She served us supper. She is the prettiest woman I ever seen."

Berry interrupted him. "He wanted to have a better look at her. And he dared me to come with him."

"And did you like the women?"

"They was all pretty," Berry said.

I puffed on my cigar. "How about a cigar?" I asked. The two boys looked at one another, then I gave each one a cigar, my last two. After I lit the two cigars and we sat in a whirl of smoke, I said, "Now I will grant that Mr. King is surrounded by beautiful young women, but none of them are as radiant as the Empress Carlotta."

"Who?" George asked as he coughed up cigar smoke.

"The wife of Maximilian, the former emperor of Mexico." I looked at the two of them and their eyes narrowed. "Why, the empress Carlotta was so smooth on her feet that she floated, and her blonde curls floated like a wave around her face."

"You danced with this queen?" George said. Berry shifted his attention between his lit cigar and me.

"Why, yes, when I was in Mexico City I met the deceased emperor and his wife, and I danced with her. In fact," I looked at one, then the other, "I did more than dance with her."

"A queen? You bedded a queen?" George asked.

"An empress," I said.

"All Mexico's got is bandits." Berry Smith said.

"For a while, Mexico had an emperor," I said.

"If you wasn't so ignorant and would read more, you'd know Mexico was invaded by the French," George said to Berry and then coughed on some more smoke.

"But," I said, and leaned toward Berry so that George had to lean closer also, "she was not as beautiful or as good a dancer as the French whores that General Mejía brought with him to Matamoros when he invaded." George started coughing on his smoke. Berry just looked up at me. "Mejía had his own coach, drawn by six white mules. And in this coach he shipped around four French whores, women chosen for their beauty and trained and refined just to please the Imperial generals."

"And you said you danced with one?" George asked.

I blew a smoke ring out in front of my face. I waited, looked at both, then said, "Yes, I danced, and I learned things only a French whore can teach a young man. It was a formative period of my youth."

Berry's cigar was turning to ash, and George looked as if he tried to believe me. "What's a fella who dances with French whores doing serving with McNelly? Captain McNelly wouldn't hire a man who consorted with whores."

I slapped his knees. "It's time for this fella to get some sleep. I suggest you two get some sleep too. Otherwise, we may all be falling off our horses."

"Wait a second," George said. "You think you could show us how to dance?"

"What?" Berry said.

George returned Berry's disdainful look. "You saw how those women in there took to dancing. Maybe he could teach us."

I faced the two of them. "Well, let's see, you two grab onto each other."

"I ain't about to," Berry said.

"Come on. Who's looking?"

Hesitantly, Berry stepped up to George. "You be the girl," I said to Berry.

"Why do I have to be the girl?"

"You're smaller. Then you can take turns being the girl," I said. George raised his arms, and I said, "Go on," and Berry stepped into George's grasp. "Now take his hand in your left hand and hold it away from you." Both hesitated, then George slowly took Berry's hand.

"Oh my God, if my daddy was to see this."

"Shut up," George said.

"Now put your right hand up under and to the back of his shoulder. That's your driving hand." George nodded. "Now pull him a little closer."

And as George pulled Berry closer, another voice came out of the dark. "When you two going to start kissing?"

They pushed each other away and spun around. A small, wiry man stepped out of the dark. He was dressed like a vaquero with boots and a frayed black vest. He had on a new Colt and a long knife in a scabbard around his waist. When he stepped into the light, I saw a crooked smile made even more crooked by the way he shoved it into a corner of his face. "I thought McNelly wanted men, not girls. I didn't know we were gonna dance those bandits into submission."

"You just shut up, Boyd," George said.

Boyd jerked his head toward me. "Is this King's dance tutor? I guess he trains all his hands in dancing."

I stepped toward the man. He was not much taller than me, but lighter. "He's just joined up," George said.

Boyd laughed. "I got you two and a dance tutor to help me shoot greasers."

"Well, maybe I'll teach you to dance later," I said.

"And I could teach you a thing or two about dancing, I imagine," Boyd said. In the dark, I strained to see his crooked, thin-lipped smile that he used to try to disguise his meanness. So I kept my mouth shut, and Boyd walked away from us into the darkness. "I'm surrounded by a bunch of Miss Mollies," Boyd said just loud enough for us to hear him.

"That's Boyd," Smith said. "Be careful of him."

George nodded his head. "I seen him sharpening and playing with that knife of his. He can stick it in your gizzard before you know it."

"Some of us thinks he's got a record," Berry said.

"And don't play no poker with him," George Durham said. They both tipped their heads to me, like kids to their elder. George smiled, "Thanks for the dance lesson, but I don't think I got the hang of it." Berry chuckled. I watched as the two of them walked out of the porch light and into the shadows on their way to their cots in the bunkhouse. I walked away from the comfortable mansion to my bunk in a smaller bunkhouse.

A woman once told me that riding a horse was a lot like dancing.

You have to refine the moves and then relax and use them. I knew how to dance and to ride, but I knew that I wasn't very good at either. Of course, as close as I had ever gotten to an empress was Addie Ford, and as close as I had ever gotten to an Imperialista's concubine was Catalina Taracón.

CHAPTER 9

On the Trail

WHEN I came out the next morning to join my comrades-in-arms, the ragged group of Rangers, the defenders of the pride and integrity of the great state of Texas, stared at me. Even Captain King, who was out on the front porch of his house, stared at me. I checked myself, then McNelly came out of the ranch house. As I had noted the day before, with his canvas jacket, trousers, and leggings, we could have been doubles. As though to go one better than me, he wore a black tie. No one stared at McNelly.

George Durham had on his patched jeans, brogans, and a hat drooping in folds about his face. Berry Smith at least had a pair of boots, but his hat, which once had a rolled and curled brim, drooped in front and back. Boyd had spent some money for his checkered shirt, crisply blocked hat, and wool vest. Most of the rest were dressed like poor vaqueros or lost farm boys.

King, now in a homespun shirt and thick jeans with holes at the knees and stuffed into high boots, was off the porch before McNelly and talking to the huddled Rangers, who didn't seem to know how to act. "I got a surprise for you boys." King limped through them. "Come on, come on." He chuckled, "Y'all slept late." They followed and led their horses after King. McNelly brought up the rear. I spotted George Durham and scooted next to him.

"You just fall in behind me," he said. "We got us a pretty good patrol squad. You met Boyd and Berry Smith last night. Bill Callicott works with us sometimes." He jerked his head around to look for him. "That's him," he pointed. I saw a boy, not much older than George, with a leather strap across his chest, a Sharps carbine on the end of it, walking across the compound with a bow-legged swagger that suggested he was far older than his tender, whiskerless face showed him to be. Then George said, "There's our sergeant." I looked and saw an older man with a turkey neck, complete with the wattle. He looked like a farmer. "That's Sergeant Orrill. He was in the war with Captain McNelly."

I spotted the thin, dashing man whom I had mistaken for McNelly. "Who is that?" I asked George and jerked my chin toward him.

"You must mean Lieutenant Robinson," George said. "He and Sergeant Armstrong kind of second command this outfit."

King led us to a corral with several horses swirling around it, being roped and taunted by several of his Kineños. "Take your pick," King shouted and laughed. "Presents from the Santa Gertrudis ranch. Evidently up in East Texas you don't have much good horse flesh to choose from." In the midst of King's men was Lee, and soon Caroline Chamberlain came from the ranch house to look at the horse roundup.

The Rangers and the Kineños started roping mounts and saddling and bridling them. King shouted again, "I took the liberty of throwing out some of your tack. Disgusting for a representative of the state to be sitting on such leather. I got you new saddles and rifle scabbards if you need them."

McNelly and I both edged up to King. I spoke first. "Captain King, I'd prefer to hold on to my mare. She was a gift from my uncle."

"Then go saddle her, Andrew."

McNelly added. "We can't pay for these mounts. The state can't reimburse you."

"Goddamn to hell, McNelly," King said, and the preacher recoiled. "I'd rather give them to you than lose them to bandits."

I walked along the side of the corral and saw George Durham's patched-bottom jeans. He had his elbows spread over a top rail and his left foot resting on the bottom. I leaned against the rail next to him. "Spotting you a good one?"

"I got my eye on a gelding," he said. But his eyes were really on Caroline Chamberlain.

I continued around the corral until I saw an old Kineño with his back against the slats of the corral, clumsily trying to roll a cigarette. His face looked like wrinkled brown leather. His bowed legs made him look diminutive. He was not at all an impressive-looking figure, but on a horse, in his wide-brimmed sombrero, Spanish leather chaps clasped around his legs with silver buckles, heavy rowel spurs, and drooping gray moustache, he would look as romantic as a Virginia cavalier, as though he, and not an ex-steamboat captain, were the ruler of this grassland. I rested my elbows on the top slat of the corral and my foot on the bottom slat. He turned his head with just the barest movement as though to conserve all his energy for rolling the cigarette. "These are good horses, huh?" I asked.

He looked at me like I was stupid and nodded, "The best on the ranch." He sounded disgusted.

"Have any of the vaqueros here thought about joining McNelly?" He smiled as though chuckling to himself and shook his head. I tried again. "Won't they be glad to see the thieving stop?"

This time he just squinted at me. I don't believe he could have done anything else. The sun had burned his eyes into that squint. He looked around himself to see who was listening. "We live next to the bandits. Some of the Kineños have bandits for friends, neighbors, or relatives." He chuckled. "Some of the old Kineños used to be bandits. Somebody helps McNelly, he or his family could be dead."

I wished that I had a pencil and paper. "What about the vaqueros who work for other ranchers?"

He shrugged. "Stealing cows to sell. Rescuing cows. It's a rich man's business. Poor people are glad to eat cow. Vaqueros are loyal to who has paid them the longest. Vaqueros have a good life. Worse is to be a poor Mexican without a gun or a horse."

"Well, what about Captain King? What do you think of him?"

"He's a good man."

"What about Juan Cortina?"

"He's a good man, too."

He scooted away from me because talking to me was probably dangerous, and I watched as the vaqueros in the corral roped the healthiest-looking animal for McNelly, and Richard King shouted, "That's a fine animal, Captain McNelly. You'll look good sitting on him."

AFTER several hours, we were on the trail with King's tower fading behind us, and I was fighting with my mare. I was trying to hang to the rear of the column of twos with George, but my mare would not stand for it. She kicked, twisted her head, and pulled at the bit. She no longer heeded the pressure of the rein on her neck, but obeyed only my jerks on the bit. I had to take the reins in both hands and pull her head to one side or the other. "Good goddamn," Boyd said. "What kind of animal is that?"

"Nevin, you need some help?" George asked. My mare puffed and upset the geldings and mares around her.

"Rein that bitch in," Sergeant Orrill yelled.

I shrugged to George and gave her rein, and she immediately ran to the head of the column, putting me beside Captain McNelly and the tall, dashing man I had mistaken for McNelly. That man was Lieutenant Robinson. Then my mare bit at McNelly's fine gelding— Segal, McNelly had begun calling him. McNelly and Robinson both looked at me, and I discerned a slight smile on Robinson's face. But my mare was still not content. She pushed ahead of the two leaders.

McNelly had an unlit cigar in his mouth, and as I twisted in the saddle to look at him, I noticed that his jaw clenched tightly and the cigar fell out of his mouth. Lieutenant Robinson saw too, and he looked at me as though I was about to be struck. "By God, what is wrong with you?" McNelly said in a barely audible whisper.

"It's the horse," I said.

"Nevin, I want men who will jump when I shout, but not until. Now if you can't get that horse back to the end of this column, I'll shoot it and you."

I dismounted and held tightly on to the reins. I curled them up in my fist until it was a ball under my mare's chin. She could have dragged me through the brush if she wanted to, but she had yet to figure out that she was that strong. If she tried to move, I yanked and let the bit cut into her mouth. I waited until the end of the column and mounted. As soon as I was in the saddle, the mare ran for the lead. I jerked up on the reins and saw McNelly turn to scowl at me. Jerking on one rein then the next, I got her back into place beside George Durham. "I ain't never seen nothing like that," George said. I now knew why the mare had scared John William so badly.

"That horse has been alone too long or something. She ain't used to other horses," Sergeant Orrill said, his head swiveling around on his scrawny neck, just like a turkey's head, as he tried to settle his horse.

Boyd, next to Berry Smith in front of us, tried to calm his horse and looked back at me. "You ignorant bastard." He said to me. "She ain't trail broke. She wants to lead this whole herd." I jerked and leaned to get her pointed around the other way. Then I dug my heels into her flanks and held on as she galloped down the trail in the opposite direction, making my gunnysack pound my thigh and her shoulder. After about a mile, I pulled up to Dad Smith's converted ambulance. My mare politely led the two mules.

"What the hell you doing?" Dad Smith yelled at me.

"My horse won't cooperate."

"You better make her or the Captain'll skin you."

So for the rest of the way, I tried to pull her behind the wagon's two mules, and when she tried to get ahead of them, I yelled, kicked, and slapped at her. After several hours of fighting me, she was content to walk alongside the wagon. "You don't ride much do you?" Dad Smith asked.

"I'd prefer to be up there with you. Better yet, I'd like a buggy with good springs, not just leather slats."

"I'm with you there. This thing hasn't got much give."

He was beaded with sweat, which plopped onto the wooden footrest, and flies buzzed around his head, but he'd blow between his pursed lips, and once in a while, he would switch the reins to his left hand while he pulled out a bandana with his right and wiped at his face. He didn't talk.

"Tomorrow, I'll see if she can tolerate the back of the column," I said.

"You want, you can borrow my whip tonight. Let her see you and then just tickle her with that whip. She'll like it at first. If she acts up, snap her a couple of times. It's how I plow-break a mule."

He blew wind from between his lips as the flies settled on his face. "Hope nothing is rotting back there," he said and jerked his head toward the cargo portion of the ambulance. Then he chuckled, "Even if it is, it's all we got to eat tonight."

"You're Berry's father, right?"

"Good boy, ain't he?"

"How old is he?"

"Just turned sixteen." He had a proud but almost idiotic-looking smile.

"Why did you let him join?"

"He wanted to."

"But you let him?"

"His momma didn't want him to join, but I knew if I told him 'no,' he'd just run away and do it. Gets boring on a farm for a boy his age. Hell, I went out to shoot some Comanches when I was his age."

I nodded and wondered if I was the only one in this state with an aversion to the ritualized blood-letting of young men. Only King's oldest son, the one named for him, Richard, like me seemed to want to escape all the dust, gore, and blood for some refinement. I began to think that I would have been much better off writing about McNelly from reports sent in to Brownsville.

Toward sundown, a figure came galloping out of the sun toward me. The front brim of his hat was turned back; his powder-blue, silk bandana trailed behind him, and the setting sun made an orange halo around him. When he reigned up in front of me and kicked up a fog of dust, making me cough and my mare snort, I saw my mare's ear twitch, and I jerked on the reins. She watched Lieutenant Robinson's gelding, and he leaned over to pat her head. His gelding look frightened. I dismounted. So did he. His gelding shied away, and my mare eyed the gelding, a certain wicked delight in her eyes, but she held her pace.

Robinson wore the long, wide, silk bandanas favored by the Anglo vaqueros. The upturned brim of his hat had left a permanent red sunburn stripe across his forehead. His pistol was on his left side, as was the fashion with the older percussion revolvers, and like most Rangers, he had a Bowie knife on his right side. "Nevin, you're not much for rangering, are you?" I glanced at him and just sort of growled.

"Neither am I. Not really, but we are brothers of a sort." He stuck out his hand, and I carefully let go of my reins with my right hand, and mechanically shook his hand. "Pidge Robinson," he said. Pidge had a habit of not waiting for an answer. He just kept talking. "The secret is to unlearn some things. If you'd been at our little skirmish, you might have seen how to act."

"What skirmish?"

"Nothing. Nothing much. More important is that we're brothers of the pen. I'm sending dispatches to the *Austin State Daily Gazette* of my, excuse me, *our* exploits. Captain tells me you're a journalist also."

"We seem to have ample coverage of this expedition," I said.

"A journalist has to take his opportunities where he can."

In the distance, I heard the first owls and coyotes, and around me, I heard and felt the buzz of mosquitos. I was just starting to cool down, and I could feel the dirt in my clothes. "I hope that Captain McNelly isn't going to ride through the night," I said.

"He'll camp soon. Still some daylight." I nodded and glanced over at the tall, thin Robinson. "I'm hoping to produce a book out of this. It will be all about my exploits, excuse me, *our* exploits, and give me the appearance of being a brave and capable man."

Now, with a compatriot of sorts, walking instead of riding, I felt comfortable for the first time that day. "I haven't thought about a book on McNelly as much as one on my uncle, John S. 'Rip' Ford," I said.

"A lucky man, you are," Robinson said. "I am sure it will be popular."

"I'd settle for written and published."

"Isn't that always the case. Genius unrecognized." He hesitated to look into the darkness and chuckled, "And love unrequited."

I had not had the company of an intelligent and cultivated man in some time. I looked at this strange Ranger. "How did you end up a lieutenant?"

"When McNelly started his Special Forces to clean up the Sutton-Taylor feud in DeWitt County, I left Austin, a mere typesetter, with some other young fellows desperate to get a name and maybe some reputation and thus a stake in the world. Captain immediately saw my greatest attributes: I could read and write. I became his clerk, his secretary. I advanced to sergeant, and then when Captain thought that he needed another officer, why there I was, a man among men, the paper pusher, the wordsmith, the man requisitioning the supplies." He slapped at my shoulder. "Why, Nevin, the pen is indeed a mighty sword and a good companion."

I dared not slap at his shoulder. He was still, in my eyes, McNelly's second-in-command, but I said, "Especially in this area where so few know what to do with a pen."

"But Nevin." His brows wrinkled. "You've got to control that horse. Better yet, control your attitude. For, you see, you must fool them. You must make them think you breathe fire. McNelly is a master. I'm an apprentice with a sense of my own ridiculousness and pretense. You sir, as a brother of the pen, must adopt the same attitude."

As I considered his words, he stopped to mount his horse. But as the journalist, I had another question, "Why 'Pidge'?"

Robinson continued to walk with me. "Because we are brothers, because I should trust you, but mostly because I have no one else in this company or in this state to confide in, I will continue to walk instead of ride, and I will tell you." He breathed in. His brows wrinkled. His short moustache twitched along with his mouth. "My lady love is nicknamed Pidgie," he said.

"A strange name for the lady fair," I said.

Robinson shifted his joking manner to a mournful look highlighted by the orange tint from the setting sun. "Back in Campbell County in my beloved Virginia, I had words with her brother." He looked away from me, down the road, and I saw that intense stare that accompanied the intellectual, literarily ambitious young men whom I had met in college. Was that look, was that awful sentimentality, an attribute of the trade? Was it feigned? Why was I immune to it, and if so, shouldn't I give up my own vague literary aspirations? "It seems he objected to everything about my nature. Nothing that I could do or say satisfied him. I told him that I would eventually take Pidgie from him and his family, and I told him that, if we had to go into hiding, we would."

"Why even tell him? Why not just take her? Just leave with her?"

He looked at me as though shocked. "I have an education, such as it is. My parents raised me to be a moral, decent man. I was a gentleman. It was only right to tell the man."

"And so?"

"And so, he said that he would kill me. The only way to settle the right to take Pidgie was a death: his or mine." He hung his head.

"So you got out."

"My parents and Pidgie herself urged me to go. Demanded, actually. So I left. I became a coward. I would not stand up for my love or for my honor." We were indeed brothers, in more ways than Robinson knew. "So where do dishonored men go but Texas? I've been a vaquero. I found the work disgusting. So I began work at the *Austin State Daily Gazette.* Now, I can claim to be a writer, but I'm a coward. I deserted the love of my life. Writing is hardly a replacement for lost love."

"No, it is not," I said, staring into the darkness. "But I, for one, think that you may have made the right decision. I've run from love myself."

"Brother," Robinson said, "I hope like me, someday, you will go back and cure the problems."

"I don't know that I have a cure." He looked at me as though pressing me for more information. He had made his confession. Now I owed him mine. Looking at the tears that were welling in his eyes, I said, "I love two women. One is married . . . to a . . . a friend. Another is . . . is . . . she makes her living loving rich men. Where is my gentlemanly act? All I can do is watch."

"Oh, my," he said. "Maybe I am the lucky one."

"Sometimes we have to live with our problems."

"I plan to kill mine. Someday, when I have the nerve, and this expedition may be the means for that, I shall go back to Virginia and kill Jesse Mitchell, my love's brother."

"And what will you do then? How will you survive?"

"I'll still be shamed perhaps, but I'll have Pidgie."

I found myself nodding with him, but then I stopped nodding. "And what if he kills you?"

"Then I will simply be dead," he said, but his great spark of life lit his eyes back up and made him smile. "But listen," he said. "We'll have to compare stories. Perhaps we'll both have time to write that book." He slapped me on the back, and in one fluid move pushed himself back in the saddle, pulled his gelding's head back toward the sun, and galloped away from me.

After I got my feet back under me, when my mare tried to pull away from me to outpace Pidge's gelding, I watched him ride away and shouted, "What skirmish?" He pulled his hat off to wave back at me. As I carefully mounted my mare once Pidge was out of sight, I felt glad to be a part of the literary contingent of McNelly's Special Forces.

WHEN Dad Smith and I caught up to the camped Rangers and I dismounted, my body sagged. I had only known a bit of saddle soreness before. Now, from my day-long fight with my horse, not only did my crotch and the two bones that formed the points of my rump ache, but my back and shoulders had a throb in them that beat along with my heart. All I could do was slump. Berry Smith came up beside me, smiling, looking like he was even younger than sixteen, and I asked him to unsaddle my mare for me. He was only one I would have dared to ask.

"Tired are you there, Dandy?" Boyd asked.

"I'm accustomed to using different parts of my body," I said.

"Who taught you to talk?" Boyd asked.

"People who were good at it."

"I'd of liked to seen you talk as good as McNelly in our first little encounter today." He could make that crooked smile of his go from one side of his mouth to the other. Before I could ask, I felt a nudge in my back and turned to see Berry holding my saddle. He handed it to me, and the throb in my back sent tremors to my head and hips. With the Winchester in the scabbard banging against my leg, I took a few steps and dropped my saddle. Then with one hand, I unfastened my gunbelt, held it out like a snake, and curled it around my saddle. Without its weight, I felt like I would float away. I started to spread out a blanket. As soon as I had a pallet, I lay on my stomach, and I looked up to see McNelly standing in front of me. I held the preacher's gaze with my own. He wouldn't let his eyes leave mine. "You want to see me now, Captain?"

"Stay sprawled out there, Nevin. But I like my men to keep their guns ready."

Soon, like puppies, George and Berry had their blankets and pallets beside mine. Then Boyd, probably wanting to torment them, just as he would torment puppies, spread a blanket alongside them and pulled a deck of cards from his saddlebags and began shuffling. Then, like the bitch watching her puppies, Sergeant Orrill spread his blanket next to us. Pretty soon, short, ragged Bill Callicott had his bedroll laid out beside ours as well. He was the bow-legged boy with the frontiersman swagger that I had seen earlier in the day.

George eyed the deck of cards. Orrill watched as Dad Smith unloaded the ambulance and muttered, "Supper." I realized that I had not eaten all day.

I turned to George. "What did I miss today?"

George pulled his eyes away from the cards. "Damn, you missed it."

Berry piped in. "Captain faced down a whole goddamn posse."

"By himself?" I asked.

"Vittles," Orrill uttered.

"We was behind him," George said. "Just like we was 'little McNellys.'"

"'Little McNellys,'" Boyd sneered and dealt himself a hand. "Damn that's a name to strike fear into those greaser bandits."

"Who is this?" Bill Callicott asked and looked at me.

"He's the dandy," Boyd said.

"Hell," George said. "He's the man gonna write all this down and explain."

Bill smiled and said, "You shoulda seen it."

I turned to George. "George, slow down. What happened?"

"I got a game or two I can play you before we eat," Boyd said to George.

"Goddamn, wait," I said, and they all looked at me. "I'm a reporter. I want a report. George, what happened?"

George shook his head as though to clear it. Berry Smith got in the first words. "First thing is Sergeant Armstrong, out on scout, gives us a signal that riders was approaching. Down the trail comes this posse. And quick as you please, Lieutenant Robinson, he motions and shouts, and we form this skirmish line, quick as you please. Just like we was supposed to do." I was a little angry that Pidge Robinson hadn't filled me in.

"Just like in the war. Proper military maneuvers," Orrill said. He scooted closer to me and grew excited. "We were straight across the trail in a line, so we had a better angle on them, seeing they were strung out down the trail. They wanted to help us kill bandits. But McNelly said he had enough men. And said that if they didn't go back home, they were in violation of state law, and he'd be obliged to arrest them."

I groaned as I twisted around, moved Rip's old converted Dragoon out of the way and pulled a pencil and a tablet out of my gunnysack. "Just what did McNelly say?"

"First this man leading the posse says real friendly, 'Captain we got about a hundred men. All white men. Nary a Yankee, nigger, or Mexican amongst us,'" George said.

"Don't see why if we're facing half of Mexico, we couldn't have got some all-white reinforcements," Boyd said.

"They was out killing bandits or Mexicans or something and wanted to join us," George said.

Orrill looked toward Dad preparing supper, then jerked his head to me to shake the skin hanging loosely under his neck. "They was a posse out of Corpus. That Corpus sheriff was leading 'em."

"What did McNelly say?" I asked.

But Bill Callicott interrupted him. "I was right beside him. Captain says, in his real slow voice. . . ."

"Slow down. What did he say?" I said to the squeaky-voiced Callicott and got ready to scribble.

The young Callicott, who—with his Sharps carbine hanging from a leather strap—looked more like a Ranger than the others, smiled at his good fortune at the one being asked to tell what really happened. "Captain up and says to that sheriff or leader or whatever he was, 'I've got all the men I need.'"

"Yeah, just out with it. Just like that. That's what Captain is like," Orrill said, and I glared at him. "I want to tell some of it too," he said and looked at Callicott and the others.

"Captain says to us, 'Boys, we're going to disarm them and disband them and return them to their homes,' he says," Callicott continued.

George pulled on my arm. "Their leader says that they won't do it. He says they got to vote. And McNelly gives them ten minutes. And he pulls out his watch with his left hand and stares at it and fingers his pistol with his right hand. And after ten minutes, he pulls out his gun." I was scribbling as fast as I could.

Laughing and smiling, with others slapping at him, Berry added, "And we all pull out our guns."

"And not one of you young puppies would have had the sack to shoot," Boyd said.

Orrill laughed, but Callicott added, "We goddamn faced those sons of bitches down real good."

George, smiling now too, concluded the story. "Captain said he'd let them keep their guns if they'd go home. And far as we know, that's where they went."

I looked away from the men and saw McNelly watching us. He let the barest smile shift his beard. I felt like I had back during the war. Young men in armed groups are just like their horses. They have a herding instinct and began looking for a leader. The first to catch their attentions are their officers. But those leaders or officers must earn the right to command them into death or danger, to lead the herd. They need to do something extravagant or dangerous. McNelly knew this too. He had earned his right to lead this herd.

DINNER was miserable. Dad Smith got a fire going and warmed left-over beans with salt pork and hardtack. Both Berry and George, even after their good meal with real beef at the King Ranch, ate. From Rip's stories, this was usual fare for an army in the field. I realized that a soldier's or a Ranger's most important trait was not firepower or courage, but a hardy constitution.

George could no longer keep his attention away from Boyd's cards, and so he was getting another lesson in gambling. The others seemed to know enough to stay away from Boyd when he dealt cards.

McNelly had retired to a campaign tent, and I studied the shadow on the tent. It would move around and then sit on the cot, and the shoulders would curl forward and then jerk. After a while, the shadow turned into McNelly himself as he emerged from the tent and struggled to carry a trunk that was too heavy for him. He got the trunk to Dad Smith's fire, dropped it, opened it, and he, Sergeant Armstrong, and Dad Smith passed out black books that were not quite the thickness of a small New Testament. McNelly himself carried a stack to our squad.

As he handed them out, he said, "This is a list of names of wanted men. They are all wanted for some crimes. If you see one, apprehend him. Don't tarry with him. If he resists, shoot him."

I thumbed through the book, which was a long list of names followed by descriptions of the perpetrator, his crimes, and the date and locale of his crimes. I pushed myself to a sitting position and stared up at McNelly. "Some of these crimes are eight or nine years old."

"So they need to be caught," McNelly said.

"But do you have warrants? Or a charge? A sheriff, a constable, can't hold these men without warrants."

"By God, Nevin. You're about to serve the shortest stint in any unit I've ever commanded. We are the authorities."

I felt the stares of the men around me. George's mouth hung open. Boyd had stopped dealing his cards to push a smile into the corner of his mouth. McNelly turned his back to me and passed out more books. When he got them all out, he spoke quietly so that the men had to move closer to him. "This state is suffering from wild, unlawful men having their way. These books were drawn up by the old State Police of E. J. Davis to control this emergency. We have the authority to take these men in." But not to hold them, I thought, and said nothing this time.

McNelly's eyes went from man to man, then settled on me. He turned his back to me and returned to his tent. Orrill spoke first. "What the hell are you thinking? You don't talk back to the Captain or interrupt him."

I studied the shadow inside, then pushed myself up. "Where you going?" Sergeant Orrill said and grabbed my hand.

"I want to talk to McNelly."

"Lay your ass back down. Captain don't owe you no stories."

I pulled my hand away from him. "I thought he was known as a man who shared everything that his men endured."

"He'll be working on strategy. Don't disturb him."

I trudged away and walked to the tent. "Captain McNelly, may I have a word," I said, since I could not knock on a tent.

A weak voice commanded me to come in, so I shoved the tent flap to one side and stepped in. He sat on a cot with his head hanging from his shoulders; his head looked too heavy to hold up. He slowly raised it. His face was drained of almost all color. As he tried to talk, a gurgling noise started in his throat, but he swallowed it and tried again, "Nevin, don't push your luck."

"I thought I might ask you a few questions."

"About what?"

"Your life. Your past. For my story."

"You have no story," he said in a firm but soft voice, one that I imagined sounded just like his orders to the posse. "At least not yet." His voice got softer. "You signed on as a private. You are not a journalist until I say so. Now don't test my patience." The gurgling noise started in his throat once again and erupted in a spasm of coughing. McNelly kept his hand in front of his mouth as though trying to fight against the cough.

"Sir, Captain. Is something wrong?"

"Get out of here." Sweat beaded on his forehead, and his eyes became small beads in the back of his head. "Leave me be. Or better, get on your horse and ride out of here." He was breathing heavily.

Suddenly, without a sound, a thickset, balding man appeared, who looked like he could and wanted to break me in half. "You don't have the stomach for this, do you, mister?" the man asked. The tightly twisted ends of his moustache quivered as he tensed, ready to start breaking me. Instead, he escorted me out of the tent.

Once outside, the thickset man took ahold of my arm. "In the morning, turn your Winchester over to Dad Smith, and he'll give you a Sharps. Captain doesn't want any man who needs more than one shot to hit his target with a rifle."

"But it's my rifle."

"You don't seem to understand that there's a pecking order in this outfit. If you violate any more, one of us, primarily me, is going to see your face is busted in. You got me?"

"And you are?" He tensed. "I'm sorry, but I haven't met everyone."

"I'm Sergeant George Armstrong. You ain't seen me because I ride point for the Captain—in more ways than one. So remember me." The faithful Sergeant Armstrong lingered to stare at me, but then left me.

I backed up and went back to my squad. George was back to playing cards with Boyd. Berry and Bill Callicott were asleep. Sergeant Orrill was shaking his head. "Ain't you got the sense God give a goose? You better steer clear of Armstrong and McNelly as much as you can, or you going to be riding that silly mare of yours back to the King Ranch."

"I'm a reporter. I talk to people. I interview them. That's how it works."

"It ain't how this outfit works. Stop disturbing people."

I shook my head. "What makes him so special?"

"You ain't going to stop, are you?"

"You, why are you here?"

Orrill pulled off his hat and stroked his thin neck, smoothing out his wattles. "You weren't even there today to see him. He's the most fearless man I ever seen. In the war, in Galveston, that little son-of-a bitch, like a mad little terrier dog, jumped into a Yankee gunboat and took it hostage. Now, of course, I jumped in after him to help out a little, and so did some other troops. Then I was with him in Louisiana. The hardest part of the fighting. He'd outfight or fool the Yankees. Once he had us crossing and recrossing two bridges and yelling and laughing to make the Yankees think they was surrounded. Next day, five hundred men surrendered to two hundred. Some thinks it's bluff, but I think it ain't. Like today, he'd of started shooting. Hell, he'd take on a buzz saw."

"What's he got?" I lowered myself and my aches down beside Orrill. "The man is sick. Is that why he hides in that tent?"

Orrill brought his fingers to his lips to hush me. "Keep your voice down." The aging man looked around and listened. Like him, I heard the snores, hoot owls, and coyotes. He jerked his thumb toward George and Boyd. "I don't know who all knows around here. But the man is dying."

"Of what?"

"Can't you tell? He's got the consumption. Had it for years. Most of these fellows know that, but they don't know how bad it is. But I've seen it. I been with him awhile. He'll whip it for a while, but then it'll come back for him."

"He should be in a hospital."

"The man has pride. He wants to do something great before he goes. He's thinking," Orrill touched his forehead with his forefinger. "He's always thinking. He's gonna go out having done something big. That's where he gets his courage. He knows what's waiting for him, so he's got no fear."

"So you and these boys are willing to follow him as he fearlessly looks for his own death?"

Orrill hushed me again. "You best just go to sleep. Forget I even talked to you." Orrill rolled over and pulled a blanket over himself. I listened to George cussing his luck and his losings, then rolled over to get my own sleep.

I WOKE before daylight, choking to the smell of forty horsemen. In the city, I could tolerate the smell of infrequent bathers passing me by in the streets or standing by me in a bar. But I was not used to the smell of these grouped, snoring men and their tired horses. Old Rip told me that any half-blind old lady could spot an Indian camp by the circling buzzards and the smell of dung. I wondered how hard it would be for bandits to sniff out our Rangers who were dressing in their musty boots, rancid shirts, and thick trousers. Then I wondered just how hard it would be to find a stolen herd of cattle. The sightings and smell of cow spoor should lead us right to the bandits. I grew scared of what seemed an inevitable confrontation.

Only McNelly, the sentries, and Dad Smith, tending to the fire, were awake with me in the faint pre-dawn. McNelly had his back to me staring to the east. When the sun rose halfway above the flat horizon, it put a golden halo around L. H. McNelly.

Later in the morning, after coffee and more hardtack, Orrill got an idea about what to do with my horse. Overnight, my mare had gotten used to Dad Smith's mules. She'd stay quiet around them. But Orrill haltered my mare and led her to the rest of the horses. He told me to hide. If McNelly saw what he was about to do, I'd be back on the trail to the King Ranch.

Orrill led my mare to Segal, McNelly's prime King Ranch horse. My mare poked and prodded at Segal with her nose. Orrill guided her to Segal's rump out of his sight, and then Orrill kicked the gelding between the legs, and Segal in turn kicked out behind him and caught my mare in the chest. She screamed and twisted away from Segal. She watched me, Orrill, and Segal. I led her back to Segal, but she pulled away. When we all had saddled up and mounted, and although she was still touchy around the other horses, my mare was content to let Segal have the lead and would calm down if she could see him ahead of her.

That day, we turned west off the Taylor road. We marched in single or double file in a loose column, Dad Smith about a mile back, with scouts out ahead and off in the brush. We lost sight of the sandy stretches of marsh grass and entered an area with thicker motts and clumps of mesquite, prickly pear, hackberry, and chaparral mixing with the grass. Additionally, we got no sea breeze and lost some humidity, so the men's shirts darkened with sweat, and the crowns of their hats grew dark circles around them. We were all busy dabbing the blinding sweat out of our eyes with our scarves or bandanas, and we constantly blew at the mosquitos or gnats flying in front of our faces. A few of the men, bothered by Dad's cooking or bad water, continually had to pull away from the column to relieve themselves in the brush. I felt my own stomach rumbling, but I noticed that either I had gotten accustomed to my aching or that it had stopped. I correctly guessed our target to be Las Rucias, an old deserted ranch northwest of Brownsville, just north of Edinburg. It was to become McNelly's base.

The area around Las Rucias was also the area regularly patrolled by Neal Coldwell and his company of Texas Rangers. Coldwell and his company had been recalled to Austin to be reassigned or mustered out. When we met Coldwell and his Rangers, I got to see some of McNelly's bluff or courage that I had missed the previous day. Without blinking, without emotion, with the stern preacher's look, McNelly simply told Coldwell that he was there to replace him and that he would use more *severe methods* than Coldwell was using to bring the bandits to justice. Coldwell, clearly embarrassed, seemed wary of McNelly. And it must have hurt this old warrior to leave his old assignment to these forty new men. I could only imagine old Rip getting a similar order.

We camped that day just south of the ranch and, thank God, rested. McNelly started organizing scouting parties. He explained to us that he would operate out of la ley de fuga. George grimaced when I told him what that law meant. McNelly excused his decision due to the facts that he didn't have enough men to guard prisoners, that gunning people down as they fled was the method of the outlaws, and that to fight the outlaws he would use their method. I kept my mouth shut and worried that McNelly's explanation was just another excuse for more butchery.

The next morning the sun woke me, not the smell of the men. Like my aches, I had either lost my sensitivity to their smell or had grown accustomed to it. Then, as I put on my shirt, I caught whiffs of my own stink. I was becoming, whether McNelly and his men liked it or not, whether I liked it or not, indistinguishable from the little McNellys.

McNelly decided that we needed some target practice. He wanted to see what his men could do. So we shot our pistols and our Sharps. I developed a new ache in my shoulder from the kick of the .50-caliber Sharps. McNelly scoffed at George Durham, who tried to imitate Boyd by pulling his pistol quickly out of his holster and hitting a log lickety split. McNelly told Dad Smith to charge George for any more shells. He was wasting the state's money. So was I. I couldn't hit anything. So George and I, with Boyd teasing us, blasted at a tree at five paces, then ten, then fifteen. McNelly told George to pull the gun slowly, choose the target, aim, and pull the trigger slowly. Next we tried to shoot from horseback. I found that I couldn't both ride and shoot. Boyd and McNelly watched me.

By the end of the morning, with the sun heating up everybody, we were all tired of target practice, and I was on my way back to my tack, hoping I could sneak in a nap. I pulled off my dusty, now sweat-stained, rabbit-fur hat, and dropped it on my saddle. Suddenly, a pistol barked and my hat jumped up. I dove for the ground and tried to pull my small Navy Colt out of my holster. I fumbled and dropped the gun, and luckily it didn't go off. Then the laughter came from behind me. I rolled over to see Boyd laughing, and beside him were Berry and George snickering. Farther away, behind them, was McNelly.

My head starting working. I couldn't keep up with my thoughts; mostly I couldn't help thinking that McNelly had put them up to this. "Looky boys, I just shot me a plump, juicy rabbit for lunch," Boyd said. He holstered his pistol.

I forced myself to smile and reached for my hat. I held it up and poked my finger through the hole in the middle of the crown. The hat was the finest one I could find in Brownsville, part of my vanity, and now my vanity as well as my balding head would suffer. Behind them, McNelly started walking up.

"Let's skin that rabbit," George said. The brim of his floppy hat shook as he laughed.

I reached into my saddle pack and brought out Rip's old converted Dragoon Colt. I stood as well as I could, assumed a dueling position, and leveled the gun at Boyd. "Whoa. I'm just fooling," Boyd said and looked behind him.

"Nevin," I heard McNelly try to scream in a raspy voice.

"Fair is fair," I said. "Now let me have a turn at that pretty curled brim rabbit on top of your head." I deliberately closed one eye. "But this gun is surely heavy, and as you saw, I'm still not too good a shot. You better hold still, Boyd."

Boyd began backing up. "George, Berry, you two better step back."

Boyd held up his hands, "Wait, wait, wait." Rangers were gathering on either side of me, some of them fingering their revolvers in case someone had to gun me or Boyd down. Then I raised the Dragoon; it was surprisingly balanced. Boyd stuck his hands, palms up, in front of him and swished them from side to side. For a moment, I thought that he might have gone for the revolver in his holster, then I or McNelly would have had to shoot him. "Nevin, I was just kidding," he said. I shot above his head.

Boyd grabbed his head with both hands and fell to his knees. And from each side of me, starting as giggles then growing, came the Rangers' laughter. I winked at George and Berry, and then looked behind them at McNelly, and I could see by the shape of his beard that he was smiling. And then a beaming Pidge Robinson, with his hands clasped behind his back, strolled up to McNelly and whispered into his ear.

I walked up to Boyd, who jumped up, doubled his fist, and shouted, "You son of a bitch."

"Fair is fair," I said and stuck out my hand for him to shake.

"Shake it," McNelly said from behind us. And Boyd tentatively reached for my hand and shoved that evil-looking smile into one corner of his mouth.

McNelly kept his eyes on me, and again, I didn't see his mouth but only his beard move as he smiled. The little preacher must have kept his mouth constantly puckered. "Boys," he said to those close by— Boyd, George, Berry, Callicott, and me—but kept his eyes on me.

"When you're about to confront a man, keep your eyes on his. Don't blink." His eyes shifted from me to the other men. "Keep him fixed in your sight. Don't worry about getting your gun drawn. His eyes will tell you when it's time to shoot. But when you draw that gun don't hesitate. Aim where your eyes are." He, in turn, fixed his eyes for a second on each of us. "And you'll be able to take your opponent. Because you are in the right. And a man in the wrong can't stand up to a man in the right, who will just keep on coming. With right on your side, you'll be the better shot."

All except me joined in a chorus of "Yes, Captain." I bit my tongue to keep from asking what had happened to the Confederacy. I wanted to ask if I had been in the right when I bluffed Boyd.

Then McNelly stepped toward me and looked at me. He spoke hesitantly, like he was not sure of his decision. "We got good daylight left. Mount up, Nevin. We're going on a mission."

I looked around me for some answer. When I found none, Pidge sauntered up to me. "You're unlearning really well. Maybe you can unlearn some more." Pidge slapped me on the shoulder again and left me to McNelly.

CHAPTER 10

Casoose and Old Rock

WE got well down the road toward Brownsville before I allowed myself the obvious question: "So why am I with you?"

McNelly had ridden most of the way curled forward, Segal's gait, no doubt, hurting him. As for my mare, she had learned Sergeant Orrill's lesson; she stayed to one side or the other of Segal and stayed slightly in back of him. McNelly straightened his shoulders to look back at me. I clucked my tongue to get her even with McNelly and Segal. She looked warily at Segal. "Your fine rabbit fur hat has a hole in the crown," McNelly answered.

I pulled it off, the sweat gathered around the inner band running down my forehead, and looked at the frayed, uneven hole on the crown. I had finished brooding about my ruined hat, but McNelly had reminded me. "I always preferred a beaver, myself," he said. McNelly slowed Segal to a walk, and he seemed to breathe more easily. After a cough into his open palm, he straightened his head and shoulders. He reached into his jacket pocket to pull out one of his twisted cigars and stuck it unlit in his mouth.

My mare followed Segal's lead and slowed to a walk. "Nevin, if you're spying on me, I'll kill you," McNelly said and, his face beaded in sweat, turned that McNelly stare full of the righteousness of God and the state of Texas on me, as though I were one of the angels of darkness—or a Mexican. I tried to match his stare, but I was afraid that I would start laughing. So I stared at the ground. Old Rip's hesitant squint was due to caution and experience, necessary to stay alive; McNelly's was a sanctimonious dare to the world. McNelly returned that gaze to the road ahead of him.

"So why am I riding to Brownsville with you?"

McNelly did not look at me, but kept his eyes ahead. "You are not like the others. You know things. And you know Brownsville and the people I plan to see. I am meeting a Colonel Potter from Fort Brown, a Major Alexander who commands at Ringgold Barracks, and a Major Clendenin at Edinburg." McNelly looked toward me as though making one final assessment, then asked. "What are the forces at Fort Brown like?"

"I'd guess there to be one hundred and fifty to two hundred infantrymen."

"And those are Negroes," McNelly said and pulled his cigar out of his mouth to give a slight cough. Then he looked at me. "I don't trust Negroes to die for this state or this country. What about the other areas?"

"Maybe somewhere close to the same, probably less cavalry troops at Edinburg and at Ringgold Barracks over by Rio Grande City."

"Do you see the absurdity of it, Nevin? How can that few men stop this thievery?" Then he started again, "Do you know Colonel Potter at Fort Brown?"

"I know of him." McNelly jerked his head toward me to urge me to go on. "He's a big man, well, he's fat. I imagine that he's a good commander."

"Not his appearance. Will he give me support?"

"What do you mean, 'support'?"

McNelly hesitated for a moment, then he turned his stare on me. "Will he follow me into Mexico with his nigger troops?"

I pushed my brain around trying to figure what to say. "I've had several conversations with Lieutenant Commander Kells of the gunboat *Rio Bravo*, and. . . ."

McNelly's head swiveled toward me. "Can he be trusted?"

"He talks and drinks too much. He wants to start a war," I said and saw just the corner of McNelly's beard raise into one of his rare smiles.

"So as you were saying, Nevin, would they follow me into Mexico to retrieve stolen beeves?"

I dropped caution and went for McNelly's trust. "Captain, I'm a reporter. I'm supposed to record the facts. But this is what I've noticed of Union officers. For the most part, advancement in the Union army is frozen. The only way to get a promotion is to do something extravagant, something that will earn public support and thereby demand advancement. Even though Colonel Ranald Mackenzie was officially reprimanded for *pursuing* Kickapoos and Lipan Apaches into Mexico and massacring them and then facing off a regiment of Mexican soldiers, he got public praise and has a shot at becoming a general. Potter appears to me to mostly be content to sit around and command his Negroes, but Alexander looks the part of cavalry officer—sort of dashing. From what I hear, he's looking for a fight. But both men, if left to their own, would charge into Mexico with or without you. However, since the Mackenzie incident, Washington and Mexico City are really worried about American troops in Mexico."

McNelly's voice picked up slightly in volume and tone. "Why thank you, Nevin." And I felt that I had somehow betrayed someone.

"Captain, while we are in town, would you like to meet my uncle, Rip Ford?"

"I've had the privilege." I looked at him, and he correctly interpreted what was in my mind. "I was a member of the '72 investigation committee. I met him then."

"Then you know the area?"

"I made some acquaintances. People came to me and volunteered their services."

We got into Brownsville well into the evening, and I guided McNelly to a livery stable where we boarded our horses, then I guided him to the Miller Hotel. He stepped on to the porch, coughed, fought for control of himself, and then said to me, "Nevin, I imagine that you are a sporting man who enjoys *entertainment*." Both corners of the whiskers around his mouth raised. I nodded. "Do your sporting until noon tomorrow, then meet me at Fort Brown. My meeting will have concluded by then. But, Nevin, in your sporting, find me some information."

"What type?"

"No one knows you are with me. And in these places of entertainment, listen. Tell me what you hear. Maybe even ask a few questions. I'll expect something helpful." I nodded my agreement, once again, to spying.

McNelly turned and started to the Miller Hotel. He turned to look at me. "You have quarters here. No reason to waste the state's money. I'll see you tomorrow at noon."

RIP came to the door in his nightshirt holding a lamp. His gaze was long, serious, deliberate, and even after he recognized me, extended. He stepped outside. He sat in one of the rocking chairs on the front porch, set the lamp down, and motioned for me to sit, too. He rocked a bit, and then said, "You smell like you're becoming a good trail hand." He actually chuckled.

"I'm on my way home."

"McNelly didn't run you off, did he?"

"I rode into town with him. Tomorrow he's going to meet with Colonel Potter and Major Alexander." His rocking became more vigorous.

"They should have come to me. Used to they would. But I'm old now." He wasn't talking to me. Then he did address me. "So what's he going to do?"

"I think that he wants a big fight. I think that he means to cross the river and retrieve a stolen herd or shoot something up."

"You think he can do it?"

"I doubt it. He seems a little, well, puny."

"So what's this puny little fellow like?"

Rip Ford had grown far more sophisticated than McNelly. "He's a preacher, low church. Methodist or probably Baptist. And he's got God and the state of Texas on his side. All he sees is right and wrong, black and white. As far as I can tell, he pays no attention to opposing forces or anything else. He knows nothing about the problems here."

"Maybe he's just trying to fool you?" From the backyard, we heard the bell on John William's goat.

"That damn goat. Shakes his head just to annoy me. To wake me up."

"He's dangerous, Rip."

"That's why I'm going to make him into goat stew."

"Not the goat—McNelly! To him, every Mexican is a potential bandit, and every bandit should be killed. Hell, he'd probably shoot Sabas Cavazos just because he's Cortina's half-brother. He doesn't see distinctions. And he's dying. He's got a death wish. He wants to go out in some blaze of glory. And he's going to take his Rangers with him."

"So he didn't impress you too much, did he?"

"He scares me."

"Nevin, I don't know how much I can trust you on this. This is your first time out with a real force."

"I'm not an idiot."

"No. But you can get confused. Although you've picked up the smell of a horseman."

I sniffed. "What do I do, Rip?"

Rip swatted around his head at some mosquitos that had gathered.

"Let your conscience be your guide." I chuckled, then he chuckled. "Better yet, let your instinct for survival be your guide. It's always worked better than your conscience."

"What if he wants to lead his company off into an invasion of Mexico?"

Rip put his hands over his face. "He's not as smart as the old Ranger captains. Not like Jack Hayes, Sam Walker, Ben McCullough," then he chuckled, "or me. None of us would have wasted men. Didn't have the luxury. Not like the officers of a regular army." Then he said something that I wouldn't have expected from him, "Run like hell." He turned to look at me. "You'd embarrass and humiliate yourself, but go ahead and desert him if you can live with it. This ain't worth dying for. Not yet. If you got to die for something, wait for something better." He turned to look at me, and my face must have shown my surprise. "Hell, I'd miss you at Sunday dinner." He broke into a smile.

I left Rip's house to go to my apartment above McGuffey's saloon and take a glorious warm bath and scrape the smudge off me and thus become again distinct from the Rangers, rustlers, vaqueros, and soldiers. Clean, I sought my own entertainment, not McNelly's, so I walked to the levee, crossed the river on the ferry, took the mule-drawn streetcar to the edge of Matamoros, then walked the rest of the way to Catalina's cottage. On the way, I saw some perennials growing from someone's cement vase. I plucked three or four for Catalina.

A light was on in the house. I hesitated, but knocked anyway. She appeared at the door in an evening gown, the tops of her small breasts showing above the plunging neckline. As if by instinct rather than intent, she raised her hand to protect her golden chest from my sight. I tried to peek behind her, but she removed her hands from her chest and put them against mine. Her brows knitted, and a worried look filled her face that made her look every bit her age. "Andrew, go away." She glanced behind her and slowly pulled the door partially closed behind her.

"Where are you? Come on, my little chicken. Where are you?" I heard from inside.

"Go away, Andrew. You are in danger." I stepped to the side and reached for the door. She sidestepped to get in front of me. "Go away."

I stopped because my mind took control and told me that I could indeed be in danger. I looked down at the small, tough woman. What light there was caught at the high points of her face—her cheeks, forehead, and chin, and dark filled the pockets and the sags. She couldn't keep a smile, so her face drooped all the more. I looked at a woman who was fighting her age but would soon lose to it, and I loved her all the more because of her losses. "Leave him inside and come with me."

Catalina grabbed my elbow with both of her arms and pulled me across her porch to her steps. As she led me down the steps, I heard the voice from inside again, but couldn't make out what he said.

"Go away," Catalina urged.

"I could be killed any day now."

"You could be killed now if you don't go."

"Who is in there with you?"

She stopped pulling, planted her feet, and breathed in. "If I tell you, will you go away?"

I hung my head. "I'll go."

"It's Juan Flores. Now go."

My head snapped back up. "No, no, the Las Cuevas Juan Flores? The rancher, bandit?"

"Depends on how you look at him as to whether he is a bandit or not. Now go. He'll kill you."

"Maybe I'd kill him."

Catalina chuckled. "He says that he will kill McNelly. Can't you see? He's your enemy as long as you are with those Rinches."

"I can see, but I know that I want to be with you."

I backed away, and we held hands as long as we could until her fingers slipped from mine.

I backed away from her and watched her turn her back to me to go into her cottage. I planted my hands in my pants pockets as I shuffled my feet back toward the streetcar and the river. I debated whether I should return to McNelly in the morning or desert now rather than later.

Back in Brownsville, in my room above the saloon, I lay my head on my pillow, and though my head throbbed with thoughts of Catalina and then McNelly, the glory of a clean, soft bed put me to sleep.

THE next day at midmorning, after a dreamless, fear-quenching sleep in a bed, after as much breakfast as I could stuff into me, I walked to the levee and spotted the *Rio Bravo*. I asked a sailor for Lieutenant Commander Kells, but was told that he was not aboard. I walked the short way to the Bivouac. Kells was at the bar about to gulp down a beer with a raw egg floating in it. I stepped in with the sunlight coming through the front door and couldn't see anyone else in the bar's shadows.

Rose Montero noticed me and said, "Andrew, you want another goat?"

Kells saw me and held his glass of beer with the egg in it out in front of him as though to toast me. "Nevin, let me buy you a drink. They've got fresh eggs, a real pick-me-up with a beer." He raised his glass and sucked out the foam, yolk, and white. When he lowered his glass, egg and foam made a circle around his mouth on his red beard. "Expected you to be killed by now," he said and laughed.

I put my elbows on the bar. "First one is free for you, Andrew," Rose said and put a full beer in front of me.

"No egg in mine," I said. "I feel like I just ate all the eggs in Brownsville."

Before I could say anything, Rose asked, "You still got that goat or did you eat him?"

"He's pulling my young nephew around in that fine red wagon."

Rose nodded and left us. She sensed when business was about to occur. "Wipe your beard, Kells," I said, and Kells, with the flat of his hand, wiped the bottom of his beard and mostly succeeded in rubbing the egg into his whiskers. He pushed his cap to the back of his head and his wavy red hair jumped out over his forehead. "McNelly's in town," I said. "He's meeting today with Colonel Potter and Major Alexander."

Kells tapped the side of his forehead with his forefinger. "It didn't escape me. I've got eyes in this town."

"What have you heard?"

Kells held his finger to his lips and said, "*Shhh.*"

"I'll be quiet." I looked over my shoulder and caught Rose's eyes. "Let me buy you another beer."

Kells eyes brightened, either by the thought of another beer or by what was going on in his head. "I don't give a damn about what they are talking about. Probably the obvious. But they don't have the troops. This is a navy job, not an army job."

"The job is to stop the thievery."

Kells nodded, "Exactly." Rose put another beer in front of him and cracked an egg on the rim of the glass and emptied the floating yolk into the beer. Kells winked at me. Staring at his glass of beer and egg, Kells said, "Nevin, whose side you on? Surely, you're not sympathizing with those greasers against the greater good of these United States or our preserved Union?"

"To tell you the truth, since I've been here nearly fourteen years,

I'm a little sympathetic to this community. I saw it shot up enough during the war."

"You've been listening to that blowhard Sheriff Browne and those leftover disgruntled Blues." Kells looked at me. "Yeah, I know about them. I'm a student of politics."

Starting in the back of my head, a thought shot through my brain to my forehead, "Have you corresponded with McNelly?"

Kells held his fingers to his lips again and said, "*Shhh*."

I assumed that this gesture would bring some kind of explanation, so I waited while he prepared to talk, but as he did, our eyes were caught by the figure blocking the light coming in from the doorway. It was McNelly. He was in the black suit that I'd seen him wear at the King Ranch. He'd probably just come from his meeting with Potter and Alexander.

McNelly stepped in and seemed to sniff at the place. He was probably smelling the sin and the lawlessness. He sized up the place then stepped up to the bar, while Kells and I swiveled to face him. His eyes caught for a moment on Kells's beer then shifted to mine. "Commander Kells?" he asked with his eyes on me.

"Yes sir," Kells said and shook McNelly's hand. Kells turned away from him to face the bar. "Pull up a piece of bar, Captain."

"Perhaps we should find a more private place," McNelly said.

"Why this is . . ." Kells started to say, but McNelly jerked his head toward the far end of the bar. Kells straightened. He pressed between me and McNelly. But when Kells passed, I saw McNelly in front of me. I had to look down at the shorter man.

"Captain," I said and nodded. "This is how I find information."

"I hope that you have some."

"Some."

"Why don't you report to your assigned post? I'll meet you there on time."

I nodded, and McNelly stepped past me to go into a dark corner of the bar. I watched as the shadowy figures that he and Kells had become lowered themselves into chairs on either side of a table. "Funny little man," Rose said. I saw her in front of me.

I finished my beer in three gulps and slapped some change on the bar. I nodded toward the corner, not knowing if either man could see me. I whispered to Rose, "See if you can catch what they are talking about. I'll pay you for listening when I'm back in town."

"I don't know. From what I hear, you could be dead before you get back to town," Rose said.

I left Rose and stepped outside. Segal was tied to a hitching post. I walked to the livery to retrieve my mare, then walked her to the front gate of Fort Brown.

WHEN McNelly met me at the Fort Brown gates, with sentries and a mounted Colonel Potter and Major Alexander looking on, he had changed back into his brush outfit. He exchanged a salute with Alexander and Potter and then reined his horse off on the road. My mare was wary of Segal, but had grown more tolerable of him.

We were well along the trail, traveling at an easy lope, my mare nervously eying Segal, before McNelly said anything. He had remained sullen and contemplative. And I had ascertained that, if I was going to find out anything from this man, it would have to be done subtly in bits and pieces. "You promised me some information," he said. When not in front of men he needed to impress, just me, he allowed himself to droop, to become a sick, weak consumptive. And because he allowed me to see him as that, I thought that perhaps he did see me as someone nearing an equal. We were very nearly the same age. We knew the same people. We could recall the same collection of experiences. And in his world, he had mostly younger or older men. Somehow, under certain conditions, I realized, he thought that he could trust me—or use me.

"I only had one evening."

"So what did you find in one evening?" His head bobbed with the horse, and he looked like he was trying to keep a cough in his lungs.

"Juan Flores is behind the raids from Las Cuevas," I said.

"That's not exactly hard information to come by, Nevin." He lifted his head enough to stare through me and threaten me. "You can't do better?"

"He wants to kill you."

McNelly's beard shifted as he smiled underneath it. "And how did you come by this information."

"I'd prefer to keep my sources anonymous. As you well know, if I reveal them, they don't become reliable."

McNelly's beard wiggled. "Even to me?"

I thought of Rip and got some backbone. "Especially to you." McNelly nodded and drooped once again in his saddle.

"You know, Nevin. I am a good judge of a man." I looked at the drooping figure. "You could be a leader. What you did to Boyd shows some intelligence. You're older than the others. They'll look up to you. You could help me—if you wanted to."

I studied him. When he drooped, I had an advantage. I took it. "Like I said, Captain. I'm a reporter, not a leader."

After several more hours, two riders approached us from a trail leading through the brush to the road. We slowed our horses. McNelly's beard twitched. They were both older men. The one with the sombrero reined his horse some distance away from us, and the other, older man led his horse toward us, and hot as it was, he had on a Union soldier's campaign coat. I recognized him as Old Rock, the man who guided a posse to the teacher's mutilated body. "Captain McNelly," he said as he looked at McNelly and then shifted his gaze to me. I looked at the other rider.

"Old Rock?" McNelly asked.

"I'd hope that I haven't changed that much since you saw me back in '72," Rock said. I kept my eyes on the other man.

"You've, you've . . . " McNelly searched for the words.

"Gotten older, Captain. I can see it in your face as well as mine."

"You are a man of your word, Rock."

Old Rock nodded. "Like I said in '72, alls I want is a chance to defeat these thieves and murderers."

My mare started to edge up toward his, so I yanked on the reins. "Hello, Nevin. That's your name, ain't it? I tend to recall you." Rock leaned to the side of his saddle and spit a brown wad into the dust of the road.

"We both accompanied a posse to find that poor mutilated teacher," I said.

Rock looked down at his Union coat. "You ain't spooked by my outfit, are you?" I shook my head. Rock shifted his attention to McNelly. "Your men ain't gonna be spooked by a Yankee, are they?"

"They'll not mind it. I'll see to it," McNelly said.

Rock looked at his sleeves. The coat was faded, but some brighter stripes crossed the sleeves. From the size, I guessed a sergeant's chevrons had been on that sleeve until recently. "The Grand Army of the Potomac. One of the finest armies ever put together."

"And one that sustained the most casualties," I added, and both Rock and McNelly looked at me as though I had transgressed my bounds.

Rock smiled at me, and I noticed his brown-stained teeth. "That was a despicable sight, that poor teacher all cut up like that. All the more reason to kill bandits." Then he shifted his attention toward McNelly. "Captain, I figure between me and Jesús, you got the best scouting team in the area."

McNelly cocked his head, and the other man eased his paint horse forward. His sombrero made shadows on his face. He had the tight leather leggings with silver buckles like the vaqueros wore. His brown beard and shoulder-length hair were flecked and streaked with gray. Neither hair nor beard seemed to have been trimmed in months. His skin was burned into a crisp brown so that it looked like old, over-treated leather. But his clear, nearly transparent blue eyes were the most unsettling part of the man. They were out of place, eerie, deep. He moved them around, looking constantly from place to place, as though afraid to let them rest, and they gave the impression that, if they did rest on a poor soul for too long, they cursed that soul. "This here is Jesús Sandoval," Old Rock said. "His disposition ain't as good as mine." Sandoval had several coiled ropes hanging from his saddle. He nodded to McNelly and then me.

"Does he understand English?" McNelly said.

"When he has to," Rock said. "But mostly he don't want to."

"I heard about him," I added, and again both Rock and McNelly looked at me as though I had spoken out of turn. And then slowly, like an owl, Sandoval turned his gaze toward me.

"I'll presume that he ain't gonna talk. So I'll tell you, Captain. No one but him truly knows his history." While Rock explained, Jesús Sandoval sat stoically on his horse and shifted his gaze between us. "Some say his whole family was wiped out during the Mexican War. Some say his wife was raped and killed. All he wants to do now is kill bandits. You don't even have to pay him."

"He'll do," McNelly said, and I jerked my head to look at him. Rock, in turn, looked at me. McNelly repeated for my benefit, "He'll do fine." McNelly urged Segal onward, and Rock and Sandoval fell in behind us.

McNelly had decided to take two days to get back to camp, so we stopped for the night. He didn't have his tent, so he spread his bedroll between ours. As our campfire turned to coals, McNelly pushed himself up from his bedroll and walked into the darkness. Rock, Sandoval, and I searched each other with our eyes as we listened to McNelly coughing. I pushed myself up and started into the darkness. "Nevin," Rock said. "Nevin, I don't think Captain wants to be disturbed." I looked at Rock for just a moment, then pushed into the darkness to find McNelly.

I found McNelly with his hands on his knees, bent over, and spitting up blood. When he saw me, he straightened, turned, and faced me. He wiped at his lips with the back of his hand. "Captain, are you all right?"

"Get back to camp," he said.

I stepped forward and whispered. "Walk with me for a moment."

McNelly obliged, and we walked into the darkness. "There are legends about Sandoval. People in Brownsville use his name to scare children into acting properly. He's a villain. He's totally outside the law. Some say he's crazy." I stopped walking. "He'd be a detriment to us, Captain. He's a vicious killer."

"Aren't you overstepping your bounds, Nevin?" McNelly replied. "You heard me. He'll do." I stood looking at him, afraid to turn my back to him. He broke the standoff by softly saying, as though scolding a child, "I thought I told you to turn in that Winchester to Dad Smith and get a Sharps."

I turned, like a whipped puppy, and thought that McNelly would follow me. I stopped and looked back at him. "Captain, will you make it? This expedition can't be good for your health."

"My health is also not a concern for you," he said softly. I walked back to my bedroll.

For most of the night, I tossed and turned over the lumps in my rocky bed. After just one night on a real mattress, I felt uncomfortable on bunches of grass underneath a blanket. Finally, able to shut off my discontentment and discomfort, I entered that semiconscious state where I felt that sleep was overtaking me. But I felt a rub and tickle on my cheek.

I turned toward it, but felt a hand on my shoulder. My fright took the form of a shout that got caught in my throat as a dirty, greasy hand spread over my mouth, and a face appeared over me. Old Rock had crawled up next to me, and now he was over me. He pulled his hand away. "What the hell are you doing?"

I squirmed out from under him. He whispered. "I know you, Nevin. I know about you. And if you're spying on us, I'll gut you."

"I'm here of my own accord. I volunteered."

He nodded. I noticed that it was his coarse beard that had rubbed my cheek. "But if you've talked to Cortina or anybody else, even your uncle. I'll kill you. And now you know, I can sneak up on you anytime I want." His breath was foul, like some scavenger who had dined on rotting meat for years.

"I'm a reporter. I'm on assignment."

"Yeah, well just be sure that you record what happens and don't make anything happen."

"You misjudge me."

I saw him nod his head and then lean closer to me so that I could again feel his breath on my face. "From what I can tell, then, a lot of people around here misjudge you."

I rolled away from him and tried unsuccessfully to get some sleep.

CHAPTER 11

Palo Alto, July 1875

The same intense scarlet that spread across our cheeks as we rode into
battle, also spread across the bandit's chest, when Lt. Robinson shot him.
Like a Virginia cavalier, he led the charge across the marsh to capture the
band of bandits.

ANDREW NEVIN
Brownsville Sentinel, *July 1875*

———

AFTER a few days of coming and going in our camp, Jesús Sandoval became "Casoose." "His name is Jesús," I told Bill Callicott and George.

"That's what I said, 'Casoose,'" Bill said.

And we soon saw Casoose's purpose. McNelly organized small squads to scout the countryside. He told us not to harm or harass good, decent citizens, but to bring in any suspicious bandits. He didn't tell us how to distinguish between the two.

George Durham and Sergeant Orrill brought in one suspect. He was suspect because he had a wide-brimmed sombrero and a sash, like mine, around his waist and because he couldn't speak English. McNelly, George, Orrill, Callicott, and I gathered around him while he sat in between us. The man's quick eyes shifted from one of us to the next, but he wouldn't let himself show any emotion. His eyes steadied on Casoose when he walked to the group.

McNelly looked around to see who was in camp, then he looked at me. "McGovern is gone. Nevin, you go with Casoose in case we need an interpreter." Then McNelly looked at George as though sizing him up. "Durham, you go with him and stand guard."

Casoose stepped through the ring we had made around the man

and jerked him up. As he untied the man's hands, our suspect backed away from Casoose as though he smelled bad. Rubbing his wrists, the man's eyes shifted from me to George, and we could see what he was thinking about: should he run? I would have just let him run. Casoose jerked the suspect's arms behind him and tied the suspect's hands behind his back. He jerked and pulled the man with one hand while he led his paint horse with the other. George and I, like boys, followed behind.

At some distance from the group, Casoose looked up at the branch of a low oak and jerked the man and his paint horse to a stop. His light blue eyes set deep in his brown, furrowed face came to life. He pulled his coiled lariat from his saddle horn and threw it over the tree branch. "Wait a minute," I said. "McNelly said to interrogate him." Casoose's blue eyes, almost like a pretty blonde girl's, made me freeze. George grabbed me as though I were about to step on a rattler.

The man looked at the rope hanging over the bough, then looked at me. His eyes now filled with fright. The bandit begged me, even as Casoose knocked the man's sombrero off his head and put the looped end of the lariat around his neck. Then Casoose asked the first question. "Where are you from?"

The man swung his head toward Casoose. "McAllen ranch," he said. Casoose jerked on the rope and the man went up on his tiptoes. He tried to talk but only made gurgling sounds.

"He can't answer if he's choking," I said and stepped toward Casoose, who merely turned his eyes toward me.

"Back off, there, Andrew," George said. "Captain knows what he's doing. That's why he hired ol' Casoose here."

With his chin sticking up, unable to turn his head, the man pushed his eyes into the corners of his sockets to keep begging me. His toes gave out, and he slumped, and just as he did, Casoose yanked on the rope. I stepped forward to help the man to a standing position. Casoose asked in a low voice, almost like McNelly's whisper, "You want to be next?"

Casoose eased up on the rope and asked again where the man was from. This time he said, "Mier."

Casoose nodded and asked, "Where are the cattle that you are stealing?" The man hesitated, Casoose looked at the bough of the tree with the rope over it. He repeated the question.

The suspect halfheartedly said, as though he was just trying to accept his fate, "I have no stolen cattle."

I translated to George, and all of us knew what would come next. Casoose tugged on the rope. Again, as his breathing turned to gargling, the man shifted his eyes to the corners of his sockets to beg me. Casoose let up on the rope, and the suspect fell to his knees; then he fell forward to let his forehead hit the ground

"Please," I said and stepped forward. Casoose's eyes pushed me back to George, and I saw the man, his rump in the air, his tied hands, just above his waist, twisting against the rawhide thong until blood dripped down his fingers. Casoose pulled on the rope so that the man had to rise first to his knees, then to his feet, choking the whole time. As soon as he could get the words out, he said that a cattle herd was being crossed. Casoose asked him where. Shaking, the man mentioned a point just south of our camp.

I translated for George, and Casoose's face grew calm and his eyes lost their sparkle. He took the loop from around the man's neck. "Let's go tell the Captain," George said.

"Wait," I said. I stood my ground and stared at Casoose as he started putting a hangman's knot in the lariat.

"What's he going to do?" George asked me, not Casoose, as though Casoose were beyond all human communication.

"Don't, don't," I muttered.

"Cabrón," the bandit said.

"Look," I said. "You got the information you wanted."

"Go tell the Captain. If you got no guts for what's coming." Casoose looked up from the noose he was knitting. George backed away from me.

Casoose completed his knot, then put the noose over the man's head. The man began shouting: "Cabrón, I told you. I told you. I promise. I'll ride away. I'll leave." I saw George backing away from me, not even minding the brush that he backed through.

"No, no. Let's think about this." Casoose paid no attention to me.

"I've got a family. Three little girls," the man said.

Casoose looked at the man, and the soft blue drained from his eyes, replaced by hard turquoise glint. "I had a family, too."

Then, as he led his paint horse to the man, and helped him onto the horse's back, Casoose muttered not so much to the man but to the landscape, the tree, the hot summer air, or God, "Think about your family. Remember their faces. Think about what's going to happen to them." The man began shaking his head against the slack rope. I looked at George. "Tell McNelly," I said. "Go." George turned and began running.

"Wait," I said and drew my revolver.

The man looked at me and stopped his begging. Casoose stopped muttering, looked at me, and laughed. "Go away," he said. He pushed the man and told him to stand—so it would be quick. Struggling, slipping, the suspect stood in the saddle and once again begged me with his eyes. Once the man was at his full height, one boot slipped on the slick leather of Casoose's saddle, and the bandit nearly hanged himself. Casoose studied the lariat, the slack in it by the man's head, then tied the rope securely around the trunk of the tree.

"Por favor, mis niñas," the man said. I put my pistol back in my holster, and Casoose hit the paint with his flat hand. The man's neck broke just as he shifted his eyes to me. McNelly had wanted me to see this.

TWO hours later, after a mad ride to the river, we saw that the cattle had crossed sometime before. That night, over a campfire, I caught McNelly's eyes with mine. He ducked his head, then lifted it to meet my accusation. "We can't spare the men to guard prisoners. The sheriff wouldn't hold them, so they'd be able to inform the others of our movements."

"That's not good enough," I whispered.

Casoose came up and squatted beside McNelly, and the firelight made patches of light and dark on each man's face. McNelly let his eyes meet mine. "And now they'll be scared of us," he said.

"As rough as this country may look, we still have civilization. We are still governed by civilized society," I said.

McNelly shook his head. "We can't afford civilization out here. In Louisiana, during the war, with my few scouts, we survived only through intimidation."

I wondered for a moment just what McNelly had done during the war before I said, "But this isn't war."

"Don't fool yourself," McNelly said. Before I could say more, with Casoose staring at me, McNelly said, "I don't hold myself separate from my men. But you better get some distance between you and me, Nevin."

I'd been warned again. So I stood and walked away from the campfire. As I got into the dark, I heard a voice, then made out Pidge's cocked hat. He walked up to me so that I could just barely make out his face. "Well, brother, I think maybe you need to work on the art of being discreet."

"Hell, I was a spy during the war. I thought I was discreet."

He hung his head. "McNelly's been talking about you. Let your foot fall lightly around him. I'd hate to lose a comrade of the pen."

"I'll pretend that I'm back in the war."

"You are back in the war," Pidge said. "You know why you rode with him into Brownsville?"

"You told him about our conversation. Pidge, I thought that was confidential."

"I told him he could trust you," Pidge said. "Don't prove me wrong. Just be careful now, and write what you want later."

"Pidge, you're a civilized man. You're above all this. You know what's going on."

"No, I don't know."

"You choose not to know."

"I know I don't want to choose between you and McNelly. Don't make me."

I was about to turn away from him because he too was a part of the barbarity. But then a thought hit me: I too was now a part of it. Together, when we finished our respective reports, we would have to strain the grit from the truth. So I stuck out my hand to a fellow conspirator.

I think that Pidge gave that warm, confident, comforting smile of his before he clasped my hand. When we pulled our hands apart, Pidge stepped back into the darkness to go back where he camped: close to McNelly and his confidence.

CASOOSE had several more informants, and we had another near miss. Though he was generally careful and skilled at killing the informants quickly, on one interrogation, Casoose's knot popped the man's head off his neck. Berry, George, and I saw the blood gush out and the body fall out from under the noose. Then Casoose got us news that a group of rustlers was going to cross east of Brownsville and were making their way near the Laguna Madre marshes. We rode hard and gained on them, right near Palmito Ranch, the site of Rip's fight with Yankees, and Palo Alto, the site of Zach Taylor's opening battle of the Mexican War. Now we were going to have our war in this area.

We left before daybreak with Casoose and Rock scouting ahead and with McNelly riding at the head of our double column, looking stiff and tense. We spotted the cow manure, some floating in the standing water. Rock rode up and circled his arm, and McNelly stopped and rode to Rock. Then, he just broke into a gallop, and we followed.

With the morning haze and fog lifting, we saw the tail end of the herd just as the thieves saw us. They abandoned the herd to gallop away and look for defensive ground. McNelly spurred Segal, and we did likewise, and I held my bridle in both hands, ready to jerk hard to hold my mare up. The bandits splashed through water and cleared a shallow resaca. They reined up, dismounted, and prepared to repel our charge. McNelly stopped us on the near side of the resaca, then turned to us.

I was in between George Durham and Berry Smith. Both were breathing hard, and Berry had big eyes. George's drooping hat almost covered his eyes, so I couldn't see them. "Boys," McNelly said to get our attention. "Those bandits have mistreated our women and carried off some into slavery. They claim to be bigger than the law, than Washington law, bigger than Texas law. So we're about to find out if they are." I lost track of his speech and focused on the men. They had pulled their horses around McNelly, and horses and men were all breathing heavily. Bill Callicott was smiling, as though this was finally the adventure he had waited for. Rock was smiling, too, but this was a knowing smile, a sarcastic smile, one that said he had been through these skirmishes before and was just tolerating the ceremony. Sergeant Orrill let his jaw go slack, as though he were listening through his opened mouth. Boyd had his mean grin, which threatened some senseless, useless violence. Berry's big eyes showed him to be confused, overwhelmed, too much to absorb, but I saw the reins on George's horse vibrate. I followed the reins to his left fist and saw that fist shiver. I looked for Casoose but didn't see him, and if I could have broken their attention from McNelly's speech, I would have asked one of them what I looked like.

Even when I was that young, I cringed when I heard the forced rhetoric of patriotism. I became a coward during the war out of fear and indifference. I just couldn't stand a less educated, less civilized man urging me and other young men to suppress my natural inclination toward self-preservation to uphold some transitory belief. But then I thought that McNelly might be mixing tactics or advice in with his inspiration, so I forced myself to listen. All I heard was, "When you get among them, pick out one and stay with him. Ride him down. And don't check to see if he's dead or alive. Put a slug in him, then check."

Segal lunged and broke the talk. And as soon as Segal hit the resaca, my mare ran behind him. Sergeant Orrill yelled at me, "Don't rush it, rein that horse."

But as McNelly pushed Segal, my mare pushed ahead. The shallow water and mud were splashing all around me, and then I saw splashes where the bullets from the bandits fizzled and just dropped. "Don't waste your shots," Orrill screamed from behind me. I wasn't about to draw my gun. I raised both hands to my reins and leaned forward to ease my mare's gallop and so I wouldn't roll over backward. As the saddle pounded my inner thighs and rear end, as my gunnysack alternately pounded against my mare's shoulder and my thigh, I looked to my left, and through the spray of mud and water I saw McNelly looking at me. Segal and my mare were in a race.

"Rein up," McNelly said. And I tried, first with one-handed jerks, then by taking a rein in both hands and jerking one way or the other. I squeezed my mare with my knees. But she only turned her head from left to right to absorb some of the pull in her mouth and kept outrunning Segal. I looked over my shoulder and saw the Rangers in a skirmish line, five paces apart, following orders, while I was gaining distance from them and gaining ground on the bandits. I felt something whiz past my ear and swung my head around. The bandits' bullets were no longer falling short and splashing water. Even McNelly was behind me, but still my mare didn't slow up. Now she wanted to get to the bandits' horses. From my position I could see McNelly's face twist with his disappointment. I could tell that he assumed I was a dead man because I couldn't control my horse.

I said what the hell to myself and didn't resist my mare. I heard shots from behind me and risked falling to look behind me at McNelly and the Rangers shooting. Still I didn't dare draw my pistol because I was using both hands to hang on. I looked to my right. Nearly even with me, leading several men to cut off a retreat in that direction, rode Pidge Robinson, his hat brim pushed against his forehead, his silk bandana waving behind him, his revolver drawn. He was the very image of what I and every young man of the South envisioned as the ideal cavalier gentlemen. I believe he saw me and smiled.

Then I was going faster as my mare hit less waterlogged, spongy ground. I had made it to the rise and the mud that the bandits were standing in. I was in amongst them. She could see no other horses to chase, so my mare just stopped.

I heard shouts in Spanish, knew only that the words were Spanish, but could not interpret any words, English or Spanish. My mare began to spin, and as I tried to shift my reins back to one hand, I dropped a rein, so she was now in control, not me. I got my revolver out of my holster, tried to count shots, but got only as high as three, as I pointed my revolver in the general direction of a blur that looked like a man—a sombrero, a sash, waving arms—and squeezed the trigger. From the smoke that swirled around me, I couldn't see anything distinct, but I heard their shots both from the snap of their firing pins igniting powder and from the bullets zipping around me. If riding a horse was like a dance, then this wild twirling through smoke and haze was a fast, spinning, uncontrollable, Mexican polka.

I felt something splatter in my face, and I feared that it was my own blood and brains, but as my mare crumpled, I realized that it was her blood and brains. She shrieked, and her legs gave out. She went straight down, me still on top. Who knows, she took a bullet meant for me, or maybe I shot her myself? Maybe she got her head in between my pistol and a bandit, or maybe I deliberately shot her to end the dance.

I crawled away from my mare as she rolled to one side and felt the mulch on my palms and knees. The smoke partially hid me and hid the circling bandits from my sight. And then, to verify the thought, I checked my empty palms to see that I had lost or thrown away my Navy revolver. Never thinking to stand up, since I hadn't been supported by my own legs in several long hours, I crawled on hands, knees, and elbows to the body of my mare. I jumped behind her, risking that she'd use her last breath to kick me. I put my head against her chest to hear and feel the last strained beatings of her heart, and grabbed Rip's converted .44 Dragoon revolver, which luckily had ended up on the top of my mare instead of under her.

As I rolled, to aim, I felt thuds in my mare's body as the bandits' bullets ceased her breathing and beating heart. Even though I had just led McNelly's charge at Palo Alto, I had proved myself to be a poor rider, unable to control my horse. And based on my past actions and my present panic, I certainly did not have any courage. But I did prove myself to be a good shot.

The pressure, the confusion, the balanced revolver in my hand, the combination—all allowed me to hit two people in four shots. I hoped that none of the people were my fellow Rangers, or God forbid, McNelly.

With my marksmanship or luck, the bandits backed away from me, and I heard no more thumps into my mare's body. The smoke cleared, and there was McNelly, dismounted, firing into the brush, glancing at me, and shouting, "Good job, Nevin."

Since McNelly was standing, I thought that it would be safe for me to stand. I stood, telling myself, "two shots, two shots." McNelly walked a few yards away from me, stopped, then turned to face me. "Nevin, I'm out. Bring me some more cartridges."

Before I could ask, "From where?" A bandit charged out of the brush, yelling, "Got you now," and raised a Bowie knife. I raised my revolver, but McNelly was between me and the charging bandit, so even with my newfound confidence, I couldn't risk a shot. McNelly actually smiled at me before he turned, calmly raised his revolver, and put a bullet, his last one, through the teeth of the smiling bandit. I saw chunks of bone and brain blow out of the back of the bandit's head, but like a charging tiger, the bandit kept coming. McNelly stood his ground, and just as the bandit got close to McNelly, his life and momentum left him, and he skidded to a stop and crumpled.

McNelly let his beard shift from one side of his face to the other with that smile of his as he turned his back to the dead bandit and walked toward me. And I noticed, behind me, still mounted, was George. "Good God almighty, damn," George said. "That man has a full sack on him."

I looked up at George. "Are you okay, George?"

"I just imagined I was squirrel-hunting back in Georgia. You ever had squirrel-head gumbo?"

McNelly surprisingly nodded, "We ate a lot in Louisiana during the war."

"But George, are you all right?" I asked again.

George couldn't answer because McNelly interrupted. "We've got a running fight now. Durham, pick out a bandit and follow him. Shoot what's left. Nevin, find a horse then do the same."

McNelly went back to his well-trained, obedient horse and mounted. He and George galloped away, leaving me with several dead bandits and my dead horse. For a moment I just stared at my mare. She never had a name; I never gave her one. I felt as though I had betrayed her.

I spotted my Navy Colt, picked it up, holstered it, and stuck the Dragoon Colt in my still-intact belt. I began looking for another horse and walked past several corpses. Then I saw a hatless Bill Calli-cott, tentatively reaching toward the sombrero on the head of a dead bandit. I reached up to check the top of my head to see if I still had my rabbit-fur hat with the hole in the crown still on my head. Bill snatched at the hat and quickly pulled it off the dead bandit. He pulled on the sombrero until it fit on his head and jerked up on the chin strap. "Do I look like a greaser now?" he asked.

I nodded. His comment reminded me that I hadn't looked closely at any of the corpses. I didn't want to, I didn't want to know, for besides not liking the barbarity of looking at ruined bodies, I didn't want to see anyone whom I recognized. "Bet I could pass for one of them," Bill said. "Hell, Captain might shoot me."

"Mind if I get a ride?"

Bill walked back to his horse and then helped me jump up behind him. As I grabbed his waist for balance, he said, "We sure gave 'em hell, didn't we? Goddamn, it was almost fun, huh?"

No, I told myself, it was in no way fun. But I kept that thought to myself.

I HAD to dip my head to fit it under Bill Callicott's sombrero's brim, and when he spurred his horse into a trot, I nearly slid off. I tried to wrap my arms around him, but he was slippery from sweat. And then I noticed just how hot it was. My eyes stung from the sweat in them; my hat seemed to slide further down on my forehead. Without danger, I began to concentrate, once again, on the miserableness of being on the trail. I wanted to be curled up on a down mattress beside Catalina.

We heard shots from off in the distance. "These bandits ain't like Comanch," Bill said. "When I was with Major Jones up around Jacksboro, them Comanches would charge us. They'd never get off a horse." He couldn't have been much over twenty and already he was or thought himself to be a veteran Ranger.

As we moved on, Callicott guided his horse toward two figures. The short, thin McNelly stared at the ground, then knelt. Callicott got close enough to see that McNelly knelt over a wounded bandit. From somewhere out of his canvas jacket McNelly pulled a thin New Testament. It must have rested right next to the black book with the Reconstruction outlaws' names. The Ranger turned into a preacher, held the Testament next to the heaving chest of the dying bandit, and started to pray. Callicott pulled his horse to a stop, then pulled off his sombrero, swiping me across the face with its brim.

The other figure, the one behind McNelly, was George. He didn't remove his slouching, shapeless hat but gawked at McNelly's transformation from warrior to preacher.

Shouting interrupted McNelly's prayer. McNelly was up and back on his horse as was George, and Callicott and I were galloping after them. I managed to twist my head around to look back at the bandit or a possible Brownsville neighbor. He was still trying to die, but now he no longer had McNelly's Testament, comfort, or prayer. He'd have to die alone.

We all reined up next to a thick mott. Out in front of the mott, a shirtless Boyd jerked his head toward a shallow, grassy marsh. He had a Ranger on either side of him, and more Rangers were riding up.

Boyd acknowledged McNelly, then he raised his pistol and shot into the grassy marsh. Two more rangers shot. Boyd's shirt was wrapped around his horse's neck and was becoming soaked with blood. We had more horse casualties than human. Boyd jerked his head to the other side. We walked our horses around his, and McNelly dismounted. Slowly McNelly approached a small Ranger face down in the salt grass. Callicott and George edged their horses up to the body. I saw the circle of blood pool around his upper torso.

McNelly knelt again, reached inside his jacket pocket to pull out his Testament, then turned over a dead Berry Smith. His face was smiling, but his chest was soaked in blood. McNelly held his hand under Berry's nose, then felt his throat. "He died for the state, the law, and righteousness," McNelly pronounced.

I looked to one side of me to see George curl his shoulders forward and dismount as though he were a very old man. I hopped off Callicott's horse and walked to George, who turned to me and twisted his face into a tight knot to keep from crying. I wanted to reach out to him, but I dared not.

"Someone ought to volunteer to go back to main camp and tell his daddy," George said.

"I will," I said.

"You don't have a horse," McNelly scolded me.

"We better kill that bandit that got him," Boyd said. McNelly directed his and our attention to Boyd. "He didn't listen. He got off his horse and walked to a dead man. The dead man rolled over and put a slug in him. That dead man's out floundering in that shallow pond."

We all squinted, then we saw grass move, and everybody shot. "Make a semicircle around him, and shoot at the grass, but be careful not to hit each other," McNelly said. Within fifteen minutes, I helped drag a bleeding, dead bandit out of the slush.

I looked around and walked toward a deserted horse warily watching all of us and hoping for some human to trust. The gelding let me get near him, and as I took the reins and swung up onto him, I noticed the bloodstains on the saddle and King's running *W* brand on its back. Without restating my request, without listening for an order, I clicked my tongue, moved the reins forward, and tapped the horse with my heels, intending to guide the ill-trained creature back toward our main camp, Las Rucias. "Hold on," McNelly shouted. From my perch on top of my horse, McNelly looked tiny and fragile. "It's too dangerous. We'll have to wait," McNelly shouted, and I moved the horse closer to him.

"I'm volunteering."

"Damn it, Nevin," McNelly looked around him. "There could be bandits behind us. I don't want to lose another man."

"I accept the job."

McNelly hung his head. "All right, so be it. Go back to camp and bring the entire force back to Brownsville." McNelly just stared at my face. "Can I trust you with this?"

I just smiled and pulled my new horse away from them all. "Don't get lost," McNelly yelled after me.

CHAPTER 12

The Public Market

Hideous death masks pasted to the faces of slain bandits greeted early shoppers this morning. For stacked in the Market Square were the bodies of those bandits killed by the supposed savior of the region, Captain L. H. McNelly. And as many repulsed observers noted, solid citizens saw the blood-stained bodies of friends, relatives, and neighbors.

ANDREW NEVIN
Brownsville Sentinel, *July 1875*

I FOUND my dead mare, avoided the flies that were already gathered around her eyes, looked up at the buzzards that were circling the whole scene, and replaced the bandit's bloody tack with my own. Then I forced the tired horse into a trot. He wanted to veer off the trail, kept trying to graze, stunk with sweat, but I kept pushing him. By sundown, my horse and I were exhausted, so I stopped and went to sleep without a fire or any food.

The next morning as I had my fire going for breakfast, I saw riders approaching and checked all my pistols and readied the Sharps that McNelly made me take. It was the rest of the Rangers from Las Rucias. They had been riding for half the night. McNelly had wired them from Brownsville. Either he didn't trust me, or he just figured that a wire would bring them faster, probably a little of both. Most likely he expected trouble and wanted more Rangers—and me out of the way.

Lieutenant Wright, the ranking Ranger, led them, and I asked him where Dad Smith was: a half mile or so behind in the wagon. So I stayed at my breakfast fire and waited until I saw Dad Smith's wagon rolling toward me. He pulled the wagon to a halt and could see from my face what had happened. "How bad is it?"

"He's dead," I said.

Dad Smith's head hung down and his shoulders drooped. "I guess I didn't do no good job of protecting him." I couldn't bring myself to look at the man who seemed to be withering in front of me. "Now I got to tell his momma." I dismounted and tied my horse behind his ambulance, then climbed into the seat with him.

As he shook the reins to the mules, he said, "You're an educated man. You help me write a good letter to his mother." So Dad Smith dictated, and I, in my usual manner, embellished. I wrote with a pencil on a sheet of tablet paper. We went through three sheets before Dad Smith was satisfied.

We pressed on, looking at the mules' rumps and swishing away flies. Dad said nothing, just tried to keep his jowls and eyelids from drooping. It was sundown, just outside of Brownsville, in the Ranger camp, before Dad Smith cried.

Dragging my tack, I found George just as he was spreading out a blanket. Boyd rested his head against his saddle, Bill Callicott was already asleep, and Sergeant Orrill was scooping up some beans with his fingers and then licking them. "Lost my spoon," he said when I looked at him. We all turned to Callicott when he snorted and blew. "That little fella can snore," Orrill said. "He didn't even wait to eat. Just plopped his ass down and went sleeping."

"You ain't eat yet either, huh?" George walked to the cooking-pots.

"These Mexican ladies brought a couple of pots of frijoles by," Orrill continued. "Captain said the state was good for the beans. Put them down in his ledger book."

"Be a tuneful night," Boyd said from his makeshift bed. Callicott's snore became a low whistle.

George came back, smiling from underneath his shapeless hat. "I guess you ain't had no more sleep than us either." I took the beans and thanked George. "Poor Berry. They got him over at the Yankee fort. A Major Alexander hisself promised to give him a Yankee-style funeral."

Orrill, sucking his fingers, slurred, "Least they could do."

I looked at the beans and realized that I didn't have a spoon either. I looked at George. "Have you got a spoon?"

"Ain't you got fingers? Or is eating with your fingers too good for a gentleman?" Boyd asked. I hesitantly dipped my fingers into the beans, mashed them with the tips of my dirty fingers, and then sucked some of the mashed beans.

George began scratching. "Being around all these cows is given me some fleas."

"Ticks, more likely," Orrill said.

George sat beside me and began scratching more vigorously. "You should of seen him, Andrew. He let me come with him into town. Set up headquarters in Miller's Hotel and began giving orders. And that Major Alexander, he just listened and nodded. They closed the ferry across to Matamoros. And everywhere we went, they just looked at us like we was mean dogs. Like they dared not touch us or even sniff us."

"Captain means to do that. They'll be scared of us now," Orrill said.

"Mean sons of bitches," Boyd muttered. I gulped down some more of my beans and relaxed, I realized, for the first time in two days. I felt the Gulf breeze pick up and cool the area, just a bit, and in the breeze was the smell of the salt and sea and of these dirty men, horses, and cattle. Like a barbarian, like these men, I raised the bowl of beans to my mouth, rested the edge against my lip, then poured the juice and beans into my mouth; I paid no attention as a stream ran down my cheek and on farther down my face and neck to stain my once white shirt. I looked around at my rough companions. Bill Callicott sucked in for more air. "Why ain't we in town in the Miller Hotel?"

"McNelly's scared of a reprisal. Wants us here. All together. Ready to rush in if need be," Orrill explained.

"That sheriff and everybody else is madder than hornets with them bodies stacked up in their market," George said.

I jerked up. "What bodies?"

"Them bandits," George said and looked from one face to the other. He had a stupid smile on his face. "Captain had a marshal fetch 'em to town in an ox cart. Then he had 'em piled in their market. And I stood first watch to see that nobody drug off their kin. Bodies stacked up like that, with guts and blood dripping and flies buzzing. It's an awful sight."

I threw the plate down and picked up my saddle and blanket. I started for my new horse. "Where you going?" I heard Orrill shout from behind me. "We got orders to stay put," George yelled.

I swung my saddle onto my horse as Lieutenant Wright came up to me, "Where are you going, Ranger?"

"To town."

"We've got strict orders," Lieutenant Wright said. I heaved my shoulder back and looked at the face of the taller man. He was not budging. "Don't mount that horse." While I thought, Orrill, George, and Boyd had come up behind me.

"Forget, it Andrew," George urged.

"Ain't nothing you can do," Orrill said as he leaned his long neck toward me and thus shook the loose skin under his chin.

"Ranger, you mount that horse, I'll have to shoot you," Lieutenant Wright said.

"And that horse is tired," Orrill declared. "He'd never make it to town. He'll quit on you. You watch."

I tied my cinch and pulled it tight. Wright pulled his revolver. "Ranger, I'm warning you."

"You'll be shooting a civilian. I just resigned. The state can keep my pay." I delayed myself just a bit to look at the sweaty, dirty faces looking at me. I swung up into the saddle, backed the horse up, turned him, and waited for the bullet in my back.

I GOT to the streets of Brownsville at the same time as the lamp-lighters. The growing glow of the kerosene lamps, one small flame after the other until they became two nearly solid yellow snakes on either side of the street, led me down Eleventh Street to the Public Market and Town Hall. I pulled my horse to a stop. I was afraid to look at the bodies, so I first kept my eyes on the offices up above. The vendors, packing their leftover goods, and the piperos, returning to their jacales farther west, passed by me. And I slowly lowered my eyes to a stack of bodies.

George was right. Entrails and blood stained the stones under the overhanging awning. Vacant eyes stared out of puffy faces. Some of the bodies had already begun to bloat. Death in the bodies and faces of these bandits, perhaps one that I had killed, looked like a great, sudden, and unbearable indignity. And McNelly was displaying that indignity.

The passers-by stared more at me than at the bodies. They had had a day to get used to the bodies, and so the staring horseman was out of place. Then my logic kicked in. Perhaps the passers-by recognized me as a Ranger, not as a fellow citizen, and their stares were threats to me. So I backed and turned my horse once again and hurried through the lamplights' glow to the Miller Hotel. I was scared, just as I had been all during the war, thinking of the long, huddled wait with Addie, worrying that I was again going to be crossing and recrossing the river as I switched sides and waited with my fear, but without Addie this time.

I half expected to see Rip in the lobby of the hotel, but instead I saw Sergeant Armstrong. He slouched in a sofa, hatless, a couple of strands of his thinning hair stretching across his head. He smoked his cigar and smoothed his moustache. I said nothing to him, but he turned to see me. "What are you doing here?"

Armstrong, the man who would later capture John Wesley Hardin, was the most fearless and loyal McNelly supporter. He was also the most ruthless. As with McNelly, he saw the world divided between his own right and truthful side and the other side. To him, I was about to step across the line. I turned my back to him, and he quickly crossed the lobby to grab my arm. "Get back to your outfit."

"Where's McNelly?"

"I swear, I'll kill you if I have to."

I turned, but suddenly he spun me around, and his fist knocked the air out of my stomach. I fell to my knees, then his knee caught my forehead and knocked me backward. I grabbed my head and started to stand and heard voices. The clerk at the desk was running up to the scene. A woman was watching. We were in civilization. Even Armstrong realized that he couldn't thrash me in this lobby. So just as suddenly as he knocked me down, he jerked me up and pulled me up the stairs, my legs barely able to keep themselves under me.

With my eyes full of stars, I focused on Armstrong's face. He looked as though he were ready to beat me to death. Then I saw a hand place itself in the middle of Armstrong's chest and push him back. I forced myself to straighten up and see Pidge Robinson. "Nevin, what are you doing here?" he asked.

"Pidge," I whispered, but Robinson's look stopped me.

"Lieutenant Robinson, sir, I want a word with Captain McNelly."

"He's not to be disturbed."

"I understand he will always welcome his men."

"Not now."

Robinson pulled me to one side and whispered into my ear, "Nevin, don't do this. Leave this part out. Write about it if you must, but not now. Think."

"I thought the whole way over here. Please, as a writer, as a cultured man, you must realize that stacked bodies can't be good for anyone."

Robinson looked back at Armstrong, then back at me, to whisper again, "Forget it, Andrew."

"I can't. Just as you can't forget Pidgie." His face reddened, and for a moment I thought that this man, who was essentially a gentleman, but who could let himself be pushed to violent extremes and allow himself to look the other way when seeing atrocities, would also hit me. Instead he nodded to Armstrong.

Armstrong knocked on a door. A weak voice answered. Then Armstrong opened the door. Pidge led me to Armstrong, who pushed me in, stepped in himself, then closed the door behind him. McNelly and Major Alexander sat at a table with a lamp in the middle of it. Alexander, with his jet black hair and moustache slicked and in his navy dress tunic with the gold epaulets and bars, was the picture of a cavalry officer. McNelly, in his black coat that he wore at the King Ranch, but with a bloodless face and hollow eyes, was the picture of a consumptive, already dressed as a corpse. He could barely speak. "Nevin, what are you doing here? I didn't send for you."

"I'm here on my own accord."

"You've deserted, then," McNelly said.

"What kind of outfit do you run?" Alexander asked. "Shoot him if you want."

Alexander stood. McNelly tried to stand but couldn't. The color had even left his silky dark hair and beard. "I caught him outside," Armstrong said.

I stepped away from Armstrong and toward the two officers. "What role do you have in this?" I asked Alexander.

"What makes you think that you have a right to an answer?" Alexander responded.

"Get out," McNelly whispered.

"Who ordered those bodies stacked up like that? What kind of butchery is that?"

McNelly closed his eyes and swallowed hard, and for a second I thought that he would pass out. "Leave us, Ranger."

"I'm here as a reporter now. As a Brownsville citizen. Who started this?"

"Colonel Potter is currently out of town. And as ranking officer at Fort Brown, I have given my full support," Major Alexander said.

"Neither of you understands," I said. "You don't understand these people. Some of those dead are citizens of Brownsville. You could start a riot. You could start an invasion."

Alexander smiled, "Oh no, sir. We do understand."

I had no answer, but turned to look at McNelly. "What is your intention?"

McNelly pushed himself up, then he coughed, then coughed some more and spat into a handkerchief, and just as quickly he tucked his handkerchief into his black coat. "I will not have a man of mine desert his post." His glare held mine. He was in the right and was going to just keep coming—after me. But I felt myself stiffen my back and my resolve.

"Under the circumstances, I believe that I have a moral right to ask about this display of butchery. I am still a citizen of Brownsville."

"But you are no longer a Ranger," McNelly said, breathed, then tried to continue. "Nevin, I tried to excuse you. But now you have put my command in danger. You may draw your pay."

"You can keep that blood-tainted pay. I'm a reporter for the *Brownsville Sentinel,* and you will. . . ." Before I could spout more of my indignation, I felt Armstrong's arms again around me. A smaller man, knowing I couldn't fight, I protected myself by not resisting. He opened the door, flung me out of the door, and slammed it after me.

Back outside, Pidge Robinson was waiting for me. "You just couldn't let it go?" he said.

"Can you?" I said.

"Come on, Andrew, you probably saw worse during the war. This is no great matter."

"It is not something a gentleman would do."

Pidge hung his head. "The East can afford gentlemen. Not the West."

I pulled my hat firmly onto my head and left Pidge and the service of the Texas Rangers.

AFTER McNelly fired me, I rode to the office of the *Brownsville Sentinel* and walked in smelling like the trail, cattle, blood, and death. The office was well lit, and as I stepped in, Jesse Dougherty walked into our storefront from the press room. He had on the leather pressman's apron and the garters on his sleeves, but still his white shirt, and even his beard, was stained with ink. "You reporting back to work?" he said and sniffed the air.

"Yes."

"Where's your story?"

We had just one desk at the *Sentinel*—behind the wooden railing that separated it from the small receiving room. So I grabbed the edge of the desk and pulled our wheeled chair up to the desk, opened up a drawer, and pulled out a pencil and a pad of paper. "I'm working on my story."

"Why don't you come back and help me with the press?" Jesse pulled his forearm across his sweating forehead and left a streak of ink and grime.

"I'm writing my story."

"Some good being an editor is. All I do is the printing, the sweeping, the bill paying." I looked over my shoulder and saw his brows knit. "You could have gone home first, put on a tie, a clean shirt."

"I just got fired from the Texas Rangers."

"I'm not surprised. I never thought you'd convince McNelly or the state into letting you be a Texas Ranger. You're not at all like your uncle."

"No, I am not. Nor am I like McNelly."

Jesse left me to myself, but I didn't or couldn't write. Instead, I stared at my calloused, blistered, dirty hands. Two half-moons of dried sweat and grime covered the front of my white shirt. When I peered closer, I saw specks of blood. As I stared at my pad, a drop of sweat from my forehead splattered on it. *A Texas Ranger*. Already the words meant something, not only to Texans but to the country as a whole. They also meant something to a Mexican soldado, peón, or even haciendado. I was not my uncle, but was I a Texas Ranger? I shifted to pen and ink. The easier flow of ink rather than lead on paper might help the words come.

"Barbarism does not excuse further barbarism," I found myself writing. "If the situation in this valley is ever to be cured of violence and theft, then the greatest virtue won't be reparation but forgiveness." I stopped to think about whom I should forgive and for what. Cortina? McNelly? Rip? I may have killed a man. "We can still hear the echo of L. H. McNelly's heroic shots on Palo Alto Prairie. The citizens of Texas and this valley should appreciate a decisive action to stop thievery." A drop of my sweat stained the ink, and I blotted at it with the sleeve of my ruined shirt. "But the stench of those bodies and the stench of his subsequent actions warrant our indignation."

And then the front door opened. I saw Sheriff Browne and City Marshal Joseph O'Shaughnessey. "Gentlemen," I said.

Browne stopped and pointed at me. He was so mad that his big belly, sticking through his coat, shook. "So what are you going to do about him? You've seen those bodies." Like me, Sheriff Browne and Marshal O'Shaughnessey hadn't changed clothes. They had been in the field, rounding up bodies, saddles, cows, and horses. So both were stained with blood, sweat, and manure.

"I'm not a Ranger anymore. What can I do?"

"It's rubbing our noses in it. It's . . . It's . . ." He blew at his wide, bushy moustache.

"It's uncivilized," O'Shaughnessey said. He stepped from behind Browne. "It's a health hazard. It's in violation of city ordinance."

"So why don't one of you go remove the bodies?"

"He's got armed Rangers guarding them." O'Shaughnessey said in an indignant way, as though someone actually expected him to do his job.

"So who has the authority?" I asked. "Can't you enforce a city ordinance?"

O'Shaughnessey looked shocked and held his hands to his chest. "He's a Texas Ranger. And he's got the army behind him. Why, I can't go against. . . ."

Browne opened the wooden gate and walked to my desk. "Exactly. McNelly has no authority." Browne pounded a fist on my desk. He smelled as bad as I did.

"So order him to remove the bodies," I said.

Browne and O'Shaughnessey looked at each other. "He's got armed guards," O'Shaughnessey said. "Didn't you hear me?"

"Sounds like you have the authority, but he has the arms."

"You gotta do something," Browne said, then looked around.

Jesse Dougherty came to the door. "I'd think that you were looking for me instead of Andrew."

"I am, excuse me, *was*, a Texas Ranger," I added.

"You're both members of this community," Browne switched his gaze between me and Jesse and started breathing heavily, as though he would soon collapse.

"And our job is to report what happened and to give the official opinion of the *Sentinel*," Jesse said.

"That is precisely what we are doing," I replied.

"Are we going to have to call on your uncle?" Browne asked.

"Don't bother Rip yet." I looked at Browne with his long moustache covering the lower half of his face and O'Shaughnessey with his trimmed moustache and chin whiskers. Both faces seemed to plead with me.

"You should have seen that little shit-ass preacher, Nevin," Browne said. "You should have seen him. Giving me orders. Telling me to do this or that. If you'd have been there . . ."

O'Shaughnessy cut in, "Telling me to go out and fetch bodies."

But Browne went right on. "He's not an elected official. He doesn't know these people. He comes in here with orders from Austin, with his East Texas, State Police attitudes. He's going to . . ."

I filled in for Browne, "Cost you an election." Browne's face formed a sneer, but then he let himself smile when he saw my smile. "I think that you two will like my report."

"What's it going to say?" Browne asked.

"It's going to say that McNelly doesn't understand the region."

That answer seemed to appease both men. They smiled at each other in a congratulatory way and left me to my work.

What I did was to write a report which appeared that week, and then I wrote an editorial for the following week, which went counter to every English newspaper in the state and condemned McNelly for his barbarous act. I thought that I should become a Cortinista.

The other exceptional report was written by Pidge Robinson for the *Austin Daily State Gazette*. It wasn't so much a journalistic report but a satire on Robinson. He was a fine writer with a gift for making himself the target of his humor. He had the facts and the figures and the occurrences, but mixed in were self-deprecating comments about his thoughts and actions, all of which were contrary to his heroic and dashing thoughts and actions—so unlike my desertion. In short, I envied him for his bravery, his talent, and his disposition.

THE next morning ahead of a hearse from the Fort Brown morgue marched two bands: one a military band, the other a local band, both trying to coordinate their dirges. In the flag-draped coffin was Berry Smith. Behind the hearse leading the processional were L. H. McNelly, Major Alexander, and one of the city's processional marshals, Rip Ford. Behind them were the Rangers, as scrubbed and as dressed as they could possibly get. Some even wore new shirts. They tried to march in as orderly a fashion as they knew how. But dismounted, wavering in their boots, unused to military custom or ceremony, they had no precision or timing. They didn't make rows; they made clumps of men. Some even tried to rest their Sharps on their shoulders, some on their right shoulders, some on their left. And behind them was the company of Negro infantrymen, some probably for the first time wearing the full dress uniform complete with the Prussian-style helmets. I was surprised that an outpost like Fort Brown even had these uniforms available. They marched in a manner that was a mixture of U.S. military parade with Negro rhythm. McNelly had coordinated this event. He was letting Cortina know that the Rangers, on this side of the border, were considered American military men.

I watched with the crowd that followed behind or beside them. I saw fists tighten around rocks or old fruit, readying to heave a missile at the *Rinches,* but fear or numbers and the presence of Rip Ford kept the missiles in tightened fists. Rip Ford, straight and tall, a pillar of restraint and dignity, occasionally glanced at the crowd and warned them not to interfere with this show.

I hadn't said anything to Rip. I hadn't sought him out. I hadn't told him that I had been fired. As we had done since the war, we just gravitated to each other. Half the time I didn't like the man, but he was related to me in more ways than in blood.

As I watched Rip, sweating into his black suit, remove his hat and so command others in the crowd to remove their hats out of respect, not just for Berry, but for all the dead, I left the crowd, crossed that empty demarcation space between the procession and the crowd, and marched with the Rangers. I added a fifth man to a row that included George Durham, Sergeant Orrill, Bill Boyd, and Bill Callicott.

I walked beside George Durham, and he looked at me with an open mouth. George had a new hat and shirt and looked tall and handsome, every inch a Ranger, instead of a stooped and confused Georgia farm boy. Boyd sneered. Orrill kept a stony look on his face. Callicott waved. I took off my hat and put it over my heart. The others in my row looked around at the other Rangers, all with their hats on, and then they took off their hats, then a few hats ahead of us and behind came off.

At the newly dug grave, between the graves of two Mexican War heroes, while several Negro troops lowered the casket, McNelly spotted me. I'm sure he spotted me well before. He was too wary to have not noticed me, to have not paid attention to the crowd and thus have been ready for a riot, just as he had done with the State Police. He held my glance with his, his mouth twitching behind his newly trimmed beard, as though trying to smile. And I think that he both admonished me and thanked me for rejoining the Rangers for Berry's funeral.

ON that Saturday, Catalina Taracón sneaked away from any obligations or trysts promised to Juan Flores and asked me to escort her to a wedding in Brownsville. Feeling clean for maybe the first time since I had joined McNelly, I felt my heart skip beats in anticipation of seeing this petite woman with the grace, well-worn age, and charm to command admiration and appreciation as well as incite lust. After a service at Immaculate Conception Church, Catalina let the outside of her hand brush mine, so I turned my hand palm out so that we could discreetly hold hands, like two adolescents. Hand in hand, we walked with the parade of friends and relatives to Washington Square.

The bride's well-to-do father had gorditas and tamales, iced kegs of beer, and good tequila. And despite the father's status on both sides of the border, he allowed several layers of Mexican society to the baile.

Trumpets and guitars provided the polkas and waltzes. And a drunken man stood in front of the band and tried to sing his newly composed corrido, one about the villainous McNelly who murdered the good citizens of Brownsville. And warmed by good liquor and the secure feeling that just the right amount gives, I got to put my arms around Catalina and practice my dancing. As with horse riding, my dancing was clumsy, but Catalina didn't mind, and she counted to me so that I could keep step, and sometimes she took the lead. But mostly, when she got a chance, she would lean her head into my shoulder, just below my ear (she was that small), and tell me that she had missed me.

And then it was that George Durham and Bill Callicott, led by a drunken Boyd, showed up on the edge of the square. I halted my attempted dance with Catalina and led her by the elbow away from the dancing to a bench. I excused myself and stood on the bench to see the Rangers watching. George tried to tap his foot to the music. His head bobbed as though he tried to remember the dancing lessons that I had given him and Berry Smith. I caught his attention, since I was higher than the crowd and the dancers, and waved him away. He waved to me.

Boyd spotted me, and even in the kerosene-lighted dark, I saw his flushed cheeks. In his face, I could see the swagger, the meanness, the disobedience. McNelly, I knew, had warned them to stay away from the locals and parties such as this, but the drunken Boyd led the two youths into the crowd.

Boyd made the mistake of smiling at a young woman, whose fingers then fluttered up to her face like small birds. It was a ritual on both sides of the borders. The gesture could be interpreted as flirtation or embarrassment. But because she was with a man who wanted to please and protect her, he chose to interpret it as embarrassment. I felt Catalina's hand tighten around my forearm. She had stepped up onto the bench to watch, and to rescue me. I stepped down and then helped her down, and she held on to my arm the whole time. Even when were standing on level ground, she still held my arm. I tried to pull away from her, but she held on. "Andrew, this is not your business."

I looked around me at the guests in linen suits or their best dress shirts and trousers. I saw no Anglos. "It's got to be mine." She looked at me and slowly shook her head. But I pulled away from her and pushed through the crowd that was starting to surround the three foolish gringos.

I got through the crowd and into a semicircle around the three

Rangers, who nearly had their backs pressed together, trying to cover four sides with just three men. The suitor or would-be suitor of the upset girl was asking what their intentions were, but none of the Rangers could speak Spanish. For once, now that George had a new hat with a stiff brim, I could see his eyes. And I saw fright and then a glitter of recognition. "No le hace," I said. "Nothing is wrong. Relax." The stiffness went out of the crowd and out of the three Rangers' backs.

"Maybe you need to choose a side, Nevin," Boyd muttered.

I looked at him and said only, "Shut up." As I did, the offended man slipped past me to swing at Boyd, and suddenly some of his compañeros were beside him. Boyd sidestepped the attack, reached into his boot, pulled out a knife, and poked the tip under the man's armpit. The man stepped back like he had been stung by a bee. He reached under his arm, felt the blood, and then crumpled. His friends caught him.

I stepped in between Boyd and the man's friends, who began to look like snarling dogs. I saw the brown faces bobbing around me and circling me and my former compatriots. I smiled to the snarling faces and said just loud enough to the Rangers, "Back up, just back out of here. Keep backing on up."

"Whose side are you on?" Boyd asked.

"Goddamn, will you shut the hell up?" Callicott said.

We cleared the crowd, stepped out of the light of the square, then I faced the three of them. "Get out of here," I said.

"You going to come with us?" George asked.

I looked over my shoulder at the people standing over the wounded man. "No," I said. "Get," I yelled at the Rangers. I faced the crowd, and out of the linen and the crinoline one small figure emerged. Catalina walked from the crowd and up to me. She took my arm and pulled me down the street, away from danger.

That night, as we held each other waiting to go to sleep in each other's arms, Catalina rolled to face me and stroked my cheek. "Andrew, I'm going to show you how much I care for you. I'm going to tell you something no one else knows."

I couldn't see her eyes, but I could feel the way she looked at me. "Like you, I have a child . . . that is estranged from me."

"Where? We'll go get him, or her, or we'll . . ." She held a finger to my lips and shushed me.

"She was . . . was . . . *unprepared for,* seven years ago." I felt Catalina's gaze leave as though she wanted to look into the dark. "The Americanos are crass, barbaric, and crude. Mexicanos, at least a few, still have some European restraint, sometimes. But the United States is going to be richer than poor Mexico. Mexicanos will always have hard times. So I gave her to the nuns at Incarnate Word in Brownsville to be raised as an American. Then, just two years ago, I sent her to a convent in San Antonio, farther away, where I would not be tempted to take her back. I pay for her upkeep."

"Do you ever see her?"

"She doesn't know where she came from. She won't. She'll be a nun."

"My God, we'll go to San Antonio and get her. We'll cross the border and rescue her. . . ." Catalina *shushed* me again.

"With what, Andrew? You aren't a rich man. And you see that I need rich men."

"Then, I will. . . ."

"Tonight just confirmed that I've made the right decision. This border is too rough, violent. The men on both sides of the river have been fighting a war for nearly thirty years. They may never stop. She'll grow up an American, a Catholic, and a nun."

I couldn't even rescue my own child, so I could see how Catalina could doubt that I could rescue her and her child. But still I pledged my devotion, my efforts, and my money to Catalina. She just laughed at my impracticality. Her daughter was already off to San Antonio.

THROUGHOUT that miserable week I had avoided Rip. After Saturday's rescue by Catalina, I found some courage. The next morning, I forced myself to intercept Rip, who was on the way home from church with his family. He had lately started going to the Episcopal church—for reasons that I could only wonder about. John William bounced on the balls of his feet when he saw me, little Addie ran circles around me, and Lula remained aloof.

Sunday supper was to be a big affair. I got invited. During supper, little Addie and John William listened as I told a sanitized version of my adventures with McNelly. Lula kept her indifference. Addie listened but didn't have the excited look of little Addie or John William; instead, she could not keep the concerned look from her face. After dinner, Addie, without a cue from her husband or me, knowing that much had not been said, hustled the children outside to enjoy the evening breeze and to fight the mosquitos. John William said, "I want to stay with Uncle Andrew and Daddy."

"Run along, son," Rip said.

Addie pushed him out of the dining room and through the

kitchen to the small yard outside. Long shadows stretched across the dining room while Rip and I tried to think of what to say. Rip's suit was nearly as white as his beard, but his white collar and cuffs were darkened a bit from sweat. He had not removed his jacket the entire day. From outside, I heard the bell from John William's goat. I let myself smile. "He's still rides in his goat wagon?"

"He likes it."

"Usually kids get bored with things. I'm glad that you haven't eaten the goat yet."

"Too stringy."

Rip stared at me, but I would not be intimidated by this statue. So I reached inside my coat, pulled out a tiny flask, and set it on the table. Next, I slipped my arms out of the sleeves of my coat and loosened my tie. Rip watched me, then did the same. And when he took off his coat, I saw that his shirt was drenched in sweat. "It's warm in here. You want to take a walk?" Rip asked.

"I don't plan to stay long." I took a long sip from my flask.

"That liquor will one day ruin you," the temperance man said.

"I know. I know, just a waste of time. But I feel as though I need a little boost right now." I took another drink. "Have you taken up religion again?"

"I'm going to the state's constitutional convention. We're going to write a new one. No more Reconstruction. If going to church can help me help this state out of its godawful mess, then I'll go to church." I chuckled, but he didn't loosen up. A couple of beads of sweat rolled from his forehead to his cheek and then flowed into his white beard. A beam of light from a window on the west side of the house lit his face and beard in its yellow hue.

Rip dropped his head. "That article you wrote was an embarrassment for the state."

"Stacking bodies up in a supposedly civilized state is an embarrassment."

"I understand that; essentially, McNelly fired you for disobeying orders."

"There were bodies stacked in Market Square."

"Don't you think that maybe he had a purpose?" A rush of blood was making Rip's forehead pink. Sweat was running down his face and splattering in large drops on the wooden table. I wiped the sweat from my face with my hand.

"What purpose could that indignity have?"

"If someone would have crossed the river, if Cortina would have made a move, then McNelly would have had him." Rip stopped to wipe his face with his open palm. "If Cortina would have entered Brownsville, McNelly, with the support of federal troops, would have had the fight he needed. Cortina, wisely, didn't set foot across the river. Even so, McNelly is now notorious. He's inviting a reprisal. And at the same time, he has made himself as intimidating as the devil himself. He's trying to make them make a foolish move. It's a military tactic."

"But this is not a war."

"The hell it's not. That's why the state has hired McNelly."

We both blinked when we realized that the sun had just gone down. Suddenly, it was darker and cooler. "So now what do I do, Rip? Whose side am I on?"

We waited while he thought. I could only make out his white head and white beard; I could not see details of his face. "You're far too old to still be wondering about that. One day, some day, Andrew, you are going to have to choose a side."

"What about Cortina's side?"

That statement seemed to shock Rip; his head jerked up. "No, stay away from him. He's no longer a part of the problem."

"You're just trying to outmaneuver him."

"No, no, Andrew." He grew calm. "The United States government has put pressure on Mexican president Lerdo. Lerdo doesn't like Cortina anyway. Cortina has just about reached the end of his rope. Stay away from him."

"But how did you know?

"I worry about you, Andrew."

I knew that our conversation had ended, so I left Rip and said good-bye to Addie and the children. And as though to confirm Rip's news, Cortina sent me an invitation to a party.

CHAPTER 13

Juan Cortina's Party

I HAD another duty after seeing Rip. Manners, propriety, inevitability, or just curiosity forced me to find McNelly after my editorial came out. He had been moved from the Miller to the more comfortable Brown Hotel. Colonel Potter had returned and sent for Carrie, McNelly's wife. Once she arrived, he was moved to the home of Chester Ward. His consumption had gotten worse. And with Carrie's attention, a diet of goat's milk, and the quiet of Ward's courtyard, everyone hoped that he might be spared from dying in Brownsville. Mrs. Ward and Carrie led me to him—lying in a cot under a hackberry tree and sipping some of his goat's milk.

The hero of Palo Alto wore a nightshirt and had a light cotton sheet pulled over the lower half of his body. One of his small, dainty feet poked out from under the sheet, and I found myself wondering where he found such small shoes. He had pillows and folded blankets under his back to prop him up. The consumption and fever had sucked the blood out of him. He was paler than I thought a human could be. Veins protruded from his forehead, but they were of a blue tint.

He cocked his head, and a curly strand of his untrimmed hair fell across his forehead. I took off my hat and ran my hand through my own thinning hair, pasted with my sweat against the top of my head. "Why, Andrew," he said feebly. "I thought you had deserted me."

I inched forward, half expecting him to jump from the bed and gun me down. "Captain McNelly," I said and stuck out my hand. He didn't shake my hand, not because of rudeness but weakness. He used all his strength to get his glass of goat's milk to his mouth. But he motioned with his head, and I sat in the chair beside his cot. I had made an appointment, and this chair was for his appointments.

"Are you still working for me, Nevin?" he whispered.

I leaned well into the back of the chair. "You fired me."

His lips started to move, and I could tell that air was coming from his mouth, but I heard nothing. I put my elbows on my knees and leaned forward to hear him. "I fired you as a Ranger."

He turned his head toward me, and our noses almost met. To focus, to see him, I pulled my head slightly away. I could see the untrimmed beard start to twitch and then shift to one side of his face as he allowed himself his crooked smile. "Exactly. I don't work for you anymore," I said.

He rolled his head away from me, and some quiver shook his head and shoulders. Without rolling back toward me, he said, "But if you remember our agreement, you were also to serve as the chronicler of my exploits." He now turned to look at me. "And as my spy."

I swallowed hard. "But you read my commentary?"

"I appreciate that." I had to recoil from his remarks. Had he the breath, I think he would have laughed. When he started to speak, I again had to lean forward. "According to your bombast, your 'journalism,' locally, I've become a devil. I've tortured and taunted. I'm cruel. I'm ruthless." He had to stop to catch his breath. Our eyes held a gaze for just a moment. His eyes were smiling. He had gotten the advantage over me. "So the populace hereabouts is scared. They think of me as you told them to. They'll be more scared of thirty Rangers than of two hundred Negro troopers. A little feint, a little daring, someone like you, and your enemy is scared of you. You don't need the men. You just need the will. I learned that in Louisiana during the war."

"That was not my intention." I wondered how anyone could be scared of this dying man. And there was yet another rumor. He was open about his sickness. He let people see it. Hoping perhaps, as Commander Kells told me while slurping a beer, that Cortina's men would try an attack on him or the Rangers and thereby ignite a battle in Brownsville.

"You are not a soldier, Nevin. But someday, if you study the issues, you will understand my intentions and methods."

From deep in me some whiff of indignation, of regret, of conviction, of knowledge forced a response out of my mouth. "I don't think that I want to understand your intentions or methods."

"You will. You will. You must," McNelly said. I thought of Mejía's bombardment of Matamoros, of Cortina's and Rip's treachery and kindness to each other, of my flights back and forth across the border during the war, of Addie in my arms during bombings or Rip's absences, of the armless, legless corpse of the teacher, of the body of the American customs inspector hanging just across the river, of the bodies stacked in the public square. I could find no excuse, no reason. I was not a soldier or policeman, and like most of the poor, I wanted no part of the politics, strategy, or tactics that made those images anything other than absurd savagery and horror.

McNelly still had my gaze, but now his eyes pleaded. "You write well. You have a flourish. I can't write worth a damn. If you think hard, if you see the right of our cause, if you see the future of Texas, then you will know." He lifted his left hand, the one that didn't hold the glass of goat's milk, out from under the sheet and then pushed it toward me. Afraid of all of his contaminations, I dared not touch him. "And when you understand, after I am gone, you can be my chronicler. You can tell this story."

"I'm not sure what I can do."

With one elbow, McNelly pushed himself up to a full sitting position. From the way that the sheet rose, from my position, he seemed to levitate and command me. "Will you be my chronicler and my spy?"

I found myself saying, "Yes," not knowing if I could do either.

I left him, half hoping that he would die and thus put an end to his plans and deceptions. But with the Wards' goat's milk and Cassie's care, he grew stronger. McNelly recovered and returned to the field with his Rangers, mostly living out of an ambulance and directing scouting parties. I continued with my job and my pleasures, with my halfhearted promise to him pushed to the dark part of my conscience. I decided that, out of the preacher's commanding presence, my promise could become another of my irresponsibilities and failures.

AFTER one of Addie's finer dinners, pork chops, in the middle of beef country, Rip and I sat in the hot dining room while Addie and the children went outside to catch the cool breezes. I reached into my pocket, unfolded my invitation to Juan Cortina's party at the mayor's mansion, and handed it to Rip. He sniffed at it. "I got one just like it."

"Would you like to attend together? We could rent a hack at the ferry, and then. . . ."

"Whoa, whoa. Did you hear me when I told you to stay away from him? Remember when you and I crossed the river during the war to deal with him about some artillery, and then here comes Mejía and nearly takes me prisoner? You going to trust him?"

"I don't think that he would dare betray us now. I think he just wants to have a party."

"You won't find me there. With all this tension, I'm not going to risk it." And I wondered if this was the first time the old Ranger had backed down from a potential fight. I was almost disappointed in him.

"You won't mind if I take Addie as my escort?"

"You're not listening. Why would I let my wife go if I'm wary of that old bandit?"

"But Addie. You know how he feels about Addie. He would never harm her."

"Not if he doesn't have to."

"Come on, Rip."

"Neither Addie nor I will be going." He softly patted the table with his open palm.

I reached into my suit pocket and pulled out my flask. "Sure you don't want a drink?" I asked and held the bottle toward him.

"I would love a drink. I have nothing against alcohol. But in this frontier, the consumption of alcohol leads to carelessness and laziness, and both of those vices can lead to death. So I'll not have one of your drinks just because of principle."

"Then I guess I'll have your drink." And I tilted my head back and sipped from my whiskey flask.

Rip shook his head. "Do you get your attitude from your whiskey, or does your attitude lead you to the whiskey?"

"I find that I like myself better after a drink or two."

Rip nodded his head. "I've been tempted to fall into the bottle myself. But I feared that I'd never be able to crawl back out." It was a surprising statement from Rip. And he smiled at having shocked me. I just nodded back to him and left the living room for the cooler front porch.

As I stepped out onto the porch, Addie met me. She stepped in front of me, and she put one hand lightly on my chest. "Andrew, I still worry so much about you."

"I've turned out okay so far."

"Andrew, you used to be more careful."

I looked back behind me, then turned to Addie. "I asked Rip if he would allow me to escort you to a party in Matamoros."

"Cortina's party?"

"Yes."

"Oh, it will be a wonderful party," Addie said and bounced on the balls of her feet, just as John William did.

"Rip said you couldn't go."

Addie stopped bouncing on her toes, looked down at the ground, and slowly dragged her flat palm down her chest until her hand was hanging at her side. "I could use some entertainment."

"I wish that we could go. A little time together, again, would be nice."

"Oh, Andrew, I don't mean it in that way. Oh no, not in that way."

"I don't mean it either. I would just like the pleasure of your company."

"You do stay charming, Andrew," she said.

Before she could go on, John William jumped out of his goat wagon and was by our sides and tugging on my arm. "Uncle Andrew, think you could ride in my wagon?"

"I'm too big."

"No, you're not."

"Yes, I am, but sometime, how about you and I going out on a horse?"

"I don't know."

"It'll be fun."

"I don't think that I like horses," John William said and looked at me with wide-open, begging eyes.

"Neither do I. We could both learn. And if one of us got scared, the other could help him off that horse."

John William's eyes seemed to soften. I looked into Addie's weary eyes. "Come here and hug your uncle good-bye," I said to John William.

Since Rip had forbidden Addie from going, I sent an invitation to Catalina. But she replied that she had an "engagement" for that night. So I went alone to the party at the mayor's mansion.

MATAMOROS was always more progressive than Brownsville, and despite the raids and takeovers, the rich kept the city lit with gas. Unlike the kerosene street lamps of Brownsville, the gaslights lit a steady circle beneath the lamp pole, but the edges of the circle were soft, not harsh. The constant flickering of Brownsville's kerosene lamps made for alternating tiny bursts of light. I felt more secure with gaslights. I felt more secure with progress.

Cortina had taken advantage of the city's ice factory, for in the mayor's mansion on the first floor was an ice sculpting of the Mexican

Eagle and Snake. Even some of the feathers were outlined. I wondered, even if Matamoros could make the huge block of ice, where Cortina had found the artisan to delicately outline the feathers. I stared at the sculpture and found myself wanting to lick it. Instead I drank cold beer and bourbon with chipped ice and mint in it.

Cortina's mansion had large paintings of Mexican heroes made to look like European nobility, and I wondered if Juan Cortina would have one commissioned for himself. The furniture had been pushed to the sides of the first floor to make room for the tables of food and liquor. And servants mingled in between the people with trays raised above their heads.

And on either side of the great receiving room were two smaller rooms. Each was a bedroom, and each had its own water closet. So tonight the bedrooms were converted to waiting rooms for the ladies. The men would politely excuse themselves to "pluck a rose" in the courtyard or in the plaza across the street in front of the house. Often, as gentlemen, they actually would bring a rose back for their ladies— for roses grew best over the site of an old privy, so the owners of better homes in Brownsville and Matamoros moved their privies from one spot to another in their backyards or courtyards, covered the holes, and planted roses. People in the older homes had elaborate rose gardens. At Cortina's party, with all of the drinking, the ladies' waiting rooms were filled, the rose gardens had men shoulder to shoulder, and the ladies had roses in their hair and gowns.

So I drank the good liquor and ate the tamales and the chocolates and the pan dulce until I happened upon Catalina Taracón. She was on the arm of General Juan Flores, the mayor of Camargo, the head of the ranches at Las Cuevas, the man who stole the most Texas cattle and thus had corridos being sung about him.

Catalina ducked her eyes as she saw me, but I stood in front of her and said, "Señorita Taracón." She raised her eyes to look at me and kept them on me. They smiled, and I knew that I smiled. She took too long to introduce me to Juan Flores, so he studied me too. His appearance matched his reputation more than did Rip's, Cortina's, or McNelly's. Juan Flores was tall with a slender, knife-edged nose that stopped just before it got long. His face didn't have the ravages of old wounds or disease. Commander of his own domain, not really a politician, an appointed general who had not led armies through grueling campaigns, he had retained some of his youth.

I stuck out my hand. He pumped it vigorously and said, "I've heard about you."

Catalina looked up at him—her gaze had caught his eye. He

turned to face her while he said to me, "You're that monkey I hear about." I clasped my hands behind my back and rocked on my heels.

Catalina's gaze warned me to be careful. And Rip's warning and refusal to let Addie came back into my ears. "Thank you," I said, and then, as he began to step by me, I added, "I think."

He turned to me with a smile that could have been interpreted as either pleasant or malicious. Catalina saw that smile too and tugged on his arm, trying to get him away from me. "Just like a monkey, you play everywhere, with everyone. First you ride with this McNelly and then you attack him in the newspaper."

"My job makes me a monkey," I smiled.

The taller man, his back getting stiffer, some blood rushing from his warrior's heart into his brain, stood over me and stared down at me. "And what is the monkey man doing here tonight?"

I rocked on my heels and stuffed my hands into my suit pockets, and clenched them into fists. "I'm about my usual monkey's business." I could see tension making his jawbone protrude. I could all but hear the grinding of his teeth. I chuckled, "And tonight, as monkeys occasionally do, I am attending a party." I released my fists and pulled my hands out of my pockets and held them palms up in front of me.

Juan Flores tried to smile. He tried to say something. But his mind and wit were not as glorious as his reputation. Catalina's mind and wit were much faster. "Are you here with me or to play with the monkeys?" She tugged on his arm and got him smiling at her as they turned their backs to me. Catalina was able to give me one good stare over her shoulder as her escort, her engagement for the night, led her away.

With the liquor in me, I drifted away from the people and the buzz of a foreign language. I had not yet made Spanish as natural as Rip had. I yearned for my more familiar English, so I drifted to one side of the great hall and found myself sitting on a sofa between two old Anglos.

One weaved back and forth. He tried to coordinate his weave with his hand so that he could raise his drink in time to catch his mouth. He was not succeeding. So I held out a hand to stop his weaving, and he took a long swig. "Thank you, sir," he said in English, with an English accent. His white hair flowed above his wrinkled brow; his white beard, smoothed into two directions, flowed down his chest.

I introduced myself and offered my hand. "Doctor Alexander Headley," the man said and limply shook my hand. The other man peeked, but kept as much distance as he could from us on the crowded sofa. I noticed then that Dr. Headley was not too much older than I. But the flowing, prematurely white beard and hair and his sun-dried skin made him look far older.

"Pleasure to meet you, sir. And what brings you to this fine party?"

"Goddamn, it is good to talk English. I can't remember the last time I had a conversation with an American." Headley's pink cheeks poked through a dense white beard that seemed to be growing to his eyes. His forehead was a mass of brown crevices, but his beard protected the pink, soft skin under it. His nose was the bulbous, pitted, puffy nose of a drinker. "Goddamn, Manifest Destiny. God loves America."

"And so you are a resident of Matamoros?"

Headley chuckled. "I'm a resident of whatever place will have me. Right now, I'm a Mexican citizen. Right now, through the favors of President Lerdo de Tejada, I am the military commandant of the forces at Camargo."

"Why not one of the states in America?"

Headley got his glass to his lips and tried to raise his other hand, but two hands in the air at the same time was too much for him. So he dropped the hand without the glass and steadied himself on the sofa. "Can't go back. Can't go back," he said.

I didn't ask, but he told me. "I didn't surrender. This beard turned white in the last year of the war of northern aggression against the Confederate States of America. I was a senior surgeon in those states' army. I came south with General Joe Shelby to join the Emperor Maximilian. That venture failed. So I began a medical practice and a mercantile business in Camargo."

"I believe," I said, "that all Confederate troops have been pardoned."

"I was born in England, served in the British navy, went to medical school in Ohio, rebelled with the Confederacy. Along the way through my life, I consorted with the French. Distrustful people. And I've seen Central America. Through it all, I've been happiest with my new country. I'm a Mexican." Evidently, when he needed to, he could overcome his drunkenness to find the right words. He raised his glass to his lips, but through with his speech, he grew unsteady again. As his hand shook and as he slowly raised his glass to his lips, he asked, "What are you, Mr. Nevin?"

"I'm . . . I'm . . . an American."

"If you had to, would you fight for it or Texas?"

I hesitated again. "Why, the greater good."

"Then you ought to work to get this goddamn McNelly and his

so-called Texas Rangers out of the area." He drained his drink. "Oh my," he said and looked at his empty glass. Before I could offer to get him another (an excuse to escape him), he tried to rise, and with my help, he got to his feet and waddled away.

The man on the other side of me leaned toward me and said, "Thank you, Mr. Nevin." I extended my hand and shook John F. Webber's hand. "Dr. Headley can be quite the bore. But he is quite a capable man and has shown himself to be heroic. And thanks to you, I was rescued from him."

"I can imagine." I had yet to sip my own drink, so now I stared into it, wondering if I had in any way been as contaminated by alcohol as Dr. Headley had been.

"That man purposely tries to irritate me." His beard was uneven and had bare patches as though he had been sick. Likewise he had red patches on his bald head. But he was dressed immaculately in a tan suit I wished that I could afford. I noticed too that his nails were manicured.

"I'd appreciate it if you waited just a bit longer before excusing yourself, for I fear that he may return." Both the old man and I laughed.

"Do you live here in Matamoros or are you from across the river?" I asked.

He didn't answer. And I could see through his beard that he gave me a fake smile. "My wife should soon return." He continued to eye me, as though sizing me up. "Tell me, Mr. Nevin, are you a Southerner?"

"Yes."

"Oh, oh. Me too." He hung his head for a moment, then added, "Were you a Southern sympathizer?"

Made hazy by drink, my mind nevertheless became cautious. "I wasn't too sympathetic to the war."

The tone in his voice loosened. "Me too. I'm waiting for my wife, you see." Before he could answer, a very old negress, whom I assumed was a servant, appeared in front of us. She obviously wanted to sit down too. I scooted to one side to give her room to sit, but Webber scooted to that space, then rose, to take the hand of the woman, said "Dear," and helped her sit in the spot that he had just vacated. She was a little woman and her clothes seemed to be piled on her.

"Webber, I see," I said as I looked at the attractive woman with just a tint of olive in her dark skin. She had, I judged, a white father.

"Do I hear some Southern disdain in your tone, Mr. Nevin?"

"Not in mine."

"I've learned to be careful."

I leaned back into the softness of the sofa. "Your wife is an attractive woman."

John Webber leaned on his knees so that he could see my face. "Thank you. Thank you, Mr. Nevin. She is also a very old woman. And has been my wife for thirty-six years." He stuck out his hand. I shook it again. He kept a wary eye on me, and I looked at his pleasant wife who dug in her handbag, seemingly oblivious to all around her, to her skin, to the two Southern American men sitting with her. "Jessie was a slave near my property on the Colorado. I bought her, gave her her freedom, then married her."

I stuck a hand across him and said, "Mrs. Webber, I'm pleased to make your acquaintance." She stuck one gloved hand out and smiled as I grasped her fingertips.

When I leaned back into the sofa next to him, Webber became more relaxed. "We couldn't live in that part of Texas as man and wife. They wouldn't let our children attend the schools. So we came to the border so that we could live a peaceful life. Now with a Northern army here, the American side has grown race conscious. So we've moved from my ranch and live in Matamoros. And even here we have to deal with the likes of Doc Headley. Doc Headley calls Jessie my 'nigger' wife."

"Your children?"

But Webber looked away from me as his wife patted his knee. He turned his red-splotched, bald head to her and nodded as she whispered something. The white-bearded white man and the white-headed colored woman looked almost like children or like toys that children might play with. When he was through with his short conversation with his wife, he turned back to me. "My two boys take care of the ranch. They both can pass, you know." With that he patted his wife's leg. It was a scandalous little endearment that a younger man would not have gotten away with.

"Mr. Webber, I do envy you. And if I can venture to imagine myself in your position, I think that I understand and sympathize."

Webber smiled and reached inside his coat. He handed me a card. "Come see us. We are old and get lonely. It'd be nice to have a chat with a young man." At that, his wife whispered something to him. So Webber stood and asked that I excuse them. I truly did envy him, as I envied any man who could find a woman who could turn such demands into such pleasure, who could find a wife he deemed worthy of enduring what Webber had. I hoped that I had not scared Mrs. Webber away.

As people left the party, Juan Cortina left his latest young mistress and found me. He smiled and embraced me in the typical abrazo. "Andrew," he raised a finger to shake at me, "time for another pronunciamiento." He turned from me, and I followed him. He took me upstairs then down a hall to a small office. As I stepped into the dark office, I saw his form strike a match and light a gaslight, and the light's soft, outer edges stretched to me. "Marvelous, isn't it? It is new."

He paced for a moment, forgetting me, then, as though he remembered, he turned to me and again wagged his finger. "Sit down. Sit," he said. I found a chair and sat, and he pulled a chair up to me to sit across from me. His smile dropped. His flashing green eyes stopped darting around. His red hair and beard seemed not to pick up the light they once had. It was as though the great weight of years of fighting was pushing on him, and alone with me, not in public, he could stoop under that weight. "McNelly, that barbarian," he said. "I knew some of those men. The barbarism goes on."

"You saw my article?"

"Very good," he said and let his head drop so that I saw the top of his head. He raised his head and pushed his hair away from his forehead. "But you know, Andrew, you haven't given me much good information about McNelly."

"I thought my job was just to watch him."

"It doesn't matter now." He tried to smile, but just couldn't force his mouth into a smile. "Has that old man, your uncle, told you anything about me?"

"He says that you are in trouble."

His face got a blank look. "How does he always know?"

"Like you, he has survived by knowing."

He patted my knee. "I'm going to be arrested."

I let my head drop. "So you're going to put together another army. . . ."

He squeezed my knee to stop me. "Not this time. I have no money. Not enough. I'm tired."

"Maybe, maybe if we went to the American consul again. Thomas Wilson is his name, right? We could ask again for a pardon. "

"No, no." He shook his head. "I'm going to let them take me. I'm tired. And these charges. That old uncle of yours and his commission and testimony. And this consul Thomas Wilson."

"When we met out at Palmito, I told you. Rip told you."

He nodded, but hung his head to look at the floor. "I was still arrogant, then."

"Maybe, maybe, you could just retire on your mother's ranch."

He pulled his head up to look at me. "You've forgotten? I lost my mother long ago."

"I could talk to Sabas. Rip could talk to him."

"When I knelt in front of my mother to ask for her forgiveness for my indiscretions with women, she whipped me with my own riding quirt. So she and your government say I must be a Mexican. Sabas has pledged his allegiance to your country. It is already too late. All these Americans want me gone. They complain to Lerdo. And Lerdo leads a weak country next to a stronger one. So Lerdo, sometime, somewhere, is going to have me arrested."

"And so?"

"And so I will be tried on these lies, these trumped-up charges. So you must write a pronunciamiento. It will help with my defense." He looked at me with his tired eyes, and I did not see the Red Robber Baron, the scourge of South Texas, but a middle-aged man growing older right before me. I reached out and patted his shoulder. He dropped his head. "Go now. Go on. Come back. I will tell you what to say, and then you say it in the way that you do. Go on." I slowly got up, and as I stepped out the door and it closed behind me, I saw the lit crack between the door and floor go dark, an aging man sitting in the dark getting used to his fate.

I felt like getting away, so I walked downstairs and crossed the great room, and as I did, I caught sight of Catalina. She jerked her eyes toward the front door. So I walked to the door, let the servant open it for me, and waited under a gaslight for Catalina. She came out of the door in a few moments and stepped up to me. She gently placed her flat palm against my chest. "I apologize for Juan. He was rude."

"Juan Cortina was a lot more cordial."

She smiled up at me, and I wanted to wrap my arms around her and pull her against me.

"Tonight, tonight after the party, can I meet you?" I asked.

"Tonight I go home with Juan Flores." I felt my head drop. "You know what I do."

"But tonight, maybe he will be tired."

She smiled at me and patted my chest. "He is a man of enormous appetites."

"No, don't tell me any more."

She stretched up on her toes to kiss me on the cheek. If some friend of Flores saw, I could have been beaten or killed. But I kissed her back, and she pulled away. "He was rude to you, Andrew. So if I find out something important, some news, something about cattle . . . I will let you know."

"No, no. I don't want you to do that."

She patted my chest. "You and I are in the same business." She smiled at me, then turned from me. "Enjoy this evening's breezes." She walked away.

I MET with Cortina a few times, but before I could finish his pronunciamiento, he was arrested. He was held, and Matamoros threatened to rebel, so President Lerdo shipped him from Bagdad to Vera Cruz, and then he was sent to Mexico City for a trial. He was held for a while but then paroled. And I was never able to finish his pronunciamiento; I don't know who wrote it for him.

And late in the Texas summer, in September, with Cortina safely away in Mexico City, with McNelly off my mind, I stopped by the house of John and Jessie Webber and listened to the story of their lives together. And I told Mr. Webber, once again, that I envied him and that, of all of the heroes, warriors, soldiers, merchants, and giants of business that I had associated with in these two cities, he was, to me, the most noble.

CHAPTER 14

Commander Kells

IP left in September for Austin to rewrite the state constitution, but just before he left, he became a vestryman in the Episcopal Church. "Do you really think that this will help you or the state?" I asked.

"The state may be in danger of going straight to hell, so I'm trying to keep me and the state out of that hell up in Austin," he told me, this time with a smile. He spoke just once at the convention, but by many accounts he gave the convention's most moving speech: an appeal to help develop south and west Texas.

By October, I had thought that I was free of McNelly, Rip, Cortina, and thus any misguided notions of my conscience, so feeling myself in a celebratory spirit, I planted myself at the bar in the Gem and decided to drink myself into a rosy appreciation of my newfound happiness.

I had gone from cooling gulps of hearty beer to the warming sips of a sweet bourbon with mint and lemon when Old Rock squeezed himself in between me and my nearest bar patron. He had a huge pile of meat and cheese in between two slices of bread in one hand and both a pickle and boiled egg in his other hand, all compliments of the Gem. He smelled of the trail and had a lot of it on him. Though officially autumn, south Texas was still warm, but Old Rock had his Union coat on. As he leaned his side on the bar to face me, he stuffed a large part of his sandwich in his mouth, followed it with a bite from the pickle, and then tried to chew what was a large wad of food in his mouth. I motioned to the bartender and bought him a beer, which he drained when he finished chewing. I tried to move away from his chomping and his stench.

He motioned with his head, and I followed him to a dark corner beyond the faro games. Somehow he managed to carry the sandwich, the egg, the pickle, and the beer with him. "Don't you ever take that Union coat off?" I asked.

He got in two more bites before he started talking. "And just take up space in the saddle?"

"Sweat in that wool coat makes you smell like a sheep." I remembered his last threat to me, and so, with the help of the bourbon, I couldn't resist being coarse to him.

"Quit worrying about my smell. Captain McNelly wants some information." For a moment, I wanted to disown McNelly, to say that I was no longer working for him, to tell him and Old Rock to go to hell, but the images of the sick man came to my mind. "Captain has several people working for him, but he wants to know when to expect more thievery."

"He can't contact me?"

Old Rock leaned so close to me that I could smell his breath as well as feel it and his long stiff whiskers, reminding me again of his habit of getting close to me to threaten me. "Captain, can't contact you. He's on his way back to Washington County."

I put a hand up to his chest to push him a bit farther away from me. "Why is he going there?"

Rock pushed some more of the sandwich into his mouth and began to chew. "I don't know if he'll live much longer." Pieces of sandwich hit me in the face. "He can barely sit a horse. The riding just shakes him up too much. He's lost weight and strength. It was me who wrote to Colonel Potter and Mrs. McNelly." He stopped to chew. "He's gone home to regain some of his health."

"Maybe it's a ruse. Maybe he wants to fool the bandits into making a move while he's playing sick."

"I've never seen a sicker man. I never seen a man sicker in our march through northern Virginia. I've never seen a man look worse with the cholera."

"Good Lord, why does he persist?"

"If anybody'll come back from a deathbed, I think he'll be the Captain." After stopping to chew more of the sandwich and take a long gulp of beer, he pushed the back of his hand, the hand with the sandwich, into my chest. "You've seen him. You've seen how bad he can get—and then come back from it. If ever there was a man . . ."

I shook my head. "But how am I supposed to find out anything?"

"That's your business. Something is up. I can feel it. I'm gonna take a ride across the border and just listen to the wind. Why don't you just listen here in town?"

"And suppose I can't find anything?"

He leaned close to me, so I could again smell his breath. "I ain't forgot our little conversation in the dark. Have you?"

"I've tried to forget it."

"I still ain't decided not to kill you." He chuckled.

AFTER McNelly left, Sergeant Armstrong, George Durham, and some other Rangers brought in several outlaws who were in McNelly's black book. But Sheriff Browne wouldn't hold them because the book was out of date, because the Rangers had no warrant, and because "In this state you can't just throw somebody in jail just because McNelly wants him there." I had heard that Armstrong stopped George from swinging.

I wrote my reports to both the *Sentinel* and the *Galveston News*. But then I happened upon a rumor that surely McNelly's other spies had heard. Monterrey businessmen, or those who profited from stolen cattle, had sent an order to Juan Flores for eighteen hundred head. So Flores and others would be very busy stealing in the early fall months. I wired McNelly in Burton up in Washington County. My source was Catalina Taracón. I still wonder if I had betrayed her and deserted her in this, too.

I heard nothing further about McNelly or the result of my information until mid-November. Sheriff James Browne and Marshal O'Shaughnessey came into the newspaper office. Jesse Dougherty was out, and I was running the press. I greeted Browne with ink stains on my sleeves and the old leather apron. As usual, Browne started banging the wood railing and shouting while Mike O'Shaughnessey watched with his hands in his vest pockets and his polite smile. I addressed O'Shaughnessey: "Mike, Sheriff Browne obviously has a complaint. Why are you here? For once, I'd like to hear you complain."

"I agree with Sheriff Browne." He never looked perturbed.

Browne swung open the wooden gate, hurried to me, and grabbed my forearm. I jerked it away from him. "Jim, look, let's start over. What's your point?"

He straightened, and his belly protruded out so far that I thought it would send a vest button zipping toward my face. He pointed at me with his hand, and his face grew red behind his white whiskers. "McNelly is in town."

"What? How do you know?"

O'Shaughnessey *tsked* and said, "It's our job." He raised his eyebrows when I looked at him.

"And my job is to report the news, not help make it."

"Yeah, yeah," Browne said as he shifted his gaze from me to O'Shaughnessey and back. "I saw him. And let me tell you where I saw him."

"I'm sure you will."

"Sometimes I feel like just knocking the ever-loving bejesus out of you, Nevin."

"Go on."

"He was on board that *Rio Bravo* gunboat. Him and Lieutenant Commander Kells, looking pompous and proud and staring upriver."

"Maybe you can explain?"

"Oh, hell, Nevin, you get it. Kells has been talking to you and anybody else who would listen. I wouldn't doubt it if the officers at Fort Brown are in on it."

"In on what?"

"Goddamn it, goddamn, McNelly is gonna start a war with Mexico."

I looked at O'Shaughnessey. He shrugged. "I just keep up with the city. I don't concern myself with national politics."

"Nevin, you know as goddamn well as I do that those goddamn ol' Reds. . . ." Browne dropped his head and sucked up some air to keep going. "The old Reds. The rich merchants. That goddamn Charles Stillman, sitting on his pretty ass up in New York City, and Captain King, looking down on us from his mansion up on the Santa Gertrudis, would like nothing better than another war with Mexico. They'd get even richer. But me, old man Neale, Powers, all the old Blues, we got to live here. And we don't want to see this town go through another war." I walked past him and sat down. He followed me. "You remember the Yankees and the Imperialistas and that whole goddamn awful war. We've got cannons staring at us now. I don't want this town in a war."

I swiveled the chair away from him. "Why are you telling me this?"

"Because you got to do something."

I jumped up, and Browne pulled back a fist as though to strike me. "What can I do?"

Browne let his hand fall. "You're Rip Ford's nephew. You got ties to Juan Cortina and all the bands over on the other side. I'm fat but not stupid, so I know you send information back to McNelly. And you get news. If there's anybody who can do anything, it's you."

I let myself drop back into the chair.

"Maybe you ought to think about it in private," O'Shaughnessey said and pulled at Browne. Browne shifted his head between O'Shaughnessey and me, then let O'Shaughnessey pull him away.

It was nearing sundown, so I knew where to find Lieutenant Commander Dewitt Kells.

THE Bivouac had smoke hanging in clouds illuminated by the kerosene lamps. A few colored troops had gathered, and a few of the whores were just starting to come in. In his usual place, in his shirt sleeves, his navy cap pressed down over his red curls, Kells was talking to Rose Montenero, who was on the other side of the bar. When I walked up, Rose said, "Where you been, Andrew?"

I pulled off my derby and put it on the bar. "Whew, I know where you been," Rose said. "You been worrying. More of your hair is falling out."

I ordered a shot of tequila for me and another for Kells. He looked at me. "We're comrades-in-arms. Compadres in this little affair. And it has finally come to pass. I thought that I'd buy my comrade a drink."

"What are you talking about?"

Before I could answer, Rose brought the drinks. "You want some lady company, Andrew?" I motioned her away with my hand. As Kells looked at me, all the light in the place seemed to get caught in his beard and in his eyes. The red in both made him look as though he were on fire.

I gulped down my tequila and said, "Drink." He obeyed. I ordered another, and Rose brought it, and I waved her away. "Salute," I said as we downed the next drink. "Now, maybe something a little less fiery." I slapped the bar and ordered bourbons from Rose.

We began to sip. "I saw that you were right. Just blow the hell out of some cattle thieves, and we march all the way to Mexico City."

Kells shook his big, red-filled head. "No, no. You're Cortina's man."

"Cortina's in jail. He's no longer a problem. Don't you pay attention?" Kells's brows knitted.

"Look, you know I was with McNelly, right?" He nodded. "Why do you think I'm not out in the field with his other Rangers?"

"Cause you got no heart or stomach for fighting."

"You think his firing me was for real? What do you think I've been doing the last several months?" I sipped my bourbon and urged him to sip some more. "No. It was a plan. I'm his spy."

"No, no, you ain't fooling me." Kells shifted his weight and turned away from me. "No, you're playing me for the fool." I grabbed his shoulder and pulled him back toward me.

"Who do you think came up with this plan?" He leaned his head to one side and took off his cap. His shaggy, curly locks fell out from his head and over his ears and forehead. "Remember, remember. We were in here. I was buying a goat. And you suggested it. Remember? I just told your suggestion to McNelly."

He started to nod, and he gulped down his whiskey. He shifted his eyes toward me, then away. He waited, and I let him think. Then he banged the bar with the flat of his hand. "My treat. Two more." Rose brought us two more whiskeys.

I caught my breath and my thoughts and clapped him on the shoulder, and he in turn hung his arm over my shoulder, getting so close that I could smell the bitter yet sour liquor on his breath. "Yeah, yeah, finally."

"So you going to fire at the thieves?"

"Or McNelly's men will fire at me, see?" He swiped at the air with his hand. "They'll cross, and if they can't find anybody, then they'll shoot at me. They're not going to hit anything, and wouldn't hurt anything if they did. So I return the fire, and we'll march right into the interior just like we should have done to avoid that whole ugly war to preserve the Union."

"God, that's good," I said.

He winked at me. "We're going to end the thievery by ending the country."

"Yeah, yeah, I see. But what about the troops? You're going to need more than McNelly's Rangers."

Kells raised his finger to his lips. He looked around. "The Rangers are nothing. They're gonna probably get killed over there in Mexico anyway. But when they are killed, then Major Alexander, under orders from Colonel Potter at Fort Brown is ready to charge hell for leather into Mexico. I even hear that General Ord of the Department of Texas is behind it." He stood back from me, puffed out his chest, and smiled. "Hell, I'm going to be a war hero."

"I just spoke to McNelly. I guess that stolen herd he's chasing is about to cross." Kells didn't speak. "McNelly can't get his men to the crossing until a day or two. He's a little worried."

"Day after tomorrow." Kells said to me and nodded. "You going to join them?"

"You goddamn bet I am. I'm riding out tomorrow to the narrows down from McAllen."

"No, don't be stupid. Across from Las Cuevas." He nodded his head at me and a long lock of curly, red hair danced over his eye. And suddenly a thought hit him. "Wait, wait. Don't tell anybody you talked to me. I can trust you, right?" He pulled away from me and moved farther down the bar. "I can trust you, right? You ain't played me for the fool?" But I left him because I had what I needed.

The liquor was hampering my feet, but I still ran: around the pedestrians, past the lamplighters. I wanted to get as far as I could, find out as much as I could before the liquor completely got me. I crossed Elizabeth Street and headed for Washington, and just as the street lamps made a flickering glow around the town, I bounded up the steps to the Miller Hotel. In the lobby, in a well-padded chair, looking like a prim preacher, sat Captain McNelly reading my newspaper by the glow of a bright lamp. He was pale and his eyes were red, but he looked better than the last time I saw him. With my brain bubbling from the liquor, I stepped toward him. He turned his head to face me and neatly folded the *Sentinel* and placed it in his lap. "Why, Nevin," he said.

I stepped toward him and pulled a padded chair on the other side of him closer to him. From the sideways movement of his beard, I knew that his mouth twitched. I looked at the hotel desk and nodded to the attendant, then I looked over my shoulder toward the bar and billiard room to see if anyone was looking at me from behind. Then I concentrated on McNelly. I leaned toward him. "You looked pained or confused, and you've been drinking." He pulled the paper in front of his face. "I have no time for drunkards." I pulled the paper away from him. His eyes became tiny black marbles. "If we were in the field . . ."

"We're not in the field. We're in what at least passes for civilization. So you are not a commander in this hotel lobby. So I'm begging you, for the sake of this civilization, this town, do not go into Mexico."

He blew the hair of his moustache and his beard out of his mouth. I could see his lips. "I intend to retrieve beeves. Now if you buggered my chances by announcing your stupid ideas . . ." His eyes shrank until they were just black dots. He seemed to be shaking.

"I've just spoken to Kells. As you probably know, he's not very discreet."

"I have corresponded with Kells. I thought that those wires were private."

"Nothing is private with Kells. I know why you are here. Don't take those boys into Mexico just to have them killed, so Kells and you can start a war." My head almost dropped. The liquor was pushing my brain into my skull. I was trying to stay ahead of a man who was not my intellectual or rhetorical equal. It should have been easier.

McNelly crumpled and rolled the newspaper until it was nearly a ball, and then he let it drop. "Kells is an imbecile. If he supports me, then fine. If not, I will do my job."

"And what is your job?"

"To retrieve Texas cattle." The little man nearly shook with anger, but also some cough was working its way up from his lungs and shaking his head and shoulders. He raised his hand to catch that violent cough.

"No war, just those cows?"

"Nevin, those beeves are the just property of Texas landowners. Those thieves who took them know this. I and my Rangers are in the right. A man who is in the right, and knows that he is in the right, is at an advantage."

"The 'right' in this situation is that thirty men may lose their lives over cattle."

"Don't you understand principle at all?" McNelly pushed himself up to stand over me. Short as he was, he couldn't get much higher. I rose, and short as I was, I was still taller and firmer than he. "Excuse me. I plan to be on my way in the morning."

As he left, I muttered. "Don't."

He stopped for moment, turned, and said. "Do you think Rip Ford would let those bandits get away with this?"

"Damn him, too!" I said. And McNelly turned away from me to walk up the steps.

The hotel clerk stepped toward me. "Can I help you?" I shook my head and started running for the ferry.

By the time I got to the ferry and paid a boatman to row me across to Matamoros, the liquor had caught me. It made the brighter gaslights of Matamoros garish. It was an unreal world devoid of true light, and I was stumbling through it, my feet keeping pace with the pounding in my head. I should have stopped, sat down, thought it out, reasoned. I wished that Rip were in town. I wished that I had stopped to see Addie. I wanted advice. But my feet wouldn't let me pause. That was right, I said to myself, blame it on my feet. They nearly tripped over the streetcar track, and then I stepped out of the way as a mule-drawn streetcar passed me by and the dark faces of the passengers held their eyes on me. All the citizens of Matamoros, it seemed to me, were watching.

My feet took me to the corner of Sixth and Abasolo Streets to the U.S. consul building. I knocked and knocked again, then turned my back to the door to look out across the small plaza in front of it. The door opened, and I whirled around saying, "Sanctuary." A soldier holding his rifle eyed me, then said. "This is an odd hour."

"Let me in. Consul Wilson will want to see me."

After some hesitation on the soldier's part, I was seated in front of the desk in the large office of the U.S. consul's office in Matamoros, the finest one outside of Mexico City. Behind me, U.S. Consul Thomas Wilson was adjusting the gaslight and making shadows dance on the wall.

I saw his shadow before I saw him come around to the back of the desk. He sat down. He had removed his tie and had hurriedly put on his coat. His collar was twisted. I'm not sure what I said, but I just started talking, and as I did, he felt around the top of the table until he found his spectacles. I said what I knew of McNelly and Kells, and he hooked the arms of his spectacles behind his ears.

"They're going to try to start a war," I found myself saying with some obstinacy, for it seemed that Wilson was not properly appalled and alarmed.

"Mr. Nevin," he said and leaned his elbows on his table. "On behalf of the United States, I want to thank you."

"Yes, fine, thank you. But we have to act fast. I'm not sure when, but soon." I thought, for just a moment, that he too was in on the conspiracy. "Wait. You know about this? You're not going to do anything?"

Consul Wilson adjusted his glasses and grinned. "Mr. Nevin, the next time you bring information, take your time. And drink less." With that he pulled a bottle of wine out from a drawer, then reached into another drawer to pull out a jar. He shook his head. "This will have to do." He held the jar in front of me. Then he set the jar on the table and poured a healthy amount of wine into the jar and handed it to me. "This may calm your nerves and chase away your suppositions."

I took the jar, looked down at the wine, then took a sip. "Now, Mr. Nevin. I thank you for this information. You have helped immensely. The United States has no intention of letting a war start with Mexico. I have heard of this plan. You've confirmed it. I shall visit Commander Kells." He held his hands together, and I thought of Consul Leonard Price and his schemes with Cortina, and then I remembered my past meeting with Wilson.

I interrupted. "Do you remember me? I brought you an appeal from Juan Cortina for giving his status back as an American citizen."

"I turned it down. I remember you. Are you working for that cattle thief now?"

"I'm not working for anyone now." I set my jar of wine down on the edge of his desk.

"How about working for me?"

"What? How?"

He reached into a drawer and brought out a ledger book. He opened it in front of him and took several American bills from it. He placed the bills beside the jar of wine. "That is for your information."

"No, no," my hand shook as I pushed the money toward him. "I'm not a spy. I'm no one's tool."

"Then take the money as payment up front for a service." When I brought my head up, he answered me. "Help me." He waited, but I said nothing. "Go on. Take the money."

"I don't want any money."

"It just seals the bargain is all. The money is like a contract. I don't have time to write a contract."

"Take the money away." Wilson pulled the bills toward the edge of his desk, grabbed them, pounded them on the desk, then stuck them back into his ledger book. He looked back at me. "Kells talks too much. I suspected his plan. The commander of the Department of Texas, General Ord, knows, the commander of the Division of the Missouri, Phil Sheridan, knows, and the secretary of the army, William Sherman, knows of the tense situation here. Since Mackenzie's raid into Mexico to destroy the Kickapoo camp, the Mexican government has been extremely nervous about our pursuit policy. Generals Sherman, Sheridan, and Ord have put out orders that no officer shall pursue Mexican bandits into Mexico—even if fired upon. These are not hostile Indians, but Mexican citizens. No matter how much they would like to, Colonel Potter and Major Alexander cannot lead an army into Mexico."

"So what am I doing here?" I mumbled to myself. I picked the jar of wine from his table and gulped some more.

"I can stop Kells. The chain of command can stop Potter or Alexander. But . . ." Then Consul Wilson waited until I looked at him, and when I did, he held me with his stare. I couldn't even really see his eyes, just the reflection of the gaslights from his spectacles. "Somebody needs to stop McNelly." He opened the ledger book so that I could see the money. And I rose and started backing out of the office. He came from behind his desk. "I have no military authority over McNelly. But if . . . if . . . if *somebody*, if somebody could talk to him."

"*Somebody* can't talk to him. He's got the might of God behind him." I dropped my head, but a surge from the liquor pulled it back up, so that I could see the plea in Wilson's face.

"I'm not asking you to succeed. I'm asking you to try."

I found myself saying. "Let me think."

"Think quickly."

"I'll do what I can."

Consul Wilson came from behind his desk to shake my hand. "On behalf of the United States, thank you." He jerked his head toward the money. "Your government can pay."

"I don't want that kind of money. If I take the money, it'll confirm for sure what I'm doing."

"You're helping the United States government prevent a war."

"Then don't pay me for betraying someone."

I stepped out of his office and walked to the main plaza. I paced around and around it while a dozen scenarios ran through my head. I had betrayed and helped everybody. But I still needed to do more for or to someone. I walked down Seventh Street to the suburbs and sobered up somewhat. My feet took me to Catalina's cottage.

A light was still on, so I climbed the steps and knocked. She greeted me smiling. "An unannounced but welcomed visitor," she said.

Before I stepped in, I said, "Tell Juan Flores. Tell him. Tell him that."

Catalina placed her palm softly against my chest. "Andrew, he went back to his wife. He is going to be faithful. I no longer see him."

I stepped in and closed the door behind me. With the door closed, I held out my arms, and Catalina circled her olive-skinned arms around me and pushed the side of her head against my chest, and I rested my chin on the top of her head. We stayed in our embrace for some time, and I believe that both of us wet the other with our tears.

My hangover kept me sleeping. The next morning before dawn, with her lithe, petite body pressed against my own, I wanted nothing more than to feel that I was home, that none of this was my business nor my responsibility, that I could stay here with her. But I pulled myself up from her bed and kissed her good-bye.

McNelly had checked out of the Miller Hotel. I couldn't find Kells. So I took the day to think and brood and drink some more. The next morning, with a clearer head and some sleep, with a slow, gentle, rented horse, I set out in my canvas riding pants, jacket, and leggings, with the saddle Rip had given me, with my returned Winchester and Rip's converted percussion revolvers, to stop a war.

CHAPTER 15

Las Cuevas, November 1875

McNELLY rode back to Rio Grande City, where he had left Carrie, wired Lieutenant Robinson, and then rode to Las Cuevas. As far as I could tell, McNelly had partially recovered from his latest bout with consumption, so he and Carrie had made a leisurely ride in a cotton wagon from Burton to Brownsville, then on to Rio Grande City. From that point, McNelly hoped to intercept the bandits. Carrie, I believe, was with her husband to keep him alive long enough for him to become a national hero. And if she couldn't, she would be close by to take the would-be hero's body back home.

On my slow horse and with my poor riding skills, I hoped to get to the Las Cuevas crossing just as the rest did. Too early, and I'd run into bandits. Too late, and I'd do no good.

I came across a sentry at sundown and convinced him that his commanding officer would want to see me. I rode through a ragged-looking company of cavalry troops who stared at me as though I were another complication to the whole mess. They were camped on a gentle slope to the Rio Grande, and the hoofprints of their horses mingled with the hoofprints of cattle. Farther toward the river, before the canebrakes and brush, were Lieutenant Robinson and most of my former colleagues from the Texas Rangers. I spotted Sergeant Orrill straining his turkey neck to get a view of me. Beside him, Boyd twisted his mouth into that sneer that was taking over his soul as well. Bill Callicott rose from his Indian squat when he saw me. And sure enough, walking up from the river was George, in his new hat and looking more and more like a real Ranger, but he let his mouth go slack when he saw me and became, again, the hick Georgia farm boy.

Then I spotted Lieutenant Robinson, his hat brim pushed up against his head, his silk bandana catching a little bit of breeze and fluttering up against his face.

McNelly was their leader, but as I saw in the war, these men under fire were drifting toward their elected leaders, the sergeants or the meanest or the luckiest, anyone who they thought could help them stay alive. Orrill was important for that reason. That was why McNelly had chosen him. Armstrong, Rock, and Casoose were thus important. Pidge had made himself important.

I guided my horse toward their group. I swung out of my saddle and walked up to Orrill. "Damn," I could see his lips say, though I was not close enough to hear him. "What the hell you doing back?" he asked as I got closer.

George trotted up to him. I stuck out my hand for Orrill and George, but then from the corner of my eye, I caught sight of a fist. It caught my temple and spun me around, but I got my feet under me to keep from falling. I squared to see Boyd. "You goddamn coward. You chickenshit son of a bitch. Leaving us to face those pepper belly friends of yours."

"You stabbed one of them."

"He deserved it."

I stepped toward Boyd, then caught myself as his hand reached toward his boot. From behind him I heard George, "No."

"Just what the hell do you hope to stir up?" I heard from behind me. It was Lieutenant Robinson. I saw him and the husky, dirty Sergeant Armstrong behind him, looking ready to beat me.

Pidge and I couldn't help but smile at each other, and I wanted to address him as "Pidge" but caught myself. "Lieutenant Robinson, I have some important information. As the officer in charge, you ought to know that. . . ." I hesitated because the air seemed to grow thicker, harder to breathe, and all the heads had turned away from me.

I followed the rest of the eyes. When I did, I saw McNelly riding toward us. Still scrubbed, starched, ironed, and trimmed, he said softly, "Boys." We were dressed the same in our canvas outdoors trousers and jacket. We were twins, only his clothes still had the sharp line of a press and no sweat stains. It was as though he were the archangel and I, Lucifer.

No one said a word as he swung off Segal. King must have kept the horse just for McNelly. He walked straight to me. The men started to form around us. "Captain," Robinson said and stepped in between McNelly and me.

McNelly's beard twitched. "You made good time."

Robinson puffed out his chest, "Five hours since I got your message. Some sixty miles."

McNelly eyes didn't blink. He looked at Robinson as though he expected that hard riding. "So your horses will need rest." McNelly swung his head to look at me. "You are no longer with this detachment." He seemed to stare at my swelling eye.

"I'm here as a reporter, sir." His smile twitched behind his beard.

"Boys . . . men," he said in his low voice so that the Rangers had to push behind me to hear. "I mean to retrieve those stolen Texas cattle. I will cross that river and attack those bandits' stronghold. The army can't follow me. And because of the nature of this mission, I can't ask you to go with me. This is strictly a volunteer mission. I'm asking you to follow me and let me lead you."

"No reason to even ask," I heard Orrill say. Shadows had spread across the gathered men and so hid their faces from me. But I could see George's face in the fading light. It was as though he were in the presence of myth.

"Wait, wait," I shouted and pushed past the others to McNelly. I faced the men. "You don't understand."

I felt a hand on my arm. I turned to Pidge Robinson. "Don't do this. Don't. Let it go."

I started again: "There is more at stake here than you know. This is a, a conspiracy to. . . ." I heard a swish, then a mechanical click beside me; I turned to see McNelly pointing his revolver at me.

His eyes seemed to move toward his nose, then I saw his mouth twitch behind his beard. I kept my eyes on his. "Do you mean to shoot me, sir?" McNelly didn't move. My education in rhetoric was swirling around inside my brain, but with the revolver at my head, my mouth had difficulty forming my arguments. Then I thought about my audience. "These men have a right to hear all sides. They are not your army."

McNelly slowly lowered his revolver. "Continue, Nevin. This is a volunteer mission." And I knew then that this was a tactic, how he led. It was a part of his experience as a guerrilla fighter during the war.

I turned back to the men, but my eyes caught George's, and he dropped his eyes so as not to look at me. Now was my chance. Instead of a lawyer brilliantly arguing my case, I was to convince these semi-literate men that I knew better than their leader. Felicity with language, metaphor, and rhetorical flourish deserted me. "You don't understand. You don't realize what you are being asked to do. Captain McNelly is asking you to invade Mexico. You'll be slaughtered. It's impossible." Some of the men started moving away. "Wait, wait. It's a plan. The plan is that you are all killed so a war can start." I heard McNelly *harrumph* behind me. "You don't understand. This filibustering has been going on for years. You're sacrifices. That's all." More of the men started moving away. "Please, please." McNelly walked past me and then most of the men left. Then Boyd turned his back to me, then Orrill left me. Then George, almost crying, said, "I didn't think you'd turn out to be a goddamn coward." George turned away from me.

Pidge Robinson walked up to me and nodded his head in sympathy. "Good try. But maybe we need this war."

"Are you ready to die for it?"

"I've got my report written." He smiled and tapped his head. "I'm going to describe my own shaking knees as McNelly tells me my potential fate." He chuckled, then added. "Don't worry, I'll leave you out."

"I wish you'd put me in."

"Brother, I'm not sure which of us is the coward or the hero." Pidge left me, and I wished that somehow he and I were on the same side. Then I wondered if anyone was on my side. Then I wondered just what my side was. McNelly's strength was his will, calculation, and determination. And those traits opposed the obvious. My strength was my ability to wriggle in between conflicts. McNelly was a leader. I wasn't.

I unsaddled my horse and prepared a pallet in among the Rangers eating, resting, and preparing to cross the river and the cavalry troops setting up a camp and a defensive position to cover the Rangers' return or to charge in after them. I watched as McNelly found a small, leaky rowboat and began to ferry Rangers and four horses across. As one man rowed, another bailed water. They quit trying to swim horses across; doing so would have taken hours. With thirty Rangers and five horses, he and his company disappeared into the darkness for the latest filibuster into Mexico.

ON a sentry's suggestion, I moved behind them. I led my horse back behind the army's lines, hobbled him, and spread out my blanket. The night had just a touch of a chill. I pulled my riding jacket on and then wrapped my blanket around my shoulders. I couldn't sleep, so I walked through the camp, bundled as I was, and my old instinct from the war made me record campfires, arms, horses, and numbers of men. They were at least two hundred soldiers. What caught my attention was a Gatling gun pointed toward the river. With several soldiers sleeping around the skeletal-looking creature, it seemed some long-dead god or a fetish that could no longer fully command the worshipers' attention.

As I moved through the camp, staring back at the soldiers who stared at me, I drifted to a glowing tent. It was the commander's tent, and he was still up. Just as I came up to it, a young officer pushed himself through the tent flap and nearly ran into me. "Who the hell are you?" he asked. From the faint light, I saw that he had one eye that drifted away from the other one. He looked like a divided man with two different visions calling for his attention. He looked frustrated and furious. His hair was knotted and smashed onto his head, and he had his hat in his hand. "So who the hell are you? Are you one of those Rangers?"

"No, I'm a reporter."

"Then get out of my way. I have nothing to say." I stepped to one side, and he started past me, hesitated, then turned to look at me. He started to speak, but first looked back at the tent. "Except, say this. Say that I was across the river. I was there before that McNelly. We could have moved on." He stared a bit at the tent flap. He pointed toward it. "He, Major Clendenin, called me back to this side. And now it is a defensive position." He dropped his head for a moment. "That's it. That's all I want to say." He slung his hat onto his head and walked away.

I knocked as best as I could on a tent flap, and when I heard "Enter," I stepped into the tent. Another officer sat on his cot and sipped from a pint bottle of whiskey. "Who are you and what is your business?" he said without looking at me.

"My name is Andrew Nevin. I'm a reporter from the *Brownsville Sentinel*."

The officer looked up at me. His jowls hung down from his face in folds. His eyes, I could see even in the candle glow, were streaked with red. The lines around his eyes were etched in deeply, and the bags under his eyes were puffy. "I'm not talking to any reporters."

"I'm also an ex-Ranger, a part of McNelly's Special Forces."

"Then why aren't you in Mexico?"

"I said 'ex.'"

"So what do you want with me?"

I stepped further into the tent. He had a table, a field chair, and his cot. I helped myself to his chair. He held the bottle out in front of him. "Go ahead. Take a sip," he said.

I took a sip of the cheap army whiskey. My mind shot back twelve years, to that awful war. I wanted to address this man as General Banks, commander of the Union troops who had just taken over Brownsville, my first assignment as a spy, working simultaneously for Rip Ford and Juan Cortina. In twelve years, I had not bettered myself. I handed the bottle back to him and said, "You look like you could use some sleep."

"I can't sleep. Mr. Nevin, is it?"

"And you are?"

He shifted his whiskey bottle to his left hand then stuck out his right. I shook it. "Major D. R. Clendenin. I suppose you bumped into Captain James Randlett outside my tent?"

"What happened today?"

"The army and I proved ourselves to be indecisive and hesitant." He took a sip of whiskey and looked up at me with his drooping face. He offered me another sip, and I accepted. "How did you just wander into my tent?"

"I just did."

He nodded his head then dropped it. "Typical. This isn't a unit, isn't an army, and I'm not an officer."

"What is it that you did?"

"I didn't get promoted when I should have. We're underbudget, understaffed, underfunded. So if we last long enough, without the promotions, without pay, we're eventually just drummed out. Grant knows that. He knows a war, a tiny one, might actually make us into a real army again."

"But what did you do today?"

"It is what I didn't do." He stuck his hand out for his bottle, and I gave it back to him. "Randlett got to the river in time to see the last beeves crossed. He crossed. He's not the fire-breather he thinks he is, for he stopped. He waited for a superior officer for orders. For all his arguments, he was the commanding officer. He could have taken the responsibility."

"And you?"

"I was in the field and in pursuit. And I didn't pursue."

"I take it that the 'in pursuit' policy applied only to hostile Indians."

"It could have applied here. But I hesitated. I made camp. I had orders from Colonel Potter. And tomorrow, while the army makes up its mind, Major Alexander will take command. Meantime, our chance is missed." He pulled at the whiskey. He tried to stand up but faltered and slumped back into his cot. He looked up at me. "I was in the war between the North and South, not Randlett. How much older do you think I look than that young man?"

"Sir, you look fine."

"Don't lie. Since the war, where I was a colonel, I've been to every hell-hole in this country. And this is it. This is as far as I go. No more. Retirement as a major."

"Major, you may have saved us from a war."

He pointed. "McNelly wasn't scared. I was. Why aren't you with him?"

"Because I am scared. Just like you. And thank God, Major, that there are still scared men."

He shook his head. "What kind of a reporter are you?"

"Probably no better a reporter than you are a soldier. But we do try. Don't we, sir?"

He squinted up at me and pointed. "If I weren't drunk, I'd think that you insulted me."

"No, sir, not at all," I said. "History writes about men who cause things. Those of us who stop disasters aren't very interesting. But several hesitant men just kept the United States Army out of Mexico."

"So what?" he said. "So what?"

I stood, and I did salute, and Clendenin almost chuckled when he saw my clumsy salute. I walked out of the tent.

With my blanket around me, I walked around the inside perimeter of the troops, estimated their strength and arms. I stopped by the Gatling gun with its command of the crossing. A sergeant roused from sleep and spied me, "You there. You. What's your business?"

"I'm an American, a reporter."

The sergeant pushed himself up. "You one of those Rangers?"

"Used to be."

"They'll give those bandits hell."

"I'm sure they will."

The sergeant began rubbing the sleep from his eyes. "And look here," he jerked his chin toward the Gatling gun. "We got 'em covered. Ashamed we didn't get here in time to let loose on them as they crossed."

"Probably would have killed a lot of King Ranch cows," I said.

"Yeah, but we would have got more than a couple of those bandits." He nodded to me.

"For the honor of Texas cows," I said.

The sergeant looked inquisitively at me. "The war's over. For the honor of American cows."

I nodded to myself and him. "So be it. All the more noble."

"We can't let a foreign nation intimidate our citizens."

"Or our livestock." As he shifted his head from one side to the next to catch my meaning, I said, "Good evening," and made my way back to my bedroll, feeling very much alone next to these men.

BY mid-morning, we heard shots, and the troops and I pushed forward to the point where the land sloped toward the river. I stood by the sergeant next to the Gatling gun, looked at its ugly barrels, then tried as well as possible to see movement in the brush across the river. "Bet they don't make it," the sergeant said.

I glanced at him and found myself saying, in contradiction to what I feared or knew, "I bet they do. Ten of your Yankee dollars says that they do."

I saw a figure, then another one, appear out of the brush. Several of the soldiers started cheering and waving their arms. One of the figures waved back. More figures appeared, and they all crossed the open space sloping toward the river.

Then the dapper figure, dressed as I was, appeared. And McNelly started to lead the rest of them toward the river. As soon as they got near the bank of the river, they began digging with whatever they had: fingers, rifle butts, sticks. Then volleys of shots started, one roar then another. The last of the Rangers scrambled to the bank to take position and aim, and riders appeared out of the brush. The riders and the Rangers exchanged shots that sounded like pops to us. Then one rider appeared and seemed to group the others together. Suddenly, Captain Randlett was beside me and the sergeant. His eyes were red, and his hair and beard were a mess. One eye looked one way while the other looked another way. The riders charged the Rangers.

I felt a movement of air push me forward. Randlett circled around as his men began grabbing guns and running down toward the river. Randlett didn't order them onward or backward. He just did his pirouette. He started smiling as he looked one way and then the other way. After a moment, he froze and looked behind me and beyond me. I saw what he was looking at: a hungover Clendenin stumbling out from his tent.

But the sergeant moved to his Gatling gun. He looked at me and smiled. "I'll show 'em what for." I looked back at Clendenin, and for a moment his eyes stayed on me. He was totally confused.

I ran toward my bedroll and grabbed my Navy Colt and Winchester and let the rush of moving men carry me down toward the river and then into it. The pops were more frequent, and as I got closer, the pops became booms and then a roar. I raced down the embankment, which with the recent high water and the trudging of cattle, horses, and men had turned into a slippery mud wallow. I sloshed, almost as if skating through the mud. As I neared the river, I peeled my jacket off and flung it from me. I waded into the river and saw a spray of water kick up in front of me. I saw the bullet actually float toward the bottom. Some of the troopers had shed shirts, pants, and boots to swim across. Others tried to wade and held their rifles above their heads. I pulled my hat as far down on my head as possible, held my Winchester above my head, and waded deeper. When I was chest deep, I started to kick and yet hold my Winchester out of the water with one hand, but the weight of my clothes pulled me down. Finally, I let the Winchester's barrel dip under the water and started to kick myself through the muddy water.

I was exhausted when I got to the other side. The first thing that I did was to pull off my shoes and pour the water out. Then I pulled my drooping, soaked hat off and tried to sling the water out of it. I put it back on and I tried not to pay attention to the weeds and thorns as I ran up the bank to take a place beside George Durham. And as I did, a rider jumped his horse over the bank, over our heads, the horse's hooves barely missing our legs. And almost before the horse had landed, Lieutenant Robinson, smiling, was off his horse and looking back at the pursuing bandits. "Glorious God," Pidge yelled. "Give 'em hell now." He shot his pistol at the approaching soldiers, bandits, and vaqueros.

In between the shots and the cheering, I heard George chuckle. He shot his Sharps, then turned to me. "We sure did give 'em hell," he said, then checked over his shoulder at the advancing men. He quickly turned to me to say, "But we attacked the wrong ranch," then turned his attention toward the advancing men.

"You attacked the wrong ranch? Did you hurt anyone?"

George was smiling. Beside him, I noticed Bill Boyd and Sergeant Orrill. They let George Durham do the talking. "Ol Casoose must have got lost or something. But early this morning we hit a ranch. Dropped a cook and an old woman right in their tracks. But it was the wrong damn ranch."

"Lucky thing it was," Bill Boyd said. "Las Cuevas has at least a hundred men, and then some regulars joined."

"We'd of licked 'em all," George said. And with a new cartridge in his Sharps he aimed and squeezed off a shot. "Knicked me one."

Bill held his eyes on mine for a moment. "You were right, Nevin.

If we would have attacked the right ranch, we'd all be dead by now."

"Like hell," George said. Somewhere since he crossed that river, he had become a Ranger in the old tradition. Perhaps, I thought, George was on his way to becoming the next Rip Ford or Lee H. McNelly.

"Steady aim, boys," a voice said, and I recognized it as McNelly. McNelly was standing, taking charge of Rangers and soldiers. His eyes caught for a moment on me, and then his mouth twitched beneath his beard. "That's why you got the single-shot rifles. Don't waste your shots. Keep 'em at a distance. They're going to charge."

With that statement, all the heads, soldiers' and Rangers', swung toward the line of brush some hundred yards away. I squared my shoulders onto the bank and aimed my Winchester, but I could barely see beneath the brim of my drooping hat. I saw flashes of white or tan, then the men dressed in the white or tan shirts came bursting out of the chaparral on their fast horses. One shot, then another, then horses and riders started dropping.

I aimed my rifle at a rider who looked like the leader. And as the distance closed between us, I realized that the man in my sight was Juan Flores, dressed in his alcalde's suit. I couldn't pull the trigger. But as he got closer, the sergeant with the Gatling gun opened up on the line of riders. And a spray of blood burst out from the chest of Juan Flores and stained his white shirt and fine suit. He toppled backward over his horse, dead, I guessed, before he even hit the ground.

The rest of the riders reined up and got out of the aim and distance of the soldiers, Rangers, and Gatling gun and pulled back to the cover of the brush.

I looked around me at the muddy rangers and soldiers, slipping, trying to steady themselves to get off one more shot. I looked at the bodies out beyond me, soaking in their own blood. I looked at my cleaner, drier twin, McNelly, as he studied the scene just as intently as I did. Bill Boyd yelled, "Come back for more, you goddamn pepper bellies." George let out a cowboy's yell. It was almost like it was fun for them. I looked down at my shoeless feet with my ripped and cut socks. A thought burst into my mind: I had come here to stop this.

George stood, whooped, then looked at me, "So you a Ranger again?"

"I guess so," I said.

Then I felt a slap on my back. "This is going to be one hell of a story, Nevin. Aren't you glad you're here?" Pidge Robinson asked. "We've even survived . . . so far."

* * *

LATER on, nearing noon, as the first crows flew down and started to peck at the eyeballs of the dead, Major Alexander and more troops appeared. And before long, he was across the river, looking more like a hero, more like a commander, than anybody. His uniform was pressed, his collar stretched up to his neck, the ends of a wide, drooping bow tie hung down from just under his chin, and, rather than a traditional hat, he had an English cork and canvas helmet on his head. And McNelly, smaller but dashing, in his dry, still intact, pressed canvas clothes, which mine at one time matched, walked up to Major Alexander.

I moved closer, feeling the stones and twigs beneath my stocking feet. McNelly saw me and his beard twitched, then Major Alexander looked toward me. "He used to be a Ranger," McNelly said. "But now he's a reporter, a neutral observer."

Major Alexander seemed to puff out his chest. "I've got a telegram from Colonel Potter. It comes from Washington. No federal forces are to support you as long as you remain in Mexico."

McNelly puffed out his chest. "So you will not follow me if I press the charge?"

Alexander's face twisted, and he looked back over his shoulder at me. "It's up. The government . . . the government will not support your . . . your invasion." I knew from the tone of his voice, from the tinge of sadness or regret, that Alexander was in on this, that he wanted nothing better than to charge and cross into Mexico into glorious oblivion. If he had gotten there before Clendenin, I may indeed have been a member of the surrounded, doomed, probably last group of American filibusters. "Will you return to American soil?"

By this time, the Rangers were gathering around us, and the better-trained soldiers, while trying to hold positions, turned their heads to see the two men. McNelly said as loudly as he could, loudly enough for all to hear, "No. I meant to retrieve Texas cattle." There was a silence. The Rangers wanted to cheer, but they knew, too, that staying here without American support doomed them.

"Nobody's going to like that," Alexander said.

"May I use the American wire service to notify my superiors of my intentions?" McNelly asked.

Major Alexander looked around him, then almost admiringly at McNelly. "Your men must be hungry."

The soldiers swam back across the Rio Grande to the American side, and McNelly went with them in the boat. I looked at the swimming soldiers, the tired Rangers, the small rowboat with Major Alexander and McNelly and several enlisted men squeezed into it and tried to decide which side of the river I belonged on. As the soldiers left, I saw just how few Rangers there were and how spread out they were. Maybe I didn't want to get wet again after I was beginning to dry off in the afternoon sun, so I stayed on the Mexican side.

We smelled the sizzling meat from the fires. "I could eat my shoe," George said.

"That might be what you have to eat," Bill Boyd said.

"Did you see me drop that one bandit?" George asked.

"Hell, that was my man," Bill Callicott said from a distance away.

"Maybe we got him together."

"Yeah, you two would be talking real big if we was in Cuevas surrounded and getting picked off," Bill Boyd said.

"Hell, sounds like you're the coward," George said. "And not old Andrew Nevin who swum back across to join us."

Bill Callicott nodded, but Sergeant Orrill disrupted the argument by saying, "You boys can argue later; now we got parley going on." About a hundred yards from our position were three men with a white flag on a rifle barrel.

Suddenly McNelly was back, and he started picking out people to join him: Lieutenant Robinson, Sergeants Armstrong and Orrill, Privates Bill Boyd and George Durham. George beamed. Then McNelly stiffened, looked at me, and said, "You want a story, Nevin?"

I tugged on my now dry shoes. "So give me one."

We walked out to about fifty yards. I was to interpret if we needed it. The riders approached, and as they got closer and dismounted, I saw that the man speaking for them was Doc Headley. His long white whiskers were in mats and twists and stuck out in all directions from his face and head, making him look a little like a pin cushion. His dark brown suit had a coat of dust on it, and his holster, on a gunbelt giving way to an expanding belly, hung over his crotch. With his short arms and big belly, Headley would have a hard, slow time getting to his revolver. He pulled off his hat and straightened his white hair and beard. With his beard unmatted, making a halo around him along with his hair, Headley looked like the pictures of God in the Sistine Chapel. In his free hand, he held a bottle of mescal, and he offered it to McNelly. The other two men were also in civilian clothes.

"Have a drink, please," he said to all of us.

"We don't have time for drink." McNelly said. Headley *harrumphed* and then took a drink from the bottle. His own men turned to look at him. He snorted and took another drink.

"We need to retrieve our dead," Headley said and looked at me as he tried to remember my face.

"We can let you do that," McNelly said.

"Doctor Headley," I said, and everyone turned to look at me. "We met at Juan Cortina's party."

"So now you jumped to their side?"

Headley ducked my stare long enough to take a sip from his bottle. He looked back at McNelly. "Are you McNelly?" Headley asked.

Headley handed him a letter. McNelly started to read, but Doc paraphrased. "You've invaded Mexico and killed twenty-seven citizens and left many more wounded."

"About to be another thirty," Boyd said.

"Sir," Headley said and straightened. "I may not look it to you, but I am the military commandant at Camargo. And the only person holding back an army from overtaking your position." Headley turned to look at McNelly. "The governor of Tamaulipas demands that you return to your own side of the border."

McNelly hastily read the letter, then looked at Headley, "I'm not going anywhere until I get those stolen beeves."

Headley squinted. "Tomorrow is Sunday. Let's suspend fighting and talk about it tomorrow."

"I suspend nothing. If someone advances on me or gets in my rifle sight, I'll kill him."

Headley didn't duck McNelly's gaze. "Captain McNelly, like you, I served the Confederate States of America. Unlike you, I never joined a Union police force. I came south with General Shelby and have been trying to help the citizens of this country. As a guerrilla fighter myself, I can tell you that your tactics won't work here. We can easily find out how many men you have. We have all the advantages. Your bluffing will work for the American newspapers, but not against us."

The two Confederates eyed each other. Headley pushed the bottle toward McNelly. "Sure you don't want a drink?" When McNelly showed no reaction, Headley took a drink. "The cattle are in Camargo," Headley said. "They are under the control of customs agents and inspectors. I'll need some time to do a little persuading to get those cattle to you."

McNelly thought for a moment. He pulled a pencil out of his pocket and scribbled something on a piece of paper, then he handed the paper to Headley. "That says that you will deliver all the cattle to us at the ferry across from Camargo. We will meet you there. Now you sign it. If you don't, I'll give you one hour before I charge."

Headley looked up. McNelly handed him the pencil. "Sign it."

"Why not just shoot me now and start the bloodshed?" Headley asked.

"If we don't see those cattle, we'll know who to kill."

"No, Captain, I'll return later to let you know if I can keep my pledge or not. I'll let you know if we can indeed cooperate with you. In the meantime," he looked at us, then at the rifle barrels sticking over the bank, and chuckled. "In the meantime, hold your charge into Mexico."

Headley took a step back. His two friends mounted. He looked at me. "Nevin, a word with you." He led his horse away. I looked down the line of our men at McNelly then at Pidge, who, though he made no move, seemed to shrug. I followed behind him, looking back over my shoulder at McNelly, and saw Pidge step out of line to go with me. "Lieutenant Robinson, your position is here with me," McNelly said. Pidge stepped back into place.

When we got beyond hearing range, Headley said to me, "Nevin, tell me, tell me who is in command here. What are the commanders like?"

"You'll excuse me if I'm a little hesitant to be conferring with the enemy in front of my commander."

He shook his head. "I'm only as drunk as I want to be. I want to make them think that they're facing an old drunk. That's for Mexico's sake. But I know you don't want to be involved in a charge into oblivion."

I checked back over my shoulder. "No sir, I don't."

"I've also talked to U.S. Consul Thomas Wilson. Your name came up." Headley looked at the ground. "He seems to trust you."

"I don't want to be on any side. I don't want to be in another war for the rest of my life. Right now, I'm not sure that I want to associate with you."

Headley nodded. "Right now, I could wipe him out and then charge those American troops. I have the authority, the men, and the firepower. I'd win. I'd have a statue of me built in Mexico City. But I want to live to be a doddering old man living in relative comfort. Just like you." He offered me the bottle. I checked back over my shoulder to see my compatriots. I took a drink of the mescal, and as it burned its way down my throat and into my belly, I knew I had again shifted sides, but this was a side distinct from Mexico, Texas, or the United States. It was the side of a few careful and fearful men who wanted to save a lot of innocent people from the barbarous times. "Who are we up against? What am I up against?" Headley asked.

"McNelly is dying anyway. He'll charge into hell and take his men with him. They don't know any better but to follow him. Across the river, Captain Randlett will charge. Major Clendenin won't do anything without an order. Major Alexander wants to charge but will follow orders. U.S. Consul Thomas Wilson in Matamoros is trying to help avoid this. Colonel Potter is in charge of the area and has orders not to cross."

Headley nodded. "We need this time. I'll be back."

Headley tried to mount, but he couldn't get his foot in the stirrup, so I held the reins while Headley guided his foot into the stirrup. He swung his leg over the back of the saddle, but then his holster dangling over his crotch kept him from sitting squarely in the saddle. I backed away as Doctor Alexander Manford Headley spurred his horse to join his companions, and I joined mine.

Robinson was the first to me. "Did you get that down? You've got the story. I bet you know more than all of us."

McNelly was also at my side. "Can I trust you?"

When we got back into camp, the soldiers had delivered us several pots of stew and loaves of bread, and the Rangers ate with their fingers, then dipped the bread into the gravy of the stew, and when they had no more bread, they dipped their fingers into the stew and licked their fingers, then dipped their fingers back into the stew. Meanwhile, several wagons appeared and threw the bodies, including Juan Flores's, into their beds and carted them off before the buzzards could get to them.

By dusk, a lone figure marched across the battlefield with a white flag in the hammer of his Sharps. I insisted that I help bring over Dr. Headley. With McNelly and another Ranger, we rowed him, in the leaky rowboat, across the river to confer with Major Alexander.

We walked through the soldiers, and Headley's eyes darted all around, no doubt, like me the night before, like me during the war, estimating their strength. The sergeant whom I met at the Gatling gun ran ahead to the commander's tent and held the flap open as we entered. There to greet us was Major Alexander sitting in a field chair, his pith helmet on his lap. Behind and on either side of him, looking on as though representing two sides of him, were Captain Randlett and Major Clendenin. All of them looked at me, for I was the odd man, the one who had no business hearing this.

After introductions, Headley said, "This can all be very simple. Right now, the most important thing is to get American citizens off Mexican soil."

McNelly started to speak. "I mean to get those cattle."

Headley, who kept his manners previously when McNelly was surrounded by his men, said, "And so, Captain McNelly, you are willing to exchange the lives of your men, the soldiers gathered here, and many more Mexican soldiers, civilians, and innocents for the sake of those cattle?"

"Please, gentlemen," Alexander said and held up a hand.

"It is just us. We need not be 'gentlemen' in here," Headley said and slumped.

"There is a larger principle at stake here than cattle," Alexander said. Clendenin and Randlett both twitched trying to keep their mouths shut. For once, I found it easy, even a relief, to keep quiet.

"You're damn right there is," McNelly interrupted. "Don't give me international law. International law doesn't mean that one nation can't defend its property. I'm acting on the best interests of the citizens of Texas, and no international law should deprive those citizens of their property."

"I was speaking of the United States," Alexander said. "So far, we have been very cautious in this matter."

"Then remain cautious," Headley said. "I warn you; I caution you. If you advance into Mexico, fifteen hundred men, ready to fight to the death, will be to Camargo within two days. I presently have six hundred men."

"And what do we get in return?"

Headley reached into a pocket and pulled out a piece of tablet paper, the one McNelly had written on. We all leaned forward and looked at the signatures on the piece of paper. "Withdraw from Mexico, and the cattle and property of American citizens or Texas Rangers will be returned to you across from Camargo." Headley looked at McNelly, "By tomorrow." He turned his attention to the rest of the men. "But first, you must return to this side of the river."

Everyone seemed in agreement. My mind worked with Headley's. McNelly could at least get the cattle. Major Alexander could claim credit for putting an end to this crisis. It would be forgotten. Major Clendenin could go on in his career. Captain Randlett was still young enough to advance through the ranks. Doctor Headley could go back to his position as an old-style impresario in Mexico, and I could go back to Rip and Addie.

Major Alexander looked at McNelly and stuck his hand toward Headley. Headley looked at McNelly before shaking Alexander's hand. McNelly nodded. And the two ranking "officers" shook hands. Afterwards, we all had a drink of wine that had somehow survived Alexander's march. After drinking to seal the agreement, Headley said, "I thought I'd have to offer my own," and reached into his jacket to pull out his own flask.

The men chuckled from relief. "Tell me, Doctor Headley, what would you have done if my eight hundred men in the vicinity would have followed McNelly to Camargo?" Major Alexander laughed.

I looked around. McNelly and Randlett smiled. Clendenin ducked his head. Alexander seemed genuinely curious. Headley, too, looked at everyone, and let his eyes settle on Alexander. "Sir, I'm an old filibusterer. I've always thought a good offense is best. If you'd have pushed toward Camargo, I'd have crossed my six hundred men and started a march through Texas on the way to Chicago."

No one said anything. Then Alexander started to laugh and held his wine glass up as though to toast Headley. McNelly gulped some more of his wine and looked at Headley. "As an ex-Confederate guerrilla, I would have done the same."

I walked back to the river with McNelly and Headley and crossed with them to the opposite side. McNelly started rowing his Rangers back across, and Doctor Headley pulled a flask out from his coat pocket. "Join me for a drink, Nevin." He pushed the bottle toward me. I took it, raised it to my lips, and felt the burn. "We deserve a drink, Nevin. You and me, huh? Reprobates." I looked at him. "Oh, I know of you. As you know of me. And we just saved a lot lives and prevented a war." I handed the bottle back to him. "Here's to us," he said and took another sip. I waited to cross the river and watched as Headley rode into the Mexican darkness.

CHAPTER 16

McNelly

History is full of posturing and boasting, and no more so, than on that day when heroes, warriors, and the legends-to-be bargained with bureaucrats and known reprobates. That's what happened. No matter what history may record. And history, while it is still being made, before it becomes history, is never so simple, clear, or as destined as heroes, men of action, and would-be legends would have us believe.

ANDREW NEVIN
Brownsville Sentinel, *November 1875*

BY nightfall we were mounted and headed toward Camargo. All of us were sleepy. When we loped, the jarring of my horse kept me awake, but when we slowed to a walk, more for our than our horses' sake, my eyelids grew heavy. I tried to keep George's dirty white shirt in front of me as we rode, but my head would drop for just a moment, then I'd look up to see that I had lost him. I feared that I would wander into the brush and get separated from the rest of the Rangers.

To keep myself awake, I remembered my last rides with the Rangers and thus tried to keep myself grateful for being with them again so I'd see the story completed. My soaked hat had dried to become a tight rope around my head; I couldn't find my canvas jacket when I went back across the river to look for it. My socks were still damp. And though it was not a cold night, the damp chill in the air made me shiver. Still, I reminded myself that it was not like the rides the previous summer when the sweat would sting my eyes and gnats would try to burrow their way into my eyes, my shut mouth, or my nostrils. But, back then, I wasn't cold.

Now I had a better mount. I was careful to choose a gentle, slow horse. This dim creature did not like to be pushed. Though a horse's natural gait is a lope, this one had grazed too long and wanted nothing more than to put his muzzle down into grass and slowly step to higher grass. He was hard to get started, easy to slow, certainly unlike the wild mustang mare whose life I sacrificed that summer.

I found myself sometimes twisting out of the saddle, so I got George to lend me his lariat, and I tied myself in, as best I could, by wrapping the lariat between the horn and the saddle back. By daybreak, nearing the ferry close to Camargo, the other Rangers began looking at me and laughing.

We got to the Camargo crossing and unsaddled our horses and tried to sleep, but we all watched across the river: the corral of cattle, the dust they kicked up, and the armed guards patrolling between the corral and the river. Throughout the morning, McNelly gave and got several messages. He demanded the cattle. Various officials promised to deliver them. Then, in a surprising move, he had us saddle up, and we trotted into Rio Grande City, and the state of Texas made some man's bakery a lot more financially solid when McNelly bought round after round of coffee and pan dulces for the Rangers.

Then we went back to the ferry. Still no cattle were crossing. McNelly had us all dismount, then he eyed his men and made his choices. He chose Bill Callicott and George Durham, but passed over Orrill and Boyd. "We're the suicide squad," George said. "We're going back across for those cows."

"Can I have your horse if you don't come back?" Boyd asked George and laughed.

McNelly slowly walked, his hands behind him, up to me. "You want a story?" I looked across the river at the two hundred yards between it and the corral. I looked at the armed riders. He leaned close to me and whispered. "I'm giving you the end of this story. Do you want it?"

Before I knew what I said, I heard my lips form, "I'll go."

We left our rifles behind. If there was to be shooting, it would be at short range. We loaded onto the ferry, and the ferryman poled us into the river. I found myself between McNelly and Robinson. Pidge leaned close to my ear and whispered. "I've got my first line written: 'My knees shook as I tried not to be a volunteer.' Aren't you glad you live in interesting times?"

"Let's hope that you get to use that line."

"If they get me, then I give you full rights to the line."

As we unloaded on the opposite bank of the river, we bunched up behind McNelly to let him lead us. I tried to stay close to McNelly in order to get the story, but then I thought about the distinct possibility that I might die. At such times, unlike my panic, our panic, our hurry at the river, we have time to contemplate the exact moment of death. I wanted to die next to someone whom I knew. This was not McNelly. So I scooted in between my closest companions in the Rangers: Bill and George. Though I begrudged him his safety, I was glad that Boyd was not with us. I looked for Pidge and saw him stay next to McNelly, always the able second in command.

Also at McNelly's side was Ranger McGovern, who did most of the translating. I had never been in this sort of a fight. I fingered the grip of my converted Navy Colt. I looked at Bill and George on either side of me, both taller than me. They seemed stoic. Sergeant Armstrong and Pidge Robinson, with stern looks, mustaches almost bristling like a cat's hair, deliberately stepping in unison in an unhurried pace, looked like the natural leaders. But our leader, with his hands behind his back, walking with his head down like a mild-mannered preacher, was McNelly.

Five men, a customs official and four soldiers, came walking toward us. McNelly pulled his hands from around his back and made sure that his jacket was hanging behind the grip of his revolver. When they reached us, they grouped together, and the customs agent stepped up. Not knowing what to do, I followed George and Bill, stood in between them, taking my place in the skirmish line. I fingered the grip of my revolver, and I saw one of the soldier's eyes following me. He looked stern. But I smiled at him, and his eyebrows furrowed as he tried to figure me out.

McNelly demanded that the cattle be crossed. The agreement that he had signed with Headley stated that they be drying on the American side by three o'clock. It was five minutes to three. McGovern translated.

"It is Sunday." The customs official stepped forward and held his hands out, palms up. "You must understand Mexico. We're a religious people. Tomorrow we will have the cattle across."

McNelly had his revolver out and his knee in the man's stomach before anyone knew what was happening. As the man fell, McNelly hit him in the back of the head with the barrel of his revolver, then leveled it in front of him. We were in a skirmish line. We could see what was happening. Bunched up as they were, they might shoot each other. But a man close by drew his revolver. As I tried to pull my revolver out, I heard a shot next to me and then watched the man grab his stomach, fall to his knees, then onto his face. We all leveled our revolvers. And the soldiers slowly let theirs slide back into their holsters.

McNelly bent his knees to try to pull the customs agent up. As small and as weak as he was, he couldn't get the man up. So Sergeant Armstrong was beside him, and the hefty Armstrong jerked the man up. The customs inspector's eyes were rolling, and he looked back at his companions, asking them with his eyes to help him. "Tell them sons of bitches, they'll get their jefe back when they get the cattle across. If the bastards don't start by the time we get back across, they'll get his corpse," McNelly said.

McGovern translated. Then with Armstrong and McNelly pulling the customs agent, we backed out of range from the soldiers, then turned our backs to them to walk slowly back to the ferry. As we loaded back on, we saw the survivors pick up the man who had been shot. His stomach was coated in blood, but he shook his head and screamed, so we knew that he was alive. When we got across, vaqueros started swimming the cattle across the river.

"I guess we just learned something," George said. "'If a man is in the right and just keeps on coming on, then nothing can stop him,' just like Captain says."

"I'll go with luck and bluff," I said and looked at a smiling Pidge. I could tell that he was composing his story, just as I was composing mine. Though I had tried to keep him out of Mexico, though he was dangerous to the area, though I had written one article condemning him, after this act, as audacious and as risky as it was, I couldn't help but describe McNelly as any way but heroic.

WITHIN an hour two hundred head of cattle were drying off in the Texas sun. I saw Captain King's running *W* all over the haunches of the cattle. And I watched as the ferryman poled the stunned customs officer back across the river. McNelly had the Rangers herd the cattle out to the prairie, and then he left. I began to interview those Rangers who were available to me. Some eyed the lump above my eye where Boyd had hit me and turned their backs to me. Though I was a part of the "suicide squad," to many I was still the one coward.

McNelly returned in a wagon full of oats and hay for our horses from Camp Ringgold in Rio Grande City. With him was Major Clendenin. The cattle safely tucked away, the Rangers turned their attention to their horses. Then another wagon rolled into our camp. Dad Smith pulled up his supply wagon, began a fire, and started cooking beans and bacon. I made my way to Dad Smith. "Too bad Berry couldn't have seen all this," he said.

"Too bad," I said.

I made my way up to Major Clendenin. "You again?" he asked.

"I still applaud your action."

He squatted and looked around him, as though he were perpetually confused. "I win your approval." He laughed. "I've asked about you. They say you're a coward. They'd just as soon not mention you. The two of us, unintentionally in league with each other."

"I also wanted to stop this."

"If you had, we wouldn't have a new, fire-eating, by-God, national hero." He picked up a rock and threw it at the ground.

"Would you have wanted to cross? Would you have wanted to go back across to get those cows? Would you have done that?" Clendenin, after all, was insulting me, and I owed him nothing.

"I don't like him. All his false humility. He's not a leader. He's got them fooled. I don't like these Texans. All action, no thought. They'll get us in trouble yet."

"Same as when he was twenty in Louisiana and bluffed and fooled twice as many Union troops into surrendering or retreating. Back then, we beat the Union."

Clendenin stood in front of me as though to make another lump on my eye. "This isn't a war. He's dangerous."

I shook my head because I didn't have any answers. "I don't know. I just don't know. Maybe they got us out of trouble. Maybe it takes men like you say, all action and no thought, to get us out of trouble. I just don't know."

Clendenin shook his head. "Hell. I'm West Point trained and some farmer 'wins' the battle."

As it grew dark, Clendenin got up and moved toward Dad's wagon to get a plate of beans. As much as he disliked the Rangers, he ate their beans. I followed him. Plate in hand, he sat beside McNelly, who sat on the wagon tongue. Beside him was private Bill Callicott. McNelly introduced Bill to Clendenin. I stayed my distance and listened, a good reporter.

"Captain McNelly," Clendenin said. "Do you allow one of your privates to sit down by you?"

"Yes, sir," said the captain. "I do at any time. I haven't a man in my company but what can lie down and sleep with me if he wants to do so." McNelly looked at Clendenin, then quickly his eyes darted around to find me. They stayed on me as I purposely smiled back at him, remembering our first meeting at King's Ranch and his dismissing of me and my unruly horse from the head of the column and later from his tent.

"We don't allow privates that privilege with officers and gentlemen," Clendenin said.

"I wouldn't have a man in my company that I did not think was as good as I am," McNelly said to Clendenin, then quickly searched for me. Clendenin, too, looked over at me. Callicott beamed, then he too saw me standing at the edge of the light of the fire. I pulled a small notebook from my pocket, and I scribbled what McNelly had said. I left them smiling—but guessing at what I had written. I, too, wondered what I would eventually write. I, more than anyone around me, wondered about some kind of truth, buried under layers and layers of misunderstanding.

T H E next morning, George Durham was quick to volunteer to drive King's cattle back to his ranch. Thus George got to meet Caroline, who would become the love of his life. And together with Bill Callicott and three other Rangers, he got a good meal and got to split two pound cakes made especially for the Rangers by the King girls.

Captain King sawed off the right horn of all the returned cows and let them roam his property until they died. Always grateful and gracious, he wanted to remind himself and all those who might pass through his ranch of the great things that Captain L. H. McNelly had done for the King Ranch and the great state of Texas.

McNelly let the Rangers rest and moved into town. He found a small house, and Carrie met him. I took a day to rest, to gather my nerves, to think, to take some notes. Then I decided to tell McNelly good-bye before I left for Brownsville.

Carrie, a rather plain woman, met me at the door to their house and asked me to have a seat. She went into McNelly's bedroom and returned to tell me that he would see me. "He wants to see you," she said. I nodded to her, then stepped through the door that she held open for me. She closed the door behind me.

The fire-eating hero, the Texas tiger who threatened all of Mexico, was exhausted. His face was the grayish, spoiled white of old ash. His lips retained some color, just a little pink. He had a sheet pulled up to his chin, and his beard hung over the sheet. He must have tossed and turned because his dainty white feet stuck out from under the sheet. He lifted his head when he saw me, and I went around behind him and stuffed a pillow behind his head. I sniffed. What I smelled was me. McNelly was sick, but clean. "Captain McNelly," I said and stepped back, my hat in my hand. "I guess that I should thank you."

He coughed. This was not a consumptive's cough from deep in his lungs, but a small, gasping cough. "I can't tell you what to write. But I want you to write it down."

"Sir?" I said.

"Write it. Write it. I no longer care what you write, but just let people know. You saw it all. You are the one who can write. None of the others of us have the gift. You, you, you, sir." He hesitated to look at me. His bare feet twitched. "You, sir, must tell the story. They must know."

"Who should know?"

"Texas," he said. "The nation," he added.

"I'll write my report."

"No, no." He pushed himself up on his elbow. "Not just your newspaper story. No, the whole thing. All of it. Get it all down. Write it down. Write it down." His eyes were pleading with me. He knew he was dying, and though he was a Christian man who once contemplated becoming a preacher, he wanted more than an afterlife. He wanted to leave some of himself behind. He wanted glory. He wanted to be remembered. He now was dependent upon me.

I thanked him. We chatted, almost as though we were friends, and I left him.

I found a small bar just outside Ringgold Barracks. It was an old crumbling place with sunbeams coming in through the holes in the roof. One other customer leaned against his elbows on the bar. I stepped beside him. Both of us smelled like we'd been on a long trail. "Did you talk to him?" Pidge Robinson asked.

I nodded. "He talked to me, too." Robinson sipped his bad whiskey, and I sipped my own bad whiskey from the glass that the old Mexican bartender placed in front of me. "He wants you to write it down, doesn't he?" I nodded again. "He told me that too."

"And are you?"

"I'll send in my reports. The *Austin Daily State Gazette* will have its stories. But I think that Captain wants a book."

"So he wants us to compete against each other."

"No, he wants us to both write about him. He wants as much as possible about him."

"Before he dies."

"Yes, that's right." Robinson turned from me and stared into his glass. "But you may have to be the one to do that." I looked at him. Without turning to look at me, he talked to his glass. "I'll do what the

Captain wants until we get through with this area. But then I'm going back to Virginia."

"Oh, Pidge," I said. "Don't."

He looked at me. "No, don't call me 'Pidge.' I'm going back to get 'Pidgie.' I'm going to take her away from that son of a bitch, her brother. He chased me out of Virginia. I've lived with that too long."

"So bring her back here."

"No, no. I'm going to have to kill him."

"What? Why?"

"Because I'm a gentleman. I shall challenge him to a duel. I will win my own true love, or I shall die trying."

"T.C., I'm not that much older than you, but I do know that what you are planning to do is not the answer. It won't help. Just steal her from him."

"I faced death here. Now I can face it from him."

"Pidge."

His face turned red. "Don't call me that."

"T.C., don't."

He almost had tears in his eyes. "Nevin, will you ever go back to the Rangers? Will you ever, really write this down?"

"I won't go back to the Rangers. I will try to write this down."

"Will you promise to leave this out? If I tell you this, will you promise to leave it out?" His nodding made me nod. "He violated his own sister. He said that he'd never let her leave him for me."

My whiskey burned my throat, and I almost had to cough. "Do you see now why I have to kill him?" And I found myself nodding, but saying, "Rescue her, bring her back. But leave him alone."

Pidge shook his head. "I've got to kill him."

ON my way back to Brownsville on my slow horse, I found myself wishing that if only it hadn't meant the death of George and Bill Callicott, McNelly should have been surrounded and destroyed in Las Cuevas. He would have been a national hero. He would have been greater than George Custer, who would ride into his own foolish oblivion and history the next summer. I wanted McNelly to have that fame. Texans remembered him. But he never became myth. He never became immortal or beat his destined short life.

Likewise, no one would remember that a war might have started. And certainly no one would remember the *heroes* who avoided the war, for heroes start wars; they don't avoid them. Nevertheless, a bureaucrat in the form of U.S. Consul Thomas Wilson; a drunken, filibustering ex-Confederate in the form of Alexander Manford Headley; and a reporter in the form of Andrew Nevin, yes, me, a coward, stopped a war and saved a lot of lives.

Pidge Robinson's report had his typical humor. He wrote about being unlucky enough to be chosen to ride into Mexico with McNelly and then to *invade* a second time to demand the cattle, but he claimed that he hadn't dashed in as quickly as McNelly had ordered. As usual, he made himself the butt of most of his jokes.

I wrote my report for the *Sentinel.* It was, for me, for the nature of Rip's old Democratic newspaper, surprisingly objective. I twisted McNelly around in my mind. I weighed him against the city and the citizens that I had lived with for nearly fifteen years. I didn't know how to take a stance. But I praised his heroism, for independent of any cause, conspiracy, or intention, he did act heroically.

After my article came out, I thought sometimes that McNelly might just have been the best solution to the border problem that two countries, two states, two cities, and several societies could devise. It was a rough, mean country. What I did believe was that McNelly was in a long line of Anglo Texans who looked at Mexico and saw their dreams or their best selves. Mexico inspired something in their tough Anglican characters, and they coveted what was not them. I knew two of these men: Rip and McNelly. And I knew their nemesis: Cortina. Those men were what I must write about. Writing a book about these men, not my article, was McNelly's commandment. I started thinking. It was too soon to write. And I had made promises to Pidge Robinson—and to Addie Ford.

PART THREE

*Writer and Whoremonger,
Old and Forgotten*

CHAPTER 17

Farewells

AFTER the raid at Las Cuevas, in January of 1876, McNelly went to Washington and testified to a U.S. House committee on the border problems. Governor Coke got letters of complaint about McNelly's tactics and cruelty and his old, dated black book. My article was cited as evidence. When he returned to Texas, McNelly was controversial.

Almost to get him out of the area, Governor Coke ordered him first to DeWitt County to watch over the age-old Sutton-Taylor feud, then sent him after King Fisher, the gentleman outlaw who controlled the area between Uvalde and Eagle Pass. Fisher was either a true gentleman or the most notorious Anglo bandit in the area, depending upon whom you talked to. McNelly raided Fisher's headquarters. But because the dashing, handsome Fisher controlled sheriffs and judges, he never stayed a night in jail and was never convicted.

From what I learned, McNelly could ride for only short periods of time, so he spent the time on the trail in his ambulance. In his absence, Pidge Robinson led the Rangers. But McNelly was still valuable to the state. In San Patricio County, two ranchers had their gunmen start shooting at each other. One watched while his bravo gunned down his rival at a church door. A Judge Pleasants lost control. McNelly showed up alone and demanded a speedy and fair trial.

Eventually, however, Adjunct General William Steele reorganized the company and took McNelly off the state roll. When the press and public complained about his treatment of the dying hero, Steele said that McNelly's health care took up a third of the company's budget. What's more, Texas needed a commander in the "full vigor of early manhood and health."

In April, I got a letter from Pidge. "I have taken a leave of absence from the Rangers," he wrote. "I will spend my pay and my time in Virginia, where I will tend to that business that has occupied me for so long." That summer, as I learned of McNelly, I also got a letter from George Durham. I had to read it three or four times to decipher the crude spelling and grammar. According to George, Pidge had ambushed Jesse and wounded him. Pidge's mistake, the gentleman in him no doubt causing him to make it, was to shout a warning to Jesse instead of simply gunning him down. With Pidge's bullet in him, Jesse Mitchell was able to put several bullets in Pidge. Jesse survived, but Pidge died the next day, April 3, 1876, in Campbell County, Virginia.

Though just as many cattle were stolen, it seemed quieter without McNelly or Cortina. Sheriff Browne had fewer hanged Mexicans to cut down out of trees. Old Rock returned to ranching and only dreamed about adventure. Old Casoose, Jesús Sandoval, disappeared, but the Mexicans that Sheriff Browne did find looked to be his handiwork. And I heard that in a village on the other side of the river, an old man, who was rumored to be Casoose, rode into town and attempted to water his horse from the well in the town's plaza. On cue, the citizenry opened up on him. I heard that he stood straight and absorbed all the shots, then fell to his knees, looking at his assassins. Then, with his body shredded, he just crumpled. Or so I heard.

FOR me and the Fords, Christmas in Brownsville in 1875 was full of the sight and smells of white roses and oranges. I felt relief and rest that Christmas, with the Fords. I got Lula and Addie ribbons and candy. I came to agree with Rip and decided that John William would benefit from a horse, and so I shopped for an older, gentler mare. And I rode her myself around other horses to make sure she was not like my last mare. I even asked Rip to look over the horse, and he gave his approval. Next, I found a boy-sized, ornate saddle. We had a goose for our Christmas meal, and Rip generally talked about the upcoming legislative session. He would be elected as the district's senator without ever running. After dinner, Rip and I presented John William with his handsome Christmas present. I took the reins, and with a boost from Rip, John William swung himself up into the saddle. I guided the mare around the house and into the street, and Rip followed us. Upon Rip's insistence, I let John William take the reins and lead the mare on his own. At first he frowned and worked his tongue over his top lip and from side to side in his mouth, but when he pulled the mare to stop in the front yard, he smiled triumphantly.

Christmas night, with my son fast asleep in the Fords' house, I left the Fords' to go to my room above the bar. I found a bottle, and while I thought about the looks that Rip gave me and Addie's still handsome appearance, I sipped from my bottle until the liquor put me to sleep.

IN January of 1876, while McNelly was testifying before a U.S. congressional committee, I met Porfirio Díaz in the home of Manuel Treviño, Rip's old friend, the man who saw Addie safely to Brownsville during the Civil War. Díaz was hiding in Brownsville and drawing up his Plan de Tuxtepec, whereby he would throw out President Lerdo and become president of Mexico. I shook his hand when Manuel introduced me. Rip approached him and promised him that Americans would give him money and support for his revolution if he kept Cortina out of the Rio Grande country and stopped the rustling. I saw Rip and Díaz shake on the deal. In a show of good faith, to verify Rip's word, Sabas Cavazos, still an American citizen, lent Díaz fifty thousand dollars. Other money soon followed. Díaz used some of the money to entertain the infamous but aging local courtesan, Catalina Taracón.

True to his word, Rip began translating some of Díaz's revolutionary statements for the *Galveston News* and thereby got more American support and money for him. I felt like I was a Cortinista. I wanted no part of his drawing and quartering.

Later that year, Cortina escaped from his house arrest and became a Porfirista. He fought in Central Mexico, then showed up back in Northern Mexico. In January of 1877, Cortina hadn't so much taken Reynosa, Camargo, and Mier as simply shown up and let his vaqueros rally behind him. He moved an army toward Matamoros and was going to take it for Díaz.

When the Spanish crown gave large parcels of land on its northern frontier to some political friends in Mexico instead of just letting the Indians have it, the Spanish king had created Cortina's, Flores's, and Díaz's armies and followers. The patrón controlled his lands, governed over them, and rode with his vaqueros. These vaqueros accepted their stations in life and gave their loyalty not to a government or a state, but their boss. So Cortina would always have an army waiting for him. To stop him, a Mexican government would have to kill him or convince him to stay away from the Rio Grande.

Servando Canales, Cortina's old enemy, was now Díaz's appointed governor of Tamaulipas. And he had sent his own general, Miguel Blanco, to take Matamoros. Too many Porfiristas threatened to start another battle in the streets of Matamoros. Cortina was not the favorite Porfirista. So Canales and Blanco (and probably Díaz himself) planned to let him march into town and celebrate, then they would enter with their own troops and arrest the old general.

Old Rip felt that he owed Cheno some warning. He scribbled down a message and, since I had always done his bidding, Rip and I decided that I should find Cortina and his army and deliver the message. I was, needless to say, skittish about going into Mexico. I was trying to make myself neutral and so wrote stories that no one really cared about. On the American side, I was merely a coward, and wild men will simply ostracize a coward, but on the Mexican side I was a traitor. Most men wanted to kill traitors.

So I put on my canvas pants, leather leggings, wide-brimmed hat, and a new canvas jacket—the McNelly outfit—for a trip through the brush. Rip found a gelding for me, and after a long morning bath, I led the stupid creature onto the steamship *Rio Bravo,* and the new commander steamed me upriver to drop me off. Kells had been disciplined and replaced. Wherever he had been reassigned, he was probably cussing me.

As I rested my elbows on the gunboat's railing and looked at my nervous-eyed horse on the deck, the new commander came up and leaned beside me. "You look a little weighted down with all that firepower around your hip. Even a little unnatural." I had bought a new Schofield because I liked the way it cracked open to load, a lot easier it seemed to me, and a new holster that didn't quite fit the Schofield. The holster was on a new gunbelt, and I had Rip's old 1851 converted Navy Colt stuck in the belt.

"I'd prefer one of your cannons."

"Someday, yet," he said, "we may get the order to fire on her." This new Kells pulled his pipe out of his mouth and looked south across the river.

"And then what?" I asked.

"And then we'll have us another war. We'll bring some order to this backward country."

"Give me a day or two to get in and out before you do," I said.

"It's inevitable. It's our Manifest Destiny, as they used to say," he said and nodded his head at this old conspiracy that was growing boring to me.

"Give up, sir. Forget it," I said. "Too many people are dead."

The commander pulled his boat as far to a bank as possible and tried to stretch a narrow ramp to the bank. We got the ramp to two-foot-deep water, and my horse wanted neither to go down the ramp nor get his hooves wet. I pulled on the bridle while a sailor flailed at the horse's hindquarters with a rope. The beast nearly ran over me after being whacked and dragged me through the water and up the opposite bank. I saw the commander laughing and waving, and then I saw his cannon facing this bank.

I followed a cow trail through the thick chaparral, cane, and salt cedar, just as McNelly's men had followed a cow trail to attack the wrong ranch, and emerged in more open country. I kept due south, dodging the prickly pear, yucca, and mesquite and came to the road from Matamoros to Reynosa. My choice now was west or east. I figured Cortina to be father west.

I let my horse lope rather than walk, as I would have preferred. And since the usually dusty road had been wetted by winter rain, my gelding sent up flecks of mud from his hooves. I got used to his narrow back and short-legged gait. I squeezed his sides to get him into a longer stride, but he raised his head and then shook it, so I let him guide me and renewed my conviction that horses were stupid animals, worse than pigs or goats or even cattle.

Before long, I came to a sentry. And I shouted that I had important information for General Cortina. I yelled "Viva Díaz" and hoped that I had the right camp and the right allegiance. The sentry took my bridle from me and led me past a line of tents guarded by ununiformed men with rifles. He led me to the middle of Cortina's camp.

No one had a uniform, unless the leather leggings, the sashes under their gun belts, and short jackets counted. If they squatted by a fire, they stood to look at me. Just in case a friend missed the gringo being led into camp, a man would poke a compañero and motion toward me. All of them looked at me as though I were the enemy. As in McNelly's camps, the air reeked of the rancid smell of men: open latrines, sweat, clothes worn for days without washing, and dirt. The sentry led me to a tent, and Juan Cortina stepped out of his headquarters. Prison had made him shorter.

I swung down off my horse. The sentry led him away, and I worried that I'd never see that gelding again. I also glanced over each shoulder to make sure that no one got too close to my back. I fingered the top of my new Schofield. No one tried to take either of my guns away from me.

Cortina eagerly shook my hand when I reached out to him. He squinted against a hazy winter sun so that his eyes seemed just slits in the dark pockets in his skull. His greasy hair was slicked across his head. His beard was untrimmed. He had more flecks of gray in the red beard. His black suit was powdered with dust. And his left hand shook, so he hid it behind his back. "Come in," he said. When he turned, I saw that his shoulders had begun to push him over so that he walked staring at the ground. He pushed back the flap of the tent and stepped aside for me to enter. In the tent was a lantern, a cot, a chair, a table on which was an uneaten lunch, a pot of coffee, and in one corner, a pen and paper. As soon as I walked in, he said to me, "I got word you were coming." I stared at him, then raised my eyebrows. "You can't fart here without my hearing it," he said and laughed at the old saying. "I'm so glad to see you. Please sit." And he motioned to the chair. "Another pronunciamiento." I stared. "Sit, sit, sit." I did as directed. He raised his fingers to his forehead and closed his eyes. "Gen. Juan N. Cortina to Brigade of National Guard under his command. Comrades in Arms." He turned his back to me, stepped away, turned back, then skipped up to me. "Okay, okay, now I need something with flourish. We no longer need to fight. We have won a great victory."

"General, please," I said, reached into my pocket, and pulled out the envelope from Rip. I handed it to him. He opened the envelope, pulled out the letter, looked at the signature, then handed it back to me. He placed his hands behind his back and rocked back and forth on his heels, as though listening to Rip in person. I read, "Do not trust yourself in Matamoros. Sell off everything you have which can be moved." I added to Rip's letter by detailing the atmosphere at the mouth of the Rio Grande.

His eyes grew round again inside their dark hollows. They had lost their vivid green and had turned mostly gray. They didn't flash and they didn't shift from side to side; mostly they just gazed straight ahead. He laughed and shook his head, "That old, white-headed American thinks he knows Mexicans better than I do." He looked at me, laughing, and shook his finger. "This is Matamoros. My mama's children. They'll cheer me."

"Things have changed. As your friend, I'm begging you to listen to this white-haired American."

"Why?" he asked, dropped his smile, and stared at me.

I didn't let myself direct my gaze away from him. I learned that much from McNelly. If you know you are in the right, and the other man doubts his position, then your gaze will whither him down and scare him, McNelly said. But my gaze was all bluff. I couldn't tell him about Rip's agreement with Díaz. I couldn't bring myself to tell him that Sabas Cavazos had contributed a large sum and raised other money to keep him out of Brownsville. "Things have changed. New people are in charge."

He clapped his hands and blew breath from his mouth. "Write the pronunciamiento," he pointed at the pen and ink.

"General, please, think."

"You think I don't know about that traitorous brother of mine? You think I don't know your old uncle met with Díaz? That old gringo just wants to get even with me for that time when he went running away from Mejía." He pointed a finger at me. He chuckled, and I wondered how he and Rip knew so much. They, not me, were the real spies.

"So think. Think what's lined up against you."

"I've thought. I'm a Porfirista now. Write."

"General, Colonel Ford mentioned that he sent me to you because of some agreement between the two of you. Don't you still owe him?"

He blew more of his breath through his mouth. "That business is over." He shrugged. "While in the midst of all these accusations of thievery, I came across some stolen cattle. They were Colonel Ford's." I nodded. "That's what he thinks the agreement is, but it isn't."

He sat down on his bunk and held his hands in front of him. "When I killed that Brownsville sheriff, so long ago, when so much turned bad . . ." He looked up like he was trying to clear his head. He wrung his hands and stared at them. "Colonel Ford escorted my mother back to our ranch on the American side. He assured her that she would keep her American citizenship, and he guaranteed that he would protect her and her American ranch." He looked at me, shrugged, and laughed. "She disowned me when I left my wife, but she became Rip's friend." He shook his head at the irony and gazed away from me, "That old man, he thinks he knows Mexicans better than I do. That's all right, I wanted my mamma safe." He told me what I knew, and I wondered if he remembered me only as one of the men who had written some of his pronunciamientos.

"And in turn . . . ?" I said, but he finished for me.

"When Mrs. Ford wanted to be near her parents when the Union occupied Brownsville, I found her quarters in Matamoros, made sure she had money enough to do as she pleased. I saw that her child had a good doctor. Of course, Sabas helped too. That was when I still spoke to my half-brother." He looked up at me to guarantee that he had not mistaken me for another writer: "And I helped his nephew."

"I'd say that he owes you another favor."

"We have fought each other too long not to have little agreements, not help when we can."

"And this is it. Believe him. He knows. You have too many enemies."

"Nevin, wait Nevin. You know all this. You know that he has shot at me, and I at him. It is a little game we play. This is not help. It is a ploy. That old man doesn't know as much as he thinks."

I began to think for myself. Whom should I trust, if push started to shove me? Would I count on Juan Cortina or Rip Ford? And then I wondered whom I should give my loyalty to. "Please General, trust me, then. Things have changed."

Cortina scoffed. "Sit. Write." When I hesitated, a worried look came over his face. "This is the last. It is all I have left. One more campaign, one more try to become better than I am. To become someone important to Mexico. A Mexican is what I am, what I must be. One more try. Same as Rip tried to do when he tried that crazy invasion of Mexico at the end of your Civil War." He shrugged. "'Your Civil War!' In Mexico we're always having 'a civil war.'" His mind went back to himself. "It doesn't matter if I'm killed. After this, I won't have the youth or the strength to try again."

I spent the afternoon taking down his pronunciamiento in Spanish, checking my grammar and vocabulary, then writing it in English, then copying another English version for me. I handed him the Spanish and English copies, folded the second English copy and stuffed it in my jacket pocket. I told him to have someone go over the grammar and structure before he published the Spanish version. We shared a meal of beans and tortillas with some dried beef, and I spent the night in his tent. During the night, he mumbled as though troubled by some dream, and he got up constantly to relieve himself. Once back in the tent, he paced. In the morning, I saw the lack of sleep was draining the green from his eyes and the red from his hair. I got my untouched horse back and rode out of his camp, just as he was assembling his army for the march into the trap waiting in Matamoros.

ON the way back, I turned off the road to avoid what might be another battle and followed cattle trails north. The thorns of the brush country scraped against my leggings, and my horse tried bolting several times. I coaxed the gelding into the Rio Grande, then floated, hanging on to the saddle horn, as he swam the river. I felt safe enough on the other side to follow a road. In fact, I felt safe enough for a drink, so I stopped in a tiny cantina on the edge of the Brownsville road. I tied my horse next to three others and went inside.

The bar was adobe brick and crude lumber, really no better than a jacal. The owner must have built it from whatever he could find. He wasn't in any town, but he was on the road, and he must have survived. I walked to the bar, which was a plank laid across several barrels. The bartender sat behind the bar swatting flies that were gathering on some fresh-killed carcass behind him, and three men and a woman were haggling about her services. All were Mexican.

I went to a corner of the bar, and the three men and the woman stopped arguing and looked at me. I saw that one of the men was just a boy. He stepped away and went to a dark corner of the bar. The bartender showed me his wares: a jug of sotol and bottle of U.S. bourbon. I pointed to the bourbon, and the bartender poured me a neat shot. As I raised the glass, one man put his arm around the woman, and another man asked in Spanish, "You always drink alone?"

I motioned for the bartender to spread out a round, and he neatly filled three shot glasses. The man who coerced me into buying a round grabbed a glass and said, "To Juan Flores, a Mexican hero."

I raised my glass and said, "And to Juan Cortina, a Mexican hero."

"Funny a gringo should say that," the Mexican said. I took a step back. "Hey, hey," he said back to the man with the woman. The second man looked around. The boy, from the dark corner of the bar, also looked at me. The bartender held the bottle up in case any of us wanted another round.

"What, what?" the man with the woman asked.

The other man said, "Remember when I said I was in Camargo and this McNelly threatens everybody. He had several of his rinches with him." I stepped back and reached for Rip's Navy Colt. I brought it up level to my face and noticed how balanced it felt once it was at a certain height.

I pulled the hammer back and pulled the trigger all in one motion, but I heard only a click. The old rimfire cartridge had misfired. The woman squatted, and the man with her drew his pistol and aimed it toward me. He would have hit me square in the face, but his amigo, the man who recognized me, drew a knife and charged into me just as he pulled the hammer back. The man's bullet caught the tip of my ear.

I brought the barrel of the pistol down on the back of the man's head and the gun went off. The weight of the now stunned man dragged me to the ground, and I tried to roll out from under him as his friend followed my squirming with his pointed pistol. Remembering McNelly's advice, I stopped squirming, cocked again, and aimed, while another bullet missed my head, and shot the man through the chest. I got a knee up under the man on top of me and got him off me. He grabbed his head in his hands and started shaking it. The boy ran toward the door. I followed him.

I got through the door of the bar just as the boy mounted his horse. I squinted to adjust my eyes to the sun and then shot. The horse twisted and fell onto the boy. All of the horses pulled against the hitching post and shrieked like they had been shot. The boy pulled his leg out from under the horse, and just as he got free of the horse, I put a bullet in him. I heard another shot and turned back and walked into the bar. The darkness kept me from seeing clearly, but I saw the bartender holding one of the vaqueros' smoking revolvers. He dropped the pistol and clasped his hands together, praying to God and begging me. I tried to remember how many shots I had fired: one misfire, three or four others. I pulled back the hammer, squeezed the trigger, and after a moment, the misfired cartridge went off. The bullet took off the tops of nearly all of the bartender's fingers on its way into his chest.

The vaquero whom I had beaned over the head got to his knees, then he charged at me with his knife. I pulled back the hammer, and it hit the chamber just as he got me. My revolver didn't fire. I was out of bullets. I starting twisting and felt the knife slice the back of my leg. I got away from the man and saw a spray of my blood across his face. He had a smile, almost like the man who smiled at McNelly at Palo Alto. This time, I drew the Schofield, pulled the hammer back, pulled the hammer again, and put a bullet into the man's forehead just as he charged. The bullet came out of the back of his head and took some of his brains and skull with it.

I heard the flap of the back door and ran to it to see the woman running across the cleared area. I raised my pistol, pulled the trigger, and saw a red stain spread across the back of her white blouse, but still she kept running. I saw her blouse shred as she ran into the thick brush. And I shot twice more into the brush where I thought that she would be. I went back into the dark bar, recounted what I'd done. As far as I knew, except for the woman, whom I may or may not have killed, now running hysterically through the brush and shredding herself, no one could bring help or identify me. I thought I'd have another drink.

I filled my glass with bourbon. As I sipped, I put Rip's pistol on the bar and felt my body for any wounds. The underside of my thigh had been slashed. I pulled off my silk sash and wrapped it around my ruined pants. Then I felt something on my cheek. I rubbed at it until I felt my pulverized earlobe.

It had been easy. After all, I had the same blood as Rip Ford. My great-grandparents had shot it out with the British and the Shawnees in South Carolina and Tennessee. Maybe the Mexicans would have a corrido about me: The Texas devil who murdered four people with less than ten shots. McNelly, Casoose, and Rip would have been proud of me. And then my hand started to shake my bourbon. Not only was I scared, but I remembered what Rip said when he grabbed Sheriff Krause's ears and what Bill Callicott said after the fight at Palo Alto: "It was almost fun."

As I finished another bourbon, I realized that I could live in the Rio Grande with my fear, but I decided that I should leave the Rio Grande for a place where I could be a hero for some other kind of act and feel some pride and elation in my victories. It was a mean, violent land, and I was a civilized man, even though I had just shot and killed four people. Maybe I had murdered, for I wasn't sure how much of my killing was self-defense and how much was just loss of control. Thinking of this, yet careful, I reloaded both of my revolvers and left no empty chambers.

I went out and rescued my horse from the other scared animals. When I mounted, I saw the boy I had shot. His open eyes gazed straight up, but his head jerked and then rolled to one side. I dabbed at my ear, wondering if I had been disfigured. I didn't wait to see if he was dead or alive. I swung up on my horse and started down the road. After only a quarter of a mile, I led the gelding up to the body of the woman I had shot. The top half of her torso was bright red. Her skirt was shredded and so was she, all the way up to her waist. She had tried to double back, and her blood had just drained out of her.

I T was well into the night when I got back, and I got my blood all over my saddle and horse as I rode back to Brownsville. The first thing I did was to get McGuffey to help me fill my half bath with warm water and wash myself. "Lucky you didn't get cut clean to the bone. I know a man had that happen to him, and now all he can do is drag his leg."

"How's my ear?" I asked.

"What's wrong with it?" McGuffey asked.

I washed, dried, and dressed, and McGuffey helped me to a doctor, who stitched my leg and wrapped it in bandages. And though the doctor told me to stay off the leg, I took a hack to the ferry. On the other side, I caught the mule-drawn streetcar and rode through Matamoros as the gaslights made the winter evening soft around its edges, then walked to Catalina Taracón's cottage. Had it been earlier, had I been able to walk better, I would have gone to John Webber's house and spoken to him and his wife just one more time.

I woke Catalina. She answered dressed in her sleeping gown, a sheer gossamer thing, without a breast piece or sleeves. She pointed a revolver at me. She exhaled and dropped the arm that held the revolver.

I pushed my way into her house and her arms. She heaved as I grabbed her, stayed in my embrace, then pushed herself from me. She went around the house and blew out all but one candle. She poured tequila into a shot glass and handed the glass to me, and as I sipped the smooth tequila, she went to the one candle and raised a lit cigar, a good Cuban one, to her lips and puffed long and deep. She motioned to a chair, and I sat.

Catalina walked up to me. She blew smoke in my face and turned away from me. I stood back up. Slowly, I raised a hand to her shoulder and slipped her gown off her shoulder. She shrugged the other shoulder and her gown fell to her waist. She turned to face me, puffed once, and then pulled the cigar from her lips and placed it in mine. She squirmed, and the gown fell to her ankles. She stepped out of it. By the single candle light, I studied and memorized the compact, olive-skinned body. I was afraid that I had not paid her body enough attention. I felt that I should have worshiped it. I pulled the cigar from my lips and put it over an ashtray. My hand trembled as I reached out and traced her face with the flat of my palm and then her chest, on down to the small breasts, to her flat belly.

"You're limping. Your pants leg is bloody," she said.

"I'll explain later."

"But Andrew, what did you do?"

"Is it a good time of the month?" I asked. She turned from me, picked up the cigar and inhaled once more.

The moon and candlelight caught the lighter patches of her olive skin and made tiny dots dance around her body. The smoke from the cigar circled as she exhaled, "Why should men have all the pleasures?" she asked.

"I'm through with the border, all the disputes," I said, and she walked to me, light dancing on patches of her body, a halo of smoke around her, and she held the cigar in front of my face for me to take a puff. I took my puff, exhaled more smoke around us, and followed it with a sip of her tequila.

"Soon, you won't have to ask what time of the month it is," she said. "I didn't want to become an old widow. But that's what I am becoming, and the border has a place for old widows. It's not a bad place."

"Then maybe we should get married."

"I'm a Mexican. Well no, I'm not. I'm Spanish. I won't go to Texas. I won't leave Matamoros.

"Who said anything about leaving?"

"I don't plan to become a widow all over again."

"I don't plan to die."

"You rode with the 'rinches,' you helped kill Juan Flores. Yet you condemned McNelly in your newspaper. Sometime, you will be in Brownsville or Matamoros, some night at a bar, or walking home, somebody will put a knife in you, and I'd be a widow again. You're lucky you made it a year."

"I know a man here who married a Negro lady. They've been happy for forty years. We could be happy."

"Where?"

"I think that I'm going to San Antonio. No one knows you there. We could be happy."

"And do what?"

"I've got many talents. I'll support us."

She blew through her lips. "I've heard that before."

"And what will become of you here? Whom have you got? Díaz? He's gone."

"We both have our fates."

I'm not sure if either of us was serious about the marriage proposal, but I knew then that she was sure about my chances of survival in the area and her future in the area. How ashamed I was that we couldn't interweave our futures as the daring Webbers had done. We stepped slowly toward each other, as if this were some dance, some mating ritual, and we almost floated into her bed. After our joy, she said there was blood on her pillow. I remembered my ear, and I told her how I had almost been killed.

"Then you have to run away, not just from this area and the danger you are in, but from yourself."

"What about you?"

I could have sworn that I saw a tear. "My fate is sealed. So is yours. It's time for us to separate."

I begged her to go with me until the morning. But, after her first few tears, she never shed another.

WHEN Cortina rode into town two days later, people danced in the streets, played music, and shot off guns as he marched to the main square. I was at the ferry, and I had a pint bottle of bourbon and John William with me. I sipped while we watched and listened. Addie had warned me to be careful; Rip said let the boy see. And I kept him at what I thought was a safe distance. Once in a while, when a particularly loud gun boomed, from a direction we hadn't anticipated, John William cringed. So I put my hand around his shoulder and pulled him close to me. "It's a little cool, isn't it?" I said.

"You smell like whiskey," he said.

"Not everyone is against drink, like your father. Hell," I said, while I thought, "he isn't so much against it as just opposed to the fact that a little alcohol may loosen you up. May cause you to lose a little discipline." John William put a hand around me as though to keep me straight. He was too old to be hugging his uncle, but he knew that I was leaving.

"Why are you leaving?" John William asked.

"'Cause I have to," was all I could say, and I sipped from my whiskey.

"Don't," he said, and I knelt down beside him. He turned his head away from my whiskey breath. Several guns went off in a row, like firecrackers. The moon was bright on the water beneath us. A norther had made it this far south, and the night was growing chilly. I squeezed John William.

"Maybe, someday, when you are nearly grown, I'll come back, or your parents will move to see me. But before then, I promise, I'll come see you."

"How far is San Antonio?"

I circled an arm around him. "It's not as far as New Orleans or Atlanta or New York. But it's as far as I can get."

"Maybe I could go with you."

I looked in his face, and I wanted to tell him "yes," to come with me and be my son. But instead, I said, "Now come on. What do you think your daddy and your mamma would say?" He smiled and then turned and hugged himself and listened to the guns and looked at the moon reflected in the river.

I had packed and was ready to leave the mouth of the Rio Grande forever. I had limped to Rip's house while he was out playing billiards at Miller's Hotel and the children were in school and I had caught Addie alone. Neither of us could make our mouths work. We trembled as we hugged each other and then kissed good-bye.

I turned my attention back to my son. "Don't go, Uncle Andrew," he pleaded.

Still kneeling, I took him in both my arms. "I'm not deserting you. I'll come back for you. We'll see each other again."

I could feel his chin on my shoulder as he nodded. "Of course we will," he said.

I found myself in San Antonio, living off the sale of some cattle and savings, drinking too much, and trying to chronicle the true events that transpired in McNelly's invasion of Mexico. Shortly after my arrival, I read in the *Galveston News* that Díaz had ordered Cortina back to Mexico City. And then the military Governor of Tamaulipas, General Servando Canales, who had defeated José Carbajal, ordered General Blanco to arrest and imprison Cortina. When Canales rode into town, Cortina was put on trial, found guilty, and sentenced to death. That was all I could find in the *Galveston News* or *San Antonio Express*. But the gossip in Jack Harris's saloon had it that old Rip had crossed on the ferry, walked down through town to the plaza, and up to the mayor's office, where he met General Canales. He persuaded Canales that he should send Cortina to Díaz and let Díaz do with Cortina as he pleased. Later still, a man at a bar told me the word from Brownsville was that when old Rip left Canales, the general said: "Did you hear what that white-headed old man said? If there is a man in the world more opposed to Cortina's mode of doing things than Colonel Ford, I do not know him."

I had to wait several years to find out that it was all true. Cheno Cortina, who dared to fight an Anglo sheriff for the honor of all Mexico, spent the rest of his life in virtual house arrest in a suburb of Mexico City.

CHAPTER 18

San Antonio, 1877

I got to San Antonio just in time to watch it grow into the town I loved. During my first week in town, I was wandering around the saloons and whorehouses looking for work when Jack Harris and his faro dealer, Joe Foster, with my help, ingeniously, inspiringly, got the idea of promoting a fight between two lions and a bull. A small circus had pulled out of town and left two sickly lions—an old male with one gouged-out eye and a lioness. Quickly, the lions appeared in cages outside of Jack Harris's Vaudeville Theater and Saloon. I was at the long mahogany bar of Jack Harris's saloon, in between Joe Foster and a disgusting, ignorant South Texas cowboy.

I need not say *disgusting* and *ignorant*. They are redundant when talking about cowboys. San Antonio would have been a much more delightful town had it not been for those rough misfits who were being called *cowboys*. The word, I believe, originated with those Scotch-Irish cow tenders on the tidal plains and later in the eastern forests. They didn't ride; they walked. I wish the term and the new Anglo vaqueros, or buckaroos, had stayed east of the Mississippi chasing their herds on foot. They weren't like the vaqueros or Kineños I had met in the Rio Grande Valley; they had no loyalty or identity to a hacienda. Their individualism was based on their inability to operate within any sort of refined society. Crude, ill-mannered, socially and personally inept, they were braggarts around men and shy, inarticulate cowards around women. Their faces and hands were sun dried into old leather, but their bellies and arms were baby-bottom white. But with cattle trails skirting just east and west of town and ranches developing all around, cowboys filled Main and Military Plazas.

Their clothes were as gaudy as their tastes. They preferred the violent or the sentimental. Just as they could cheer a fight between a bull and two lions, so they could weep at the most insipid, contrived melodrama. Even the prostitutes, when not working, tried to avoid them.

Though the saloon owners and gamblers may have sat downwind from the cowboys, though they certainly did not associate with them, and though the cowboys may have shot—just for sport—Chinamen and Negroes who were good, cheap labor for the saloon owners, they were welcomed into the saloons because they lost money. With such stupid bettors, gamblers and saloon owners were thriving. Every saloon around Main Plaza had faro, monte, and keno games going twenty-four hours a day—and thus they contributed to my preferred style of life.

"Those damn lions look kind of puny to me," the cowboy in the bar said.

"Can't you see their nobility?" Joe Foster asked and stepped around me to get next to the cowboy. With spectacles on the end of his nose, a simple suit, Joe Foster, who dealt games for Jack Harris, looked more like a professor than a gambler. Joe never carried firearms. He, like me, wanted no excuse to get shot. Jack Harris trusted him implicitly. Jack stepped up, and I could smell him and catch a reflection from his hair. Every day, Jack went to a barber. His hair was slicked back with some perfumed oil, his moustache was curled into two points with the same oil, and he sprinkled cologne on his face. The only thing spoiling his demeanor was his lame left arm that was always dangling at his side. Joe Foster shifted his attention to Jack Harris. "This cowboy here says your lion is puny."

"Are you saying that the king of beasts that I have posted in front of my saloon isn't noble?"

"He's only got one eye."

Jack Harris lifted his stiff, bent arm as he always did when he got excited. He used his hands to talk, but the shriveled left arm would allow him only so much leverage; he could only flap his left hand. But his right hand could go a mile a minute. "Why, sir ('sir' to a cowboy, I could see what was going on), that animal could tear your heart out with you watching."

"I ain't saying I'm so tough as to take on even a one-eyed, sickly lion, but he just don't seem so kingly."

"What do you suppose could take on my lion?" Harris said, the gaslight reflecting from his hair, his cologne spreading around room, the picture of class.

"Two lions," Joe Foster said. By this time, Billy Sims, Jack Harris's personal ruffian, joined us. Billy Sims was always armed. He had a reputation as a dangerous man with a gun, and though he didn't talk about it much, rumors circulated about a shooting feud he had gotten into with Austin's more dangerous gunman, Ben Thompson. Sims had seen the cowboy and his boss and was there in case of trouble.

The cowboy leaned his back and elbows against the bar and furrowed his eyebrows in thought. I interrupted. "Why any damn good ol' Texas bull could skewer both the lions on either side of his horns." Harris turned to me with his brows furrowed.

"You cowboys live around cows too much. No bull alive could take on a lion," Harris said.

Finally the cowboy's eyes lit. "We got a really mean bull leading our herd." Harris flashed a short grin at me.

Joe Foster looked at me and then shifted quickly to the cowboy, "You think that your friends would be as confident in that bull as you?" I was between the cowboy and Sims and getting nervous about being in the line of a punch, a night stick, or a bullet.

Jack Harris nodded his head, and very quickly the bartender had filled the cowboy's glass. "One on me," Harris said.

The cowboy took a sip of his drink and then said, "Hell, yes."

"But we ought to have some rules," I said.

"What?" the cowboy said. "Rules?"

Harris's look warned me not to go further, and Billy Sims tensed and reached inside his coat for the revolver that was rumored to be there. But as the *neutral* figure, I had a way with the cowboy's reasoning. "I was just fooling. You couldn't really expect a bull to take on two lions at once. Now come on, could you?" I asked Jack Harris. Harris raised his right hand and squeezed, then straightened his right lapel between his thumb and forefinger.

"Hell no," the cowboy answered for him.

"Who's talking to you, anyway?" Billy Sims said to me.

But Joe Foster, the consummate gambler, saw down the road that I was leading the cowboy. "Now, hold on. Let's hear this gentleman. He might know far more about lions and bulls than we do."

"I'm just trying to be fair. Why not send that scrawny old one-eyed lion at him first for round one, and then send the lioness after him . . . if he survives?"

"Hell, he'll take that scrawny lion, no problem," the cowboy said. Foster's and Harris's eyes lit up. Billy Sims had a hard time catching the ploy: two rounds of betting instead of one, with the house taking some off the top.

Harris turned to the cowboy, motioned with his head to the bartender, and suddenly both the cowboy and I had more drinks. "What do you think?"

"I'll talk to the others. We'll do it."

"Maybe a wager would be in order?" Foster asked.

"Of course, if the bull survives one round, the odds will have to change," I added.

"What odds?" The cowboy said.

Foster, glancing at me, said to the cowboy, "Odds, just to make it fairer."

Harris interrupted. "Why, that could be the biggest thing since Bet-a-Million Gates drove that herd of longhorns into his barbed wire. Did you see that, cowboy?"

"Who won?" the cowboy asked.

"The barbed wire," Harris said.

When the cowboy drank enough so that he had to have several friends position him in his saddle, Jack Harris came up to me and shook my hand. "Thank you. That was real smart getting two rounds like that. Twice as many bets."

"I didn't mean to interfere. It's just that sometimes I can see what a man is thinking before he knows what he's thinking."

"What is it that you do?" he asked.

"I'm a writer, a journalist. But I'm rather short of work right now."

Harris smiled, and Joe Foster patted my back. "Maybe we could find you some journalistic work."

I wrote the copy for the newspaper to promote the battle between two lions and a bull to take place at the old fairgrounds just south of town. I talked to people on the streets. I helped Harris figure the odds on the two rounds. Harris and Foster had bets from most of the people in town and took the top cut of the winnings, the *gravy*, so I had helped make them lots of money.

The fight was brutal. The old lion just stared at the bull with his one good eye and accepted his fate. He gave some half-hearted growls, and the terrified bull gored him and then trampled him. The lioness charged the bull and got up on his shoulders and ripped out hide and muscle with her teeth. The growling and the bawling were worse than the sight of the carnage, and eventually the bloody bull twisted until he got the lioness off his back. He gored her and slung her up over his back, then he charged and tried to trample her. She twisted and scurried away, and with broken bones waited and watched like a kitty. He charged again, and this time she was not able to get away quite so fast. Again he charged, and again, until the fairgrounds were soaked with her blood. Harris, Foster, and Sims made enough on their gravy that they didn't need the admission that they charged at the gate, so they donated it to the Society for the Prevention of Cruelty to Animals.

Jack Harris and Joe Foster were grateful. Foster introduced me to the editor of the *San Antonio Express*, and Jack Harris wrote me a recommendation. Harris's say-so ensured that I would have a job, so without John Ford's help I became a reporter again.

IN front of the Alamo and the Menger Hotel, the ex-Confederates, ex-Rangers, and other honored Texas politicians and heroes sat in Alamo Plaza and watched the Germans. Across and south from Alamo Plaza, bordering the San Antonio River, was the Little Rhine area. The businesses that the heroes saw were respectable, family-style, German beer halls. Whole families owned and operated them. Kids, opas, and omas could have lunch, usually sausages and kraut, and freshly brewed beer. Behind the beer halls, jungen could plunge into the river for a swim.

From Alamo Plaza, a person could walk or take a mule-drawn streetcar west down Commerce or the newer Houston Street and pretend that he or she were in an international city. Midway down Commerce or Houston Streets, across the wooden bridges, San Antonio's air was full of a cacophony of accents and languages. From the west came Spanish and English mixed with the sounds of cockfights, bar fights, and whiskey talk. From the north and east, mixed with the smell of laundry soap, sausage, and beer, came German, Yiddish, Syrian, Chinese, and French. The sight and smell of food was everywhere: tamales, Mexican candies, bakery goods, pickles, noodles, chicken, beef, duck, and venison.

Farther west was Main Plaza, thriving with saloons, whorehouses, gambling houses, and restaurants. It was the wildest and tawdriest city south of Denver, west of Saint Louis, and east of San Francisco. In its midst, on the corner of Soledad and Commerce Streets, made conspicuous with his crude paintings of showgirls and Indians on canvas hung from its walls, was Jack Harris's Vaudeville Theater and Saloon. Also in the midst of this sin and vice was San Fernando Cathedral, supposed burial place for the ashes of the Alamo's heroes. Three times a day its bells would ring, reminding us all of forgiveness and redemption from what we all savored. If we didn't mend our ways or sins, just south of the plaza was the Bat Cave, a rambling stone structure that housed the city jail, police department, and the Bexar County courthouse. And just in case San Fernando Cathedral and the Bat Cave were not enough to control the violence, thievery, and cons, just west of Main Plaza, in Military Plaza, left over from years of Spanish use, was the old lynching oak, which still saw plenty of use. We all thrived with the stealing, trading, gambling, drinking, and killing.

With Main Plaza's peculiar culture came a desire for vaudeville and melodrama. I convinced my editors to let me critique the tawdry shows. I had a seat in the theaters and in Jack Harris's Vaudeville Theater and Saloon. Since the theaters gave free passes and complimentary drinks to all the critics, the jugglers, melodramas, mimes, minstrels, phrenologists, and mind readers all got good reviews. I very nearly came up with a template for my glowing reviews. They were easy to write, and so when I wasn't at the saloons, I wrote my version of the whole McNelly affair, which I was determined to send to Rip.

To my delight, San Antonio had fresh springwater all around it. It was a hydropath's dream. I was surprised that the hydropaths of the world weren't making pilgrimages to my city. The Spanish had built acequias throughout the town, and the Anglos had added their wider ditches. In the house I rented on Flores Street, just south of downtown, all I had to do was step outside and fetch a few buckets of cool water from the ditch outside and fill my new copper half-tub. Or since the ditch by my house was not for drainage, if in a hurry, I could simply bathe in it. Or I could simply walk a few blocks to the river itself, or what was left of San Pedro Creek, for my baths. Naked men strolled to the river with a bar of soap, a towel, and their clothes. The more modest men, and most women, ducked into one of the bathhouses, a floor and walls floating on beer keg pontoons.

People were always carrying buckets. There was plenty of water underneath the town, so most of the major hotels and business had their own wells. Even so, there was talk of building a pumping plant to supply the water to the entire city—good, modern plumbing was on its way. With the ditches, acequias, and the river itself, San Antonio was full of wooden bridges, but a steel bridge was being constructed across Commerce Street. With water and ditches, San

Antonio, unlike comparable cities, had very few of the nighttime scavengers with their shit wagons and privy pumps.

San Antonio had an ice and gas factory. The streets were lit with the soft gaslights. I liked to follow the lamplighters as they walked down Commerce or Houston and slowly formed two snakes of lights stretching down the main streets. If you paid for the construction and bills, you could have gaslighting in your house. The streets were always full of hacks, ox carts, vendors, cattlemen, war veterans, and hustlers. This city was the heart of Texas. No wonder they died for it at the Alamo. The Galveston, Harrisburg, and San Antonio Railroad made it into town from the east. More merchants and peddlers came to town. So did more gamblers, whores, and patrons of saloons and theaters.

The railroad got to San Antonio just in time for me to take it east to McNelly's funeral. When I read of his death, I volunteered to cover his funeral. I got off at a rail stop due south of Burton in Washington County and then rented a buggy for the ride north.

Washington County had tall hardwood trees, rolling hills, and broad prairies. It was good farming land for the essentials and king cotton. It provided grazing for sheep and cattle. But it was not like the pure, rich, grassy ranch land of South Texas. Here, a man was a farmer, and so McNelly had tried to be. He seemed suddenly out of place in the thickets, marshes, and grasses of the border.

At L. H. McNelly's funeral, the Little McNellys sat in the front pew of the small Baptist church in Burton. McNelly died on September 4, 1877, not quite two years after he bluffed an invasion of Mexico. He was thirty-three years old. At the state's request, a funeral parlor packed his body in ice, brought in by railroad car from Houston, so that the funeral could be postponed to give all the mourners a chance to get to Burton, conveniently a railroad stop on a rail line being built between Houston and Austin.

True to his word, McNelly had stricken me from his rolls and from history. I never drew any pay as a Ranger. I never was one of the Little McNellys. So I sat behind them. George Durham's big shoulders hunched around his neck, then began to shake as he cried. Sergeant Orrill kept his face stone still, just staring ahead. Bill Callicott found something to smile about. He wouldn't erase the silly grin from his face. Bill Boyd wasn't there. I had heard that Ranger Bill Boyd decided there was more money to be made with King Fisher than with the Rangers and had joined him. Years later, I heard that several Rangers had found Boyd and hanged him.

On a pew on the other side of the Little McNellys were Carrie and

McNelly's ten-year-old son, Rebel, and her eleven-year-old daughter, Irene. Irene sat silently and cried. Carrie scolded Rebel, who just couldn't sit still, even at his father's funeral.

McNelly, if history were fair to a man's reputation and chances at posterity, would have been killed in Mexico, sacrificing the lives and notoriety of his Rangers, and me too, perhaps, and thus become another Custer with his luckless and nameless troops. Instead, though he remained famous in Texas for several years, the nation forgot him.

After the ceremony, the Little McNellys carried the coffin to the small cemetery beside the church and lowered it into the ground. They took turns at two shovels and covered the body. I paid my condolences to Carrie, patted Irene's shoulder, and shook Rebel's hand, and watched as the Rangers covered their leader with dirt.

As they filed past me, Sergeant Orrill dipped his head; Lee Hall, the new captain, said nothing; Sergeant Armstrong, stiff in his suit, ducked me also; Bill Callicott put his finger to the brim of his hat. Had he survived, surely, my literary brother Pidge Robinson would have spoken to me. As it was, only George Durham stopped to say anything to me. He had tears all over his face and rubbed his eyes with his big hands. He had his coat off and his shirt was wet with his sweat. "He was the best man I ever knew," he hesitated. "Better than my daddy."

"Jesus, George," I said. "It's not natural for you to look up to a man in that manner."

"He was a great man. History will remember him."

"I suppose. Why don't you and I go get drunk? I'd like to get a few dates, incidents, heroes, and adventures straight."

George pulled up, straightened, and looked at me. "The Captain didn't drink."

"George, that doesn't mean you can't drink."

"Well, hell," he said. "Just hell. I never knew what to think of you. I can't see you as a coward. You're too smart of a fellow. I just can't figure why you did what you did."

"I'm not sure if I know why I did what I did. If I knew then, what . . . what difference would it make? As it was, I think I helped stop a war. If it wasn't for me and . . . Well, skip it."

I walked with him a way, and we both decided to sit in the shade of a pecan tree on the edge of the cemetery. George looked up into the tree. "Be a good crop. I see a lot of green pecans. This isn't native pecan, though. I bet somebody brought the tree from Georgia."

I took my hat off and wiped at the sweat on my brow. "You going to stay a Ranger, George?"

George shook his head. "Ain't the same." He looked up at me, "Captain King's gonna give me a job, and I'm gonna learn the cow business." He beamed all over now.

"I never saw a man so happy to take up with cows."

He leaned close to me, "You watch, I'm going to marry that Caroline."

"Best of luck to you," I said to George, shook his hand, and rose. He pulled himself up. I thought that maybe I should see some resemblance between him and me when I was twenty-one. So my thoughts went to Addie, and I lost any feeling of resemblance between George and me. "You hold on to her, huh?"

He shook his head. "I almost wish I hadn't of come. He just didn't look natural, you know."

"No one ever does when he's dead."

I stuck out my hand again. "Please keep in touch. Let me know what happens with you and Caroline."

"Try to."

I wrote down my address and gave it to him. Then I left him, and, I hoped, McNelly behind. But McNelly was a Ranger, like my uncle, and because I could not leave my uncle behind, I could not leave McNelly. George was right. Dead, McNelly, with his white face with dabs of rouge on his cheeks, looked nothing like the sickly man. Rebel, his boy, didn't seem to recognize him. His crying wife and daughter didn't look at the corpse. I had never thought of him as a family man. I saw Carrie, Rebel, and Irene as no more than a change of clothes for him, not a part of the man I saw trying, in what little time he had, to intimidate the world into remembering him. The McNelly I knew wouldn't have had time to have a family that mourned his passing.

I could always see the family man in old Rip. He divorced his first wife in 1836, less than a year after he married her, to come to Texas and become what he was. He started out as a doctor in Tennessee, but by the time he got to Texas, he had made himself a lawyer, too. His daughter, Fannie, joined him, and married an Austin man during the war. I never heard him mention Fannie's twin brother. My mother never even mentioned him. That boy didn't just disappear to history, but to his family. Rip married a second time late in 1845, but when his wife died in 1846, after he appointed himself her physician, he joined Jack Hays in Mexico and became a part of the Diablos Tejanos. Addie was his third wife, and she got busy having children with the old man at a time when she knew me better than her husband. I knew about

Rip's earlier life from my mother, Elizabeth Ford. But both Rip and I had stopped writing her regularly, and she to us.

The boy Rip wanted, the boy to replace the lost twin of Fannie, was John William, named for Rip and Rip's father, the boy that Addie and I gave him. Earlier that year, John William found Rip's converted old Dragoon, the pistol I had used. He must have been fascinated by the history that he held in his hand, for as Addie wrote to tell me, he was becoming fascinated with his father's legend. He could read about his father in Beadle's dime novels. That liar Erastus Beadle and his writers had discovered Rip Ford and his fight against Cortina. They sent him out to conquer Cortina and other bandits over and over, complete with shoot-outs, cattle stampedes, and massacres that never happened. Pidge and I should have had the rights to that story. So John William must have fondled that descendant of Excalibur, on its own way to being a relic. Did he not know it was loaded? Had Rip let him have a loaded revolver? Hadn't Rip taught him about revolvers? The old Colt put a half-inch hole in his forehead and took most of the back of his head off.

I was glad that I had left Brownsville before this. Because of my cowardice, I did not want to be in a house with Addie and Rip after they scrubbed the blood and brains of their youngest off their white walls. I found myself thinking that someone as strong, as daring, and as great a warrior as Rip Ford should not have let this happen to his son. Addie had John William buried in her family's plot. I could not have endured my son's funeral, so I came to McNelly's instead.

As I got in my hack and left McNelly's grave, I developed a sorrow that would last for twenty years, not a sorrow for McNelly or old Rip, but for all those weak men, like me and John William and maybe some of the Little McNellys, who tried to follow their fathers or captains, but couldn't properly handle a six-shooter. I swore that I would never touch another revolver, not even to defend myself as I had in that small cantina outside of Brownsville.

WHEN I got back to San Antonio, my head started throbbing. To make it stop, I started drinking. I would wait most of the day before I would start. Then to sit through the phrenologist, the magicians, the belly dancer, or the risqué play, and to quiet my conscience, which took over because my mind wouldn't stay on the boring performance, I'd begin drinking. Then I'd keep on drinking, as my mind fought my conscience, and I'd compose my review in my head. I'd even scribble a few notes on my way to the west-side jacales and the brown arms that waited for me there. My hair started falling out in chunks until my crown and forehead became one slick pate. Even in my haziest days, though, I scribbled in my book about McNelly. Bit by bit, I wrote that story down.

What my conscience told me was that I truly was a coward. For I, not Addie and Rip, had let my son die. I was afraid to stand up to Rip Ford and claim his son as mine. And for that reason I deserved to be estranged, expelled, banished from the family I had known for the last fifteen years. I deserved my loneliness, and San Antonio and drink allowed me to live with it.

I got letters from George, and though I nearly needed someone to decipher them for me, they cheered me up. He was getting to be a good hand for Captain King, and he was making weekly visits to see Caroline. He told me that since McNelly's family could not afford a proper marker, Captain King bought one. I had already heard that several months after the burial, a gaudy granite obelisk appeared on the grave of L. H. McNelly. Captain King, as usual, always showed his gratitude.

Then the sixteenth legislature of the great state of Texas convened in January of 1879. And the state senator from the twenty-ninth district, in his second term, stopped in San Antonio for two cold nights as he made his way to Austin and the old state capitol. Rip Ford was now a hero. The *San Antonio Express* said he was on his way. He kissed babies and talked to widows, who, depending upon just how old they were, told him that their husbands served under him in the Mexican War, the Cortina War, the Comanche Wars, or the War Between the States. I think that he stayed an extra day just to soak up that adulation—and to spite me for the chronicle I had written about McNelly's Special Force. I had finished my book and mailed him a copy, and he promised to return it on his trip to Austin.

I left Jack Harris's Vaudeville Theater and Saloon and walked to the Menger. I had on two shirts and the jacket from a suit. I had sold my coat and hoped for a warm winter. A stiff wind blew across Alamo Plaza, so none of the old Confederate officers and ex-Rangers were feeding the pigeons and telling lies. I stumbled into the lobby of the Menger Hotel and stomped my feet. The lobby clerk looked at me and then toward a big man who served as a bouncer. I had been thrown out before.

In a high-backed chair shaped from cattle horns and hide with the hair still on, a gift from Captain King, sat the twenty-ninth district's state senator. Rip Ford straightened to his full height and rubbed his palm over the white beard. I looked to the bouncer and the clerk to make sure that they knew that I was here to meet the hero. "Andrew," the legend said and extended his hand. As I shook it, he looked at me. His nose wrinkled as though he were sniffing me.

"How about a drink?" I asked.

He hesitated, "I have buttermilk, courtesy of the hotel."

"I mean a real drink," I said.

He stared, went to his horn chair, grabbed his coat, a package, a cane, and his glass of buttermilk. He slung his overcoat over his shoulder, tucked the package under an arm, held his buttermilk in his hand, and tapped his cane on the wooden slats of the Menger lobby floor. He didn't need a cane. He was still as straight and as stiff-shouldered as the ladies and newspapers of San Antonio described, but since Sam Houston had sported a cane, and as a past supporter of Houston the man and a present supporter of Houston the legend, old Rip, upon his election to the sixteenth Texas state legislature, starting using a cane.

We walked to the Menger bar, a fine affair with gleaming mahogany and shining brass. It was not at all like Jack Harris's cavernous saloon with its rows of gaming tables and prostitutes mixing with cowboys and gamblers. It was an establishment for socially respectable gentlemen's drinking. I found the warmest spot in the bar, a table close to a Franklin stove, and sat down. Rip sat down next to me and put both of his hands on the handle of his cane, a golden screaming eagle. "Could I trouble you for the price of a drink? I'm a little short of cash right now." Jack Harris had insisted that I pay my drinking and gaming tab. Since Jack was a gentleman and knew uncouth, rough people, I was paying off my tab at the expense of my drinking habits.

"You haven't become a drunk, have you, Andrew?" Since he was no longer in command of rough men, he no longer went into bars, and in his first legislative session he demanded that a saloon next to the Capitol be closed down because of the number of legislators who enjoyed a long lunch at the bar and thus were in no condition to conduct the affairs of the state. He cocked his head to study me. "What is wrong with you, Andrew? What has happened?"

"A drink," I said and yelled "bourbon" toward the bar. "I like to drink, Rip. It helps me to both remember and forget. With my drink I can sort things out."

Rip said, "All I have ever gotten from you is this," and he threw the package on the table between us. "Nothing else. No news. Addie worries, you know. She has cried because she hasn't heard from you.

William's death was such a blow for us. And nothing from you. No word. So she cried." I wanted nothing more than my drink. And I was greatly relieved when the bartender brought my small, straight-up bourbon. The warmth of its first sip cooled the warmth in my brain that started when Rip mentioned John William.

"Tell her I'm fine." The bourbon also kept me from talking too much, from getting too close to the truth.

"The help here seems to stare at you."

"My associations are in a rougher part of town. Sometimes we drink too much and take a hack to this bar. I've been kicked out of here a couple of times."

I shivered and then looked at the package. The honorable senator from the twenty-ninth district pounded the end of his cane onto the floor so hard that vibrations could be felt going up the walls of the Menger bar. The bartender turned to look at the tall, white-bearded gentleman from Brownsville. "The man was in enemy territory. He was on a military expedition, not a police force. He conducted himself as any officer should."

I hung my head, "What I wrote is what happened."

He blew a little wind out between his lips. "But it's not the truth."

"It's objective."

"Given the times, he needs to be defended."

"So does Cortina."

Rip slowly nodded. "I agree with you there. Cortina does need his defense. But we disagree about history."

"Wasn't McNelly the Ranger who said, 'No man in the wrong can stand up against a man in the right who keeps on a comin'. Either he'll get there or others will follow him'?"

"Yes, he did, but you're not *right*," Ford said and leaned back as though he had just judged me. The heavens were about to shake.

"Yeah, maybe so." I sipped my whiskey, felt it burn my throat and melt my worries and my concern for this man. "But that's where you and I differ. I could never exactly figure out the *right*." I raised my glass of whiskey, "To los Tejanos sangrientos, diablos Tejanos, los rinches."

The temperance man looked at my whiskey, then me. He stroked his white beard. "Is it the whiskey that leads you to your new life here, or has your new life led you to the whiskey?"

"Maybe my whole life makes me drink."

He flipped his cane adroitly in his left hand and caught it. "I'd suggest you burn that book. No one is going to read it."

I looked at the Franklin stove. "You do it. You burn it." I reached to the package and shoved it toward him. "You just take it and throw it in that stove. Go ahead. That book has plagued me too. Just forget it, burn it. If it's not right, if it's not history, then burn it."

He looked at the manuscript, at me, and at the stove. The old man was just starting to grow concerned with a history of Texas, so he could not destroy any trace of it, even if it was a distasteful one. He was not a book-burner. He would face the future as he did his past, as he faced the Comanches and Mexicans. He pushed the book back toward me. "Do with it what you will. And good luck."

I grabbed at the manuscript and put it in my lap. Rip studied me for a while, then said, "Speaking of stories, there's corridos growing about how some gringo demon massacred everybody in a bar. Even if you were just defending your own hide, I was proud of you when you told me, because you finally fought back."

"It was just base survival."

"Still, it was something." He seemed, then, as an old man, as more heroic than the figure on a horse leading Confederates or Rangers, but I felt like a coward because I could say nothing to him about John William. My mind and hand started trembling. "What do you do to support yourself now?" he asked.

"Whatever I can."

"How are you making a living?" he asked, opening his wallet and peering inside.

"I'm a critic now. And I'm friends with Jack Harris."

"That man is a pimp, a gambler, a criminal from what I hear."

"He's also rich, and he pretty much says what happens in this town."

Rip smiled, "So things haven't changed that much." The hard times after the war, the money from Captain King still stung, but he pulled new Yankee bills, the first bills any Texan took seriously, and laid them in front of me.

"I'll buy you some more drinks then, instead of your friend Jack Harris." I trembled as I scooped up the bills and ordered another bourbon. "Don't drink all the money."

Because of family or Southern graciousness or my respect for valor and his respect for my education and writing, we were always able to pass over the uneasiness that inevitably developed between us, but when I took the money and ordered that whiskey, I think I made that uneasiness into a wall we could not climb over for another five years.

CHAPTER 19

Jack Harris

Lady Audley's Secret *brought tears to an admittedly rough crowd. Cowboys, gamblers, and their escorts unashamedly wept as the intricately timed drama came to a close. Many of these rough folks, as well as this reviewer, carried images of the delicate, subtle performances home with them. Now if we could just erase the images of the ugly shootings that occurred in the balcony—in this supposed civilized city.*

ANDREW NEVIN,
San Antonio Express, *March 1884*

N
O matter what the proper people whispered, Jack Harris was a gentleman. Though he ran a gambling house and a theater that ran tawdry shows and sold liquor and the favors of young ladies, in devotion to his friends, in his manner and appearance, and in the courtesy he showed, he was every bit a gentleman. Even those who would not acknowledge that Jack Harris was a gentleman had to acknowledge that he ran San Antonio. His money and his influence elected mayors, passed taxes, and started and paid for city projects. He had a vision of the city. He opened the first account with the new San Antonio Electric Company. He saw an electrically lighted theater followed by an entire electric city. He was San Antonio.

To me, his mistakes did not come from his line of work, but in his defense of his work. When a friend, his property, or his reputation was threatened, he'd arm himself with a sawed-off shotgun, balance the barrel on his lame left arm, and demand an apology. With his shotgun in hand, he was scared of no man. He claimed that, even with his lame arm, he could shoot a bird on the wing with a shotgun, so why not a man standing still.

A hero and adventurer, Harris fought with the Union Army against the Mormons in 1857; then he went south to join Walker's filibuster in Nicaragua. He got back to this country in time to join the Confederacy. After the war, he piloted ships and found himself first in Galveston and then San Antonio. He became a city policeman and learned the town. And since 1872, he ran the finest gaming tables and saloon in San Antonio.

Then the foundation of not just a small vaudeville theater, but a larger variety theater formed in his mind. With the help of my imagination, it took its final form. Jack Harris's new theater stood beside and over Jack Harris's Saloon. It had its own entrance and ticket booth as well as ones in the saloon. Patrons of either the theater or the saloon could thus have both theatrical entertainment and a beverage. To get to the theater itself, theater-goers went up a flight of stairs from either entrance and then descended several more stairs until they found a seat. Two boxes on either side of the theater were reached by a narrow stairwell. And if a theater-goer wished, from the box, during the show, he could order cigars or drinks from girls in short dresses and low necklines. I had my choice of seats in either box.

With memories of the old Gem, I suggested an upstairs water closet and washroom for both ladies and gentlemen. San Antonio's new water system brought San Pedro Springs water into the city, but so far, only horse troughs and fire hydrants had fresh water. Jack Harris, with enough of his own pipe, could easily tap into the modern-day wonder of fresh water. Jack was thus freed of facilities and a septic tank in the alley behind the theater and the fees to the scavengers who would clean out the tank.

Until we had actual electricity flowing into the theater and lighting it, I suggested gas-lit lamps curling out from the walls rather than chandeliers hanging from overhead. With one switch, a stagehand could dim the lights and lead the patrons to their seats; then when the show started, a stagehand could further dim the lights. The show would determine the amount of light. Phrenologists, magicians, and animal acts demanded light. Melodramas were better viewed from a dark seat.

Occupying the corner of Commerce and Soledad, Jack Harris's Vaudeville Theater became both famous and notorious. In truly democratic fashion, it brought the *best* and the *worst* of the city together. I was there at its grand opening, smiling and welcoming people along with Jack, Joe Foster, and Billy Sims.

During that time, I became the favorite critic. Since I could not indulge my critical eye and write a negative review, I amused myself with my style and my jaundiced tone. In a short time, I became popular because of my flamboyance. But I needed a personal flamboyance to fit my journalistic flamboyance and the gaudiness of the theaters. I showed a copy of a *New York Times* article about Oscar Wilde to Jack Harris. Wilde had never toured San Antonio; few people here had heard about him. So his style became my style. I became a daffodil, or at least what Texans might think a daffodil, grown middle-aged. From Wilde, I got the idea to wear velvet britches—red, green, and black— and matching frock coats, even though the style had shifted to shorter jackets. I wore only velvet in winter, along with a black cape with a gold satin lining. During the San Antonio springs and summers, I wore silk vests and sashes. I had shirts with ruffled sleeves. I had a fine beaver fur with one side of the brim pinned up, as Jeb Stuart made popular during the war, homage, in a way, to Pidge Robinson. At times, I pasted a wig to my scalp and sported my newly full head of hair. Over time, I pulled out all of my remaining strands of hair as I peeled the wig off my head. I spent extravagantly on food, drink, and Chinese tailors and launderers.

What man but a nance would have the feminine refinement to carry on a decent conversation about melodramas, opera recitals, and the fashions that society ladies read about in the *New York Times, Galveston News,* or *New Orleans Picayune?*

I got invited to parties and soon was writing in the society page about who graced what party and began quoting the wives of the Germans who found themselves on top of the economic and social heap. I was an amusement, a curiosity, a brightly colored, gelded bird, and I was, of course, no threat to wives or daughters. Once I began to dress and act the part, I got speaking engagements in San Antonio, and once I took the new train to Galveston to cover the arts scene and to talk to Galveston's own ladies and ladies' clubs in order to report back on San Antonio's financial and social betters.

Most of my days became pleasantly predictable. After a night at another melodrama in which an eternally young and dim-witted lady was oppressed by a villain in a cape similar to the one I wore and was rescued by an equally dim-witted lumberjack, after the review that I had all but written in my head, I'd go into Jack Harris's saloon for an evening's nightcap and a little gambling. Pleasant, amusing Joe Foster usually joined me.

Then I'd begin my sojourn to the Mexican side of town. I'd leave Main Plaza. I'd cross Acequia, the "fatal corner," the site of so many shoot-outs and murders, walk to San Fernando Cathedral, which watched me and the other sinners, walk down the alley beside it, and enter Military Plaza. Sometimes, in certain seasons, the vendors were just setting up, and I could smell the vegetables, fruit, and pastry. Then, I'd walk yet farther west, past the Italian and Belgian merchants and the Chinese restaurants, theaters, and one opium den, and enter the Mexican side of town. There, I bought the attention, not just the favors, of young, olive-skinned Mexican girls who couldn't afford to go to melodramas or recitals, who didn't know about society, who couldn't even read. There, with them, I could recapture my moments with my dear Catalina Taracón.

In the summer of 1882, just before a performance, just as the sun went down and a gentleman could feel a little coolness, could feel his sweat-stained back and shoulders start to dry, Jack Harris called me into his second-floor office. Shirt-sleeved, with garters keeping the sleeves off his wrists, hair oiled, moustache in two points, Jack, with his good hand, held a stack of silver dollars over his desk and dropped them on top of one another. I heard their clinking over and over. I sat across from his desk, and I could smell his imported cologne from where I sat. "Loosen your tie," he said to me. We were just starting to wear neckties in those days, but in my silk and linen costume I wore a drooping bow around my neck. I felt my damp collar as I pulled at my bow.

"Jack, I've as much as written my review. When have you ever read a bad one?"

Jack let the dollars drop, then held up his good hand. "You could find a little more to like in the shows and stop indulging that sarcastic whimsy of yours, but your reviews are not what this is about."

I took my watch from my coat pocket. "The show will start soon, and I'd like to get to my box."

Jack nodded. "Despite your journalistic liberties, you're prompt, efficient. You've even cleared up that problem you had with over-indulging in my liquor." He looked around the room and gestured with his good hand. "You helped design this theater." Something grand was about to take place. Jack didn't normally praise or make speeches. "I don't forget people. So I've decided to do you a favor. How much money do you have saved?"

Not many people in town could afford to turn down a Jack Harris favor. "I thought that you were going to do me a favor?"

"I thought that you might like an interest in the theater."

I leaned back into the chair. Jack's theater was doing very well. He pushed out an agreement. "My attorney says this is good. I've given one just like it to Joe and Billy. I'm thinking about the future. With the money from you three, I can make a start at turning this place electric, or I can maybe buy the property this place sits on."

"How much?"

"Bring what you have saved or put away for your old age. That will be fine."

"I haven't exactly thought about getting old."

Jack smoothed his waxed moustaches and raised one eyebrow. "So you'll make payments to me, and I'll give a point less than the banks on interest."

"Jack, I do have some expenses, and my rent goes up. And though I have some notoriety, I still get the salary of a newspaperman."

Jack lifted his lame arm with his shoulder. "So indulge yourself a little less."

I realized that this was not an offer but a demand. It was the part of Jack that could get him and me in trouble. So I stood and slowly, knowing that I was in no position to refuse him, extended my hand.

Jack smiled, stood, and pumped my hand. "Now sign the paper." The smell of his cologne nearly overpowered me. Thus I was pushed into the best and most profitable business decision of my life. As I stooped to sign the paper, Billy squeezed through the door to Jack's office and shut it closed behind him. "Ben Thompson is downstairs. He's drunk," Billy said.

"Sign that," Jack said to me, and I quickly signed the document. "Billy, you witnessed it."

"Hell yeah, he's down there demanding to know where your shotgun brigade is."

"No, no, I'm telling you, not asking, I mean Andrew's signature."

Billy nodded, and Jack went to a corner and pulled out his sawed-off shotgun and cradled it over his lame left arm.

"Jack, wait. There's no reason for this," I said.

Billy laughed and said to me, "You don't know that son of a bitch. He's drunk. He's been talking." Earlier that day, as I had taken the mule-drawn streetcar to St. Mary's Street, then walked the last two blocks, then stopped in for a beer, I had heard the rumors. Ben Thompson was in town and getting drunk. No one dared stop him. He was talking about Jack Harris, saying vile things. And Jack had gone looking for him with his shotgun in his good arm, but had not found him.

"Jack, don't." Jack cracked open the shotgun to look at the two chambers. "We're civilized men."

"You look extra civilized in that getup of yours," Billy laughed.

"Jack," I said.

"Maybe you don't have the stomach for this. I don't expect you to. But somebody has to take up our reputation," Jack said.

Jack held out his lame left arm and slung the barrel over it. "He's a lying killer. Those sons of bitches in Austin don't even know better than to elect him city marshal. People in San Antonio aren't as stupid."

"Jack, consider," I said.

"You're my partner now, so you consider," Jack said. "If I allow a man to accuse me of cheating and then leave his tab unpaid, then every tinhorn and bad-luck-story cowboy is going to pull the same thing on me."

"But he paid the tab," I said.

"Eventually," Billy said.

"There's still his words," Jack said.

Now Billy looked at Jack. "Be careful, Jack. I've seen him." Billy had once been Ben Thompson's partner in Austin and subsequently had fallen out with him. Ben was the reason Billy had left Austin to come to San Antonio. "The drunker he gets, the wilder he gets. And you wouldn't think it, but he gets better with his pistols when he's drunk."

Jack smiled, "I'm going to get him."

Billy held the door open for Jack to leave. Jack moved toward the door but stopped and swiveled to face me and smiled like a good-smelling gentleman. "Are you coming?"

All I could think about was Pidge Robinson and his bravery, chivalry, or foolishness. "You were right. I haven't the stomach for it."

"So be it," Jack said and smiled. "All of us have different talents. Stick with yours, Andrew Nevin." It was almost as though he had given me his blessing. "You stick with your writing. You watch and write down what others do." I became only slightly insulted.

Ben Thompson drank twice as much as me but only had half my tolerance. He was drunk most of the time. Two years before, during the year of our grand opening, he came into the saloon and lost heavily in a game that Joe Foster was dealing. He lost, gained a little, then lost more. He accused Joe of cheating. Stoic Joe Foster simply looked down at the man, held his coat open to show he had no pistol, and said that he should take his complaints up with the owner. "That goddamn pimp, Jack Harris. Hell, he mistreats those poor women he's forced into white slavery. Why, if he was in Austin, I'd run him out of town." Ben left, but Jack went out looking for him with his shotgun.

Ben Thompson had faced Wild Bill Hickok and had killed men in three states. He had come home to Austin, and after getting beat once, was elected city marshal. Jack was right, Austinites must be crazy. He liked to dress in a silk top hat and leather gloves. And we all knew that when he took off the gloves, he was prepared to start shooting.

I waited in Jack's office, sweating even as the evening cooled, thinking that I had left this all behind at the violent border. I had thought San Antonio civilized enough for me. I thought that I should have run farther away from the border: Galveston, New Orleans, or New York.

I heard shots. I waited, counted the seconds. When I heard no more, I raced down the steps and went through a side door into the saloon. Jack Harris was blocking the doorway. And my foot slipped on his blood.

Jack had fallen forward, crushing the door with its Venetian blinds, and twisting before he hit the ground so that he lay on his back. On his back, he looked up at me and gurgled. He clawed at the blood stain on his white shirt. As I stepped over him, Joe Foster was beside him, and the bartender was on this side of the bar. Joe asked what had happened before I could.

The bartender answered. "Jack came up behind the door to his office and leveled the shotgun. But somebody says to Ben, 'Jack's got his gun.' People just started running then. And Ben asks, 'What you going to do with that gun, Jack?' and Jack says, 'I'm going to shoot you, you son of a bitch.' And Ben sends two shots into the door and one at the bar."

Jack's eyes looked panicked. "Where's Billy?" Joe asked.

"He's out looking for Ben," the bartender said.

As I was pressing the bartender's whiskey-soaked towel on Jack's chest, I said, "Get him back. Get him back."

Jack's head stayed still, but his eyes shifted from Joe to me, then back again. "How does it look?"

Joe shook his head. "Lots of blood," he said.

"So you think ol' Ben's killed me?" Jack asked.

"I hope not," Joe said.

I couldn't make my eyes lie. "So I'm killed."

Joe and I strained and got Jack to his feet and dragged him, his blood filling the towel and even staining our suits. We pulled him outside the doors and stuffed him into the closest hack. We rode with him to his house, and the hack driver complained to us that he didn't care if it was "Jack Harris his own self" but that someone was going to pay to clean the blood off the leather upholstery. Joe and I got Jack Harris to his bed. Joe shook his head. And as I stepped out of Jack's bedroom, a lady I recognized as one of the city's madams rushed in through his door. I watched her go to Jack's bed, kneel, and start to cry as Jack feebly lifted one arm and patted the back of her head. As I got back into the hack with the stained leather upholstery, another hack pulled up. A doctor rushed out of it and into Jack's house. That night I reviewed *East Lynne*. As horrible as the show was, I still remember it because after the show I took a hack back to Jack's house, but he was already at the morgue.

Billy didn't catch Ben. Before the night was done, Ben surrendered to a policeman and got out on bail. He went back to Austin, and some Austin city councilmen gently, cautiously persuaded him to give up being city marshal. Those stupid goddamn Austinites even gave him a parade.

Of course he was acquitted—as happened to him time and again, as so often happened in Texas. Jack had threatened him. These were personal matters where self-defense pleas usually meant acquittal. Austin would have screamed for blood if he had been convicted.

Ben started drinking even more. He went to an Austin bar and at gunpoint brought the Negro patrons into the white part of the bar. Later, at a cattleman's convention, he kicked the table of condiments over and shot off several rounds in the air. Those tough cattlemen let him get away with it. Later yet, in an Austin theater, he loaded his revolver with blanks, jumped on stage after the show, and shot at the audience. He was lucky he wasn't shot. He was lucky that everyone in Austin and San Antonio was scared of him—everybody except for my new partner, Billy Sims.

I found some happiness amidst all the sadness of Jack Harris's death. I got a letter from George Durham. With perfect spelling and grammar, with penmanship that had loops, spacing, and design instead of a clumsy scrawl, George told me that he had married Caroline. Obviously, Caroline had written the letter. Captain Richard King, the savior for all Texas Rangers, made George the foreman of the El Sauz division of the ranch and built them a house on that ranch as a wedding present. I sent my congratulations and then received another letter inviting me to visit. Thus began a few years of correspondence between George and me. No doubt he mumbled and guffawed while Caroline shaped his comments into coherent thoughts and grammatically correct sentences. Sometimes, when I opened one of the letters, containing just a scent of Caroline's perfume, I could smell and feel the joy George had in his good fortune.

TWENTY months after Jack Harris's death, on March 11, 1884, I went to the Jack Harris Vaudeville Theater, which I now partly owned, to review yet another melodrama, *Lady Audley's Secret,* and was met in the bar, where I usually stopped for a pre-show libation, by Billy Sims. His eyes darted about, then he pulled a revolver out of his coat and pressed it into my hands. "Just keep your eyes open." I stuttered; then he added, "Ben Thompson is in town." I had heard already. Everyone who frequented the bars and brothels knew that Ben Thompson had gotten on the train from Austin with his friend King Fisher, the outlaw or lawman, depending upon your view, who had foiled McNelly, and had stopped in San Antonio.

King Fisher was a deputy sheriff of Uvalde County. He was on his way back from Austin to the county seat, Uvalde. He visited his old friend in Austin, and Ben, drunk as usual, insisted on accompanying Fisher back as far as San Antonio. Ben had drunk all the way from Austin to San Antonio. And as Billy Sims spoke to me, Ben was making his way from the train station down Commerce Street and stopping off at every bar.

I held the revolver in front of me. "Hide that thing," Billy said. I stuck the .38 caliber in my coat to make a lump in my jacket. "Have you ever shot a gun before?" he asked me with some disdain. My mind immediately went back to McNelly and my last days and last shoot-out on the border. He knew nothing of my exploits, and I had pushed them and my true account from my mind. My memory and recollection of my own killings and my adventure with McNelly rested with my manuscript in the bottom of my chest of drawers. "I didn't think you had. But don't worry. I've got help. Just fire if you get a chance or if we need you. You'll know."

"Whom do I fire at?"

Billy look disgusted. "Why, at Thompson or Fisher."

"Two of the most dangerous outlaws in Texas. Two of the best gunmen in Texas."

Billy only said, "Right. And one of them killed Jack Harris and got away with it."

"Why do you have to see him dead? Why do you have to continue the killing?"

"We go back a ways," Billy said, and he left me in the soft gaslight of the theater (we were still a few years from electricity); I faced the bar, feeling the revolver on my side, and had one more drink.

For several years, King Fisher ran his own kingdom between San Antonio and Eagle Pass. McNelly himself had turned his attention to

King Fisher after he had invaded Mexico. He had in fact arrested Fisher. But through fear, friendship, and good lawyers, no charges could stick on the King. He was corrupt but beneficent. He was also careful and spread his money and influence through the area. He was happily married and had forsaken drink. Tall, dark, with a wide moustache, he was a handsome man and could have had his pick of the Main Plaza ladies—or maybe even some of the society ladies settling in the King William area. The peace officers and monied people of San Antonio had all but forgiven and pardoned King Fisher. He had, for all practical purposes, through his outlawry, won his honesty.

Ben Thompson had given the King a gift that made him even more regal. Ben bought a tiger from a traveling circus, killed it, and had it skinned. He had the hide made into a pair of soft chaps for his friend. A tall man, wearing tiger-skinned chaps, riding anywhere west of San Antonio, was untouchable, was royalty. Now his loyalty to a drunk was pushing him into an ambush.

I took my accustomed place in a corner in the box. Two young ladies in short skirts and red stockings appeared, and one, my favorite, who from time to time came by my house, took my order for a mint julep. I felt "Southern" that night. Soon, Joe Foster, my other partner, along with Billy Sims, joined me. He adjusted his glasses on the end of his nose, pulled his watch out and looked at it. "We are running late."

"We always run late, Joe. It helps sell more liquor." From behind me, three more male guests appeared and sat down.

"Have you heard?" Joe asked me.

"Did Billy give you a revolver too?"

"He tried to, but I refused it." I looked at him. "It's illegal." I held open my coat to show him the butt of my revolver. Joe shook his head. "Billy just doesn't think sometimes. Without Jack, I can't control him. We don't need to get into any trouble."

No sooner had the words gotten out when a silk top hat entered the box. Under the silk hat was Ben Thompson. He stumbled toward a seat. Beside him, guiding him, was King Fisher. King Fisher pushed his friend into a seat, and then Ben noticed Joe Foster and me. He waved. "Joe Foster, you old son of a bitch," he said. King quickly looked in our direction, and as Ben rose, as though to join us, King pushed him back into his seat. Then twisting, King positioned himself in a seat between us and Ben's vision. "Watch the play," we heard King say.

The gaslights went down. A woman with nothing but a veil

appeared on stage, and *Lady Audley's Secret* began and took Ben's attention off us. With my mint julep in my left hand I pulled out my pad and pencil with my right and took notes on the false, easy sentiments of the play. The people behind me stretched their necks to watch me. They didn't know me, nor did they know why I was there. Something about a person, especially one dressed as I was, taking notes in the dark, was annoying to people. So I scratched down the plot, the subtleties, the nuances, the drama, or rather I tried to make them up. Ben, meantime, shouted to order more liquor.

After the play, when the flames on the gaslights grew larger and brighter, Ben again looked in our direction. "Joe Foster, Joe Foster, come on over here and let me talk to you." Joe and I both turned to look and saw that, during the performance, Billy Sims and the very large city policeman, Jacobo Coy, whom we hired after hours for security, had sat behind Ben. "Joe Foster, leave that old sister you're with and come talk to me. I want to know about Jack Harris's killing."

King Fisher, dapper, concerned, caught my eye. "Look, gentlemen," I said. "I get very bored with these all-too-common talks of killings. Everyone has a favorite story. They've become like fairy tales."

"My favorite is the one about the killing of Jack Harris," Ben Thompson said and looked behind him at Sims and Coy. Thompson tried to stare at them, but he couldn't keep his head still. The patrons who had sat behind me quickly filed out.

"Let's go to the bar and have a drink and discuss this," King Fisher said.

"I'd like to discuss this with Joe Foster," Thompson said. "Bring your Miss Molly with you and come on over here, Joe Foster."

The springs in the seat beside me squeaked as Joe Foster tensed, and I reached over to put my hand on his arm. "Don't go over there," I whispered.

Coy and Sims were up before Joe. And Fisher pulled Thompson up out of his seat and began to push him toward the exit. As Joe Foster, a small man, about my height, unarmed, stood up, I fingered the butt of my pistol. And in my mind, starting as just a tiny silhouette but growing and expanding until it became a full mural, was my memory of killing those people on the border. Panic and fright had given me the advantage, but had also pushed me into killings that may have been avoided. I had sworn that I would not touch another gun, but stuck under my belt was a revolver.

Joe stood up stiffly and stepped into the aisle, and I moved in behind him. He didn't glance at any of the others but intended, I believe, to walk out of the theater. But Ben Thompson jumped in front of him. Joe stopped, leaned his head back to peer through his glasses on the end of his nose at the belligerent drunk, and Ben Thompson slapped him. My revolver was out of my pants before I had time to think. I had a clear shot at Ben Thompson.

But I didn't shoot. Caution fought panic and fear, so I waited, and I saw Ben Thompson pull his gun out so quickly that its barrel was a blur. And then he stuck that barrel in Joe Foster's mouth. Ben Thompson, whom everyone tolerated but no one really liked, showed his sinister, despicable nature. He could have pulled that barrel out of Joe's mouth and holstered his pistol, and all might have passed. Instead he chortled, a mean sucking sound.

Jacobo Coy slapped his hand over Thompson's revolver to hold the cylinder in place, and Joe Foster, with the gun slapped out of his mouth, must have lost a tooth. Giving into his fear and panic, reacting as I probably would have done, Joe uncharacteristically lunged at Ben Thompson, and Thompson's revolver went off.

Ben and Joe were down and coiled together. Joe grabbed his thigh, and I pulled him off Ben. I looked across from me and caught King Fisher's glance. One of the new bowlers cocked to one side of his face, a diamond stickpin on his chest, just below his throat, holding his tie in place, his suit fitting his broad shoulders, Fisher pulled a revolver out of his coat. I raised mine.

In that moment, looking at one of the most feared gunmen in Texas, I saw a gentleman, and maybe King Fisher saw one, too. I hesitated, and he showed me mercy. But in thinking long enough to show me mercy, King Fisher gave Coy and Billy Sims enough time to empty their revolvers. Soon, one of the vaudeville performers, a gambler, and the bartender were in the crowded box, and with a Winchester and two shotguns, they shot, point-blank, at Fisher and Thompson.

I knelt beside Joe Foster and saw the growing bloody spot and the jagged bone sticking through his trousers just above his knee. I looked beside me. Fisher and Thompson were down, but Coy, Sims, the gambler, the barkeep, and the performer were over them and firing still.

The box filled with smoke. More people came into it. I choked and held onto Joe Foster. Before too long, Sims and Coy were beside me picking Joe up. He groaned. A woman knelt beside the prone bodies of Fisher and Thompson and asked, "Which one was Ben?"

Another woman, crying, tentatively reached toward King Fisher's face and brushed at the powder burns on it. She bent over and gently kissed the dead man's lips.

As they carried Joe Foster out, and people swirled around me, I looked in my hands to see what they held. In my left hand were Joe's spectacles, in my right was my revolver. I hadn't shot it, I hadn't even cocked it. And a face and a name appeared in my mind at the same time: John William. A civilized man, I looked at the revolver in my hand. Maybe, maybe, I too was to blame for John William's death. I swore once again that I'd never touch another gun, not even in self-defense, and dropped the revolver.

As I heard my revolver thud against the wooden floor, I looked at the tops of the stooped heads, all bent over to gape at the two bodies, thus giving me a straight view of the face on top of the tall, unstooped shoulders. The old man's eyes took it all in, watched everyone carefully. His white beard caught the light and illuminated those small, observant, careful eyes. If anything else was to happen, this man with the comforting yet dangerous gaze would stop it. For a moment, my eyes locked with my uncle's.

Rip Ford turned from me, and I pushed through the crowd to get to him, but I couldn't find him. I stepped out of the theater, and the soft glow of gaslights caught my eyes and lifted them up to the bell tower of San Fernando Cathedral.

ONCE AGAIN, I walked to the lobby of the Menger to meet Rip. I walked in between the cowmen and the ex-Rangers and generals as they were reading about Ben Thompson and King Fisher's deaths and passing their judgment, which would probably become the official opinion of Texas. I wore a white shirt, open at the collar, the sleeves ruffled, a black vest with golden fringe and designs, black britches with a velvet strip, black patent leather shoes, a green cape over my shoulder, and a hat with the brim pinned up to the side in Confederate Cavalry fashion. I rarely made appearances at the Menger.

As I placed my hand in front of John S. Ford, as he sat in the cowhide and horn chair, reading a column next to mine, he didn't even recognize me. As he shook my hand, I said, "Did you enjoy the show? Did you read my review?"

"I'm saving your review until last. I've read some others of yours though." He looked away from me. "I don't know that I like them."

"I don't either. I'm getting tired of the 'embellishing.'"

"Your style was always different from mine."

"You were more direct, bombastic. You almost had to pull a sheriff's ears off because of your style."

"People knew my opinion, in print or otherwise. I think I'm what they are calling 'Realism.'"

"William Dean Howells, he's one of my favorites."

"What newspaper does he write for?"

"He writes novels."

"So he lies."

"How about a drink, something a man would drink?"

He lowered his head to look under the brim of my hat, and I took off my hat, I didn't have my wig on. I didn't have to look to know that the old Confederates and Rangers turned away from me in disgust, but Rip Ford said, "Andrew. Why, Andrew, you've gone completely bald."

I rubbed the top of my head. "I hear baldness comes from the mother's side of the family."

He rubbed his still bushy white hair. "So it does."

"I didn't think that you would have enjoyed the show."

"I've been with enough hard men to enjoy occasional bawdiness. Of course, Addie wouldn't appreciate them, and I wouldn't dream of taking her to them."

He got up slowly. His shoulders sloped slightly forward. Now he needed the eagle-head cane by his side; he tapped it as we made our way to the Menger bar. "How is Addie?" I asked. "I've missed her so. Please tell her that."

"She's missed you too."

In the bar, we sat down at the table next to the Franklin stove. I yelled for a bourbon. Rip ordered some buttermilk. "Why are you in San Antonio?"

"Don't you read your own newspaper? I've retired. San Antonio seemed like the place for old Texans to retire. The water, I guess."

"Do you have any money?"

He dropped his head as my bourbon and his buttermilk arrived. "I've got one pension, from my last job, director of the Texas State School for the Deaf up in Austin. And I've got some friends."

I had read about his entirely political appointment as director for the school for the deaf. It was a political gift for the old warrior, just so he could have some sort of state retirement money. But true to form, old Rip attacked. He had insisted that the deaf weren't idiots, that they could hold jobs like ordinary people. When he left the school for the deaf, it was making money and finding jobs for its students. "It's a nice day with a gentle breeze. How about we sit outside?" Rip asked.

So I grabbed my liquor and Rip grabbed his buttermilk, and we stepped out of the Menger bar. Rip stopped, squinted, and checked first to his right at the old mission that was currently a grocer's warehouse, then checked the livery to the left. Content that there was no ambush, he stepped into the street, and we crossed the partially paved street to Alamo Plaza. The city was experimenting with different types of pavement, the latest was some sort of crushed gravel that washed or wore away. In Alamo Plaza, across from the crumbling old relic, amongst the old Anglo Confederates, Rangers, and ranchers who had come to this symbol of what they thought Texas was to gossip and relive some glory in a city rapidly becoming modernized around them, I sat with perhaps the most famous of the old warriors. The city was building a gazebo, but it was incomplete, so the old men sat on wooden benches under the oaks and pecans. Rip and I had one bench to ourselves. We watched the thriving businesses in the Little Rhine area. We heard the laughter that had a German accent and the *oompapa* of tuba, violin, and oboe come wafting toward us from across the street.

Rip looked at me. "So you became him? That English fella." His eyes got brighter, and he started to laugh. "You had to become a nance." He laughed until he could laugh no more. And I began to pat his back when he stopped laughing and started to cough. "I've talked to some people. I understand that you have given up the ladies." He laughed some more. "I remember telling you that you had to choose a side. I see that you have. Gamblers, prostitutes, and show people." He smiled at me.

"I understand that you are trying to write your memoirs," I said.

"You did know I was in town. I'm not hard to find."

"Nor am I."

He spread his hand across his face and rubbed his beard. "I'm writing my memoirs the way it was. But my memory is a bit faulty. I need someone to help me remember and to help me research."

"Would you like some help?"

"Lily, my adopted daughter, is helping me."

"How would you like professional help?"

"What's the charge?"

"I'm part owner of Jack Harris's theater, and I have my column. I can see to my affairs at night and help you write your memoirs during the late mornings. The charge is just to let me help."

Rip looked at me cautiously. "It won't be like your reviews—or your book about the McNelly affair."

"I will see to it that it is written as you wish."

Rip cocked his head and looked at me. "Why?"

"I've grown as concerned as you about getting 'our' history recorded. We need, oh, hell, I need . . . to leave something."

Rip nodded his head, then thought for a moment. "They've got Ben Thompson's and King Fisher's bullet-filled bodies on display. What became of your friend, the one who got wounded?"

"A doctor amputated his leg last night. He just lost too much blood. He died this morning—after the papers came out."

Rip squinted across the street at the Germans and said, "I had thought this town a better place, more civilized."

CHAPTER 20

Rip Ford

Citizens of San Antonio, I hope that you will join me in welcoming the distinguished Indian, bandit, and Yankee fighter, the honorable Colonel John S. "Rip" Ford into our community. Along with Hamilton Bee and James Slaughter, who fought with Col. Ford in the late war, and so many other notables from that war, from our western and southern ranches, and from our fights with savages, Col. Ford has chosen to retire along the banks of our fresh waters.

ANDREW NEVIN
San Antonio Express, *March 1884*

Dear patient, forgiving, and loyal readers, I wish to announce my retirement from this great publication. The city, this newspaper, and I have all grown more refined and sophisticated in my tenure here. And so it is with loyalty, fondness, and courtesy that I bid adieu *and* adios.

ANDREW NEVIN
San Antonio Express, *June 1884*

The itching which some writers seem to feel to place themselves forward on all occasions will be avoided. The writer will not endeavor to become the hero upon all extraordinary events and to let the book speak of himself alone.

RIP FORD
"Statement of Purpose," 1885, Rip Ford's Texas, *ed. Stephen B. Oates, 1963*

MY urge to quit my role as a counterfeit Oscar Wilde was well timed. The real Oscar Wilde himself came to town and appeared in Jack Harris's Vaudeville Theater. In green velvet knee britches, velvet slippers, cape, and ruffled sleeves, he held a book in front of him as he read or recited poems and lines from his plays. Some of the dirtiest, crudest cowboys cried. The prostitutes, dressed well enough to appear as society ladies, as well as the real society ladies, swooned and sighed. And when he bowed and the applause started then grew to bring the cowboys, gamblers, prostitutes, merchants, bankers, and proper wives out of their seats, I knew that I'd seen the curtain close on my nance drama. Oscar Wilde had outdone me and thus himself.

So my life took another turn. I convinced Billy Sims that my notoriety and thus my influence and profitability as a critic were failing. The years as a critic had taught me the taste of San Antonioans, so Billy agreed to allow me to book acts. Free to concentrate on the drinking and gambling at the White Elephant, his new saloon, Billy soon left the theater and the saloon operations mostly to me. As the manager of Jack Harris's Vaudeville Theater and Saloon, I found companions for the cattlemen and their cowboys. With my contacts in jacales west of town and my friendships with the various madams in town, I could find them any skin shade or nationality they might prefer. My extracurricular activities, for which I got a small percentage, became very profitable. Soon, Billy and I were able to buy the property that the saloon and theater occupied.

My life was actually pleasurable, and I thought well earned. I would rise before noon, bathe in my tub or the acequias running just yards from my house, and walk to Rip Ford's home and begin an afternoon of writing down his memoirs. He would talk, and I would write. Rip's story would have been the perfect collaboration for Pidge Robinson and me. But instead, I was joined by Rip and Addie's adopted daughter, Lily. She was just a few years older than William when Addie and Rip adopted her. I think she was a replacement for him. Addie probably wanted no boys. A girl, whose life could be proscribed, an adopted girl, no less, who would be dedicated to the parents who pulled her out of an orphanage, presented less fear and worry to her newly adopting mother than a boy. For boys, Addie must have reasoned, were constantly in danger from the attitudes and manners they acquired as they grew into men. Lily, as a woman, raised by a decent, civilized mother, would be safe. Not even a civilized mother could protect a boy from something like John William's or Pidge Robinson's fate.

But Lily, a horrible writer with bad diction and grammar, wanted to edit everything. She wouldn't write what Rip said, but what she thought he should say, and I would always steal her pages from Rip's sight when she left and correct them. Rip knew what she was doing, but what could he say? She was his new daughter. She brought a feminine sensibility to his rough world and notes and thus corrupted what Rip was.

As for Rip, even with Lily's interference and his memory and opinion, the old man convinced himself that his final mission was to leave a history of himself for Texas. He would rise early and meet with other old Confederates and Rangers at the Menger or under the oak and pecan trees at Alamo Square and reminisce. Then after lunch, he'd catch a mule-drawn streetcar (and later the new electric streetcar) and walk the rest of the way home for lunch. After lunch, he'd join Lily and me for a couple of hours of writing. First, Lily and I took notes. Sometimes, Rip couldn't always remember dates, and his fingers ached from the writing. I could figure dates with a few details. And Lily was learning shorthand and wrote with the looping penmanship that both Rip and I lacked. Later, I became the first man in town with a typewriter. Lily and I learned to type. Addie fed us all, and when the old man would drift off for a nap when the noon meal and his writing had made him sleepy, Addie would keep me company.

On an early visit, just after I met my estranged family, with daughter Addie married to a man in Corpus Christi, Lula courting a merchant named Maddox, Lily the dutiful child dusting and cleaning, and Rip taking his nap, Addie and I sat on the front porch and watched a Mexican lady dip her naked baby into the acequia for a bath. We rocked in unison and stole glimpses at each other. What we noted, with my slick pate and Addie's streaks of gray and creases in her porcelain skin, was that the two of us, a year apart, were growing older. My rocking chair creaked, then hers.

Addie spoke first. "So Andrew, where were you when we . . . *I* needed you?"

I could only hang my head. "I couldn't be there. It took me seven years to forget." I wanted Pidge to forgive me for not rescuing Addie and my son from our fates. Like him, maybe I should have come riding into Brownsville and somehow rescued everyone.

Addie rocked and nodded her head. "Are you angry at me?"

I looked back toward the house, through a window, and saw Rip, his boots off, feet sticking straight up, sleeping on his window-sill-high bed. I whispered, "I was never angry at you." I looked toward Rip. "Not at you." My hand made it halfway across the space between us. She looked at my hand. "But I was mad at him. I blamed Rip for. . . . " I found myself unable to mention John William's name or to say "death." "This state caused what happened. It is as though a man comes to Texas and something takes over his mind. Corrupts or twists all notions of common decency or self-preservation into something, something silly, some stupid myth."

Addie turned to look at her sleeping husband, then took my hand in both of hers. "Oh, don't blame Rip. He is what he is. They are just what they have always been. It isn't Texas."

"Oh, Addie," I said and leaned my head toward her as she dropped my hand and looked over my shoulder. I then looked over my shoulder. Standing in the doorway was Lily drying her hands in a towel. Lily stared at me for a moment and sensed, from my look, that she wanted no part of this family secret. She turned her back to us and went back into the kitchen.

Addie stared over my shoulder for a moment to make sure that Lily had indeed left, then said, "If anything, it is God's will."

"Oh, Addie, no," I said. "No, no, no."

"John William's death is God's punishment for our deception of Rip."

"You can't believe that. You don't believe that. You don't want to believe in a God who would hurt the innocent to punish the guilty. It is not us. We should have been together. What we did can't be wrong. Who else did we have?"

"Shh, shh, don't go on."

"It was the world Rip and McNelly and Houston and the Alamo and all the rest made."

"It *was* their world," she said in defense of them. She smiled. "It won't be for much longer. Texas is changing. So you can't blame them." I pulled my face toward her, and our eyes held each of our faces still. "A woman, to survive, must accept their world, not like it, but accept it. It is a dangerous world for a boy." I felt tears forming. My hand shook. "I've been like a spy in their world. I know it all too well. And I know that the best thing to do is simply accept it. Oh, Andrew, if you could only accept it. That, that and God's will. It must have some sense." Addie saw my hand shaking. "Seven years is such a long time."

Addie took my trembling hand. I didn't care whether Rip or Lily were watching or not. "Addie, you've been the one true love of my life," I whispered through sobs.

"Andrew, if he had lived, I would have wanted John William to have at least some of your qualities and habits of mind."

"Thank you, Addie."

Then Addie stopped all the gushing emotion, the sentimentality, the romantic notions that governed Pidge Robinson and said, "Your whore, that Taracón woman, I heard, went back to Spain."

I pulled my hand away from hers to look at her. "She deserves her dignity too."

"I heard that she could find no well-to-do gentlemen to support her." Addie stopped to look at me. I'm not sure if she wanted to condemn me or protect me with some news.

"You know something else, Addie. Go on."

"I had heard that she left because she had the pox." Addie dipped her head. "The sexual disease."

"Syphilis?" Addie pulled her head up to look at me, and her eyes almost seemed to smile. She nodded her head. All I could do was tremble. And Addie couldn't make me stop.

That night, after work, with the sun just starting to put some eerie streaks over my shoulder, I walked past the plazas, past the new Italian and Greek merchants, to the Mexican jacales. I stopped in front of one and through a window caught sight of the young girl I was looking for. She was preparing breakfast, but before I could say her name, she was moving toward me. As she made her way over the hard-packed dirt of her front yard, I finally got a name out, but it was not hers. "Catalina," I said. She wrapped her arms around me anyway, and I paid her just for that embrace that took me back to a time years before. I could see Catalina's face in hers, but she was still a girl. She often wondered why I came by only to talk and to listen to her tale about being raised by nuns. Betsy, the name the Incarnate Word nuns had given her, had forsaken the nuns and her impending vows to try her mother's profession, at a much baser level.

"Betsy," I said while looking at her face and remembering Catalina's. "I knew your mother, very well. And that is why I've been coming to see you." After her shock, I told her about her mother. I was never to see her again. She disappeared before I could help her. And over time, Catalina's face even began to fade in my memory.

AFTER a year of helping Rip, in April of 1885, several months after the completion of a rail line that could take a passenger from Galveston to San Francisco, I had joined Rip in front of the Menger and listened while he and the other ex-Rangers and Confederates, all of us in our shirt-sleeves with our coats beside us, judged well and ill of men and the times. I heard but ignored the older men's conversations in order to concentrate on the sounds and smells wafting over from the Little Rhine area, and I found myself watching one of the German's big-boned, buxom, blonde, Teutonic daughters hauling water. And while I was watching one, wondering about her creamy skin and folds of flesh, as compared to the olive skin and petite but hard bodies of the women whom I favored on the west side, a familiar figure walked to me and then stood in front of me.

George Durham's hair was matted as though he had never run a comb through it, beneath his hair was a smooth, fish-belly white forehead, and beneath the hat line was the brown, wrinkled face of a cowboy. Of all wonders, he had on a new suit and tie, not a bow but the new knotted fashion. At first, I wondered who had dressed him; then I saw that he had tears in his eyes, and like a small boy he wiped at them with the back of his hands. "Why, George Durham," I said and knew that I beamed.

Before I could go any farther, he said, "I don't think he's gonna make it."

Rip stopped his conversation with the others and stared on. "George, I don't think that you've ever met my uncle before," I said. "This is Rip Ford."

Rip stood and almost equaled George's height. I stood and could come nowhere close to matching either man's height. As they pumped each other's arms, George muttered, "Gawd." For he was indeed shaking one god's hand while another god, as he was about to tell us, was dying right behind us in the Menger Hotel.

Rip sat, and I let George have my seat and knelt to hear him. "We come up the same as always: two of us out ahead scouting, mounted men all around one of the Captain's fine Rockaway Coaches. Him inside coughing and sputtering. And I peeked inside and seen him all ghostly white and gray. But he's shouting orders to Henrietta and the rest of his family inside with him. And I think I started crying then and ain't stopped."

Rip nodded, "I had heard something of that. Someone important. Someone had summoned Dr. Ferdinand Herff himself." Rip stood and pushed the wrinkles from his pants. He slid each arm into his jacket and looked at George. "Captain King's in there now?"

"Yes, sir. He is," George said.

His back still rigid, white beard still neatly trimmed, Rip, forever the frontiersman, squinted down the plaza both ways then across Alamo Street to the Little Rhine area. He turned his back to us and took large strides toward the Menger. He entered the lobby with George and me following. Pulling his hat off, his eyes still in a squint, he looked around the lobby, didn't see what he was looking for, so strode across the lobby under the huge chandelier and entered the dining room. There for lunch were all the Kings. Henrietta stood. She wore all black, including the black enameled diamond earrings that Captain King gave her. With her dress, she must have spooked the still living Captain King.

I tried to pick out the faces. I didn't see Nettie, but I spotted Ella and Alice, and I remembered when the girls sang for me and then danced with me when I first met McNelly. They had grown to be modestly attractive women. I spotted the man who must have been Richard II and his wife. And then I spotted Robert Kleberg, the husband to King's favorite, Alice. With them, in his elaborate suit, was the ancient Dr. Ferdinand Herff. My eyes shifted as I looked at the brim of my bowler, and I pulled it off. "Mrs. King," Rip said and was about to go on when Henrietta, Etta they now called her, stepped to him and reached to him with both hands so that he could take her hands in his.

"Oh, Rip, dear Rip," she started to cry. "Those days have all gone. Where did they go?"

Rip pulled her hands to his chest. "We helped change it, Etta. We couldn't let it stay like it was, so now we don't recognize it."

"Would you like to have a cup of coffee?"

"I'd like to see your husband," Rip said, and Etta nodded and started to lead us to Captain King's room.

Rip gently reached out to touch her arm. "No, enjoy your breakfast. I'll show myself the way. What room?"

Before Etta could answer, Dr. Herff pushed himself up from his chair with both of his hands and scooted his feet toward us. He held out his finger as though to warn or scold Rip. "Do not let him have any liquor. He asks for it. But it will shorten his time on this earth." Then he turned his back to us and scooted back to his chair.

We climbed the stairs to the second floor. Rip knocked but there was no answer. After a second knock, he just shoved the door open and stepped into the room. It was a room on a corner with a view of the Alamo, still a grocery warehouse, and the plaza. In the bed, his long, now iron-gray beard outside the sheet, was the white-faced Richard King. His head slowly rose and his eyes opened. At first, he cocked his head to study us. Then he recognized Rip. He swooshed the sheet off him, draped his legs over the side of the bed, and with great effort and sucking in of air, he stood. He looked down at his night shirt. "Fetch me some pants," he said. "I'm going to have a drink with the great old warrior Rip Ford." Then he collapsed.

George, Rip, and I picked him up as best we could and stuffed him back under the sheet. "No, no. I need a drink." Then he winced and gritted his teeth. We waited until he unclenched his jaw and let his eyelids droop again. "Oh, Rip, it is an unbearable pain. The doctor tells me not to drink. Says that it will hasten my death. But the burn of sweet bourbon or rye is all that puts out the fire in my belly."

Rip pulled up a chair to the side of the bed and sat beside King, and he rolled his head so that he could look at Rip. Gently, Rip reached out and, with the flat of his hand, stroked King's face. "Oh Rip, Rip, there's so much pain."

"The liquor won't help."

"That's not the only pain." King's eyes drifted around the room. "Two years ago, Lee died alone up in Saint Louis of pneumonia, and last year, James died of typhoid. Have you ever lost a son?"

My teeth clenched as I waited on Rip's response. "Two. From my first wife, back in Tennessee, I just lost track of him; for all I know he's dead." Rip held his back stiff and his chin up. "Then I lost my boy with Addie."

"The only goddamn thing I got to remind me of a future is that little baby, Richard III, back at the Santa Gertrudis. And maybe that lawyer down there. That Robert Kleberg is the best damn cattleman's lawyer in the country. He'll see my ranch makes it. He'll see they remember me." He turned to look at Rip. "And you. He'll see to it they remember, you too." Rip turned to look at me and George. I got the cue, and I pulled George out of the room to leave the two old legends alone.

Back out in Alamo Plaza, I stood with George. "How are you doing, George?"

"Not too good. I'm taking this hard."

"But other than his death, how is your life?"

George toed some dirt. "I've got one baby, Lucy, and another on the way." He smiled through his tears. "Me and Caroline are hoping for a boy."

"You've got money?"

"Plenty. More than I ever seen," George said, and I slapped him on the back for his good luck.

"George, that's great. I've found my element here in San Antonio."

George nodded for a moment. "I'll never forget them McNelly days. And even if you was a bit of a turncoat, you done right by me, and McNelly too, I guess, so I'll never forget you neither. You need something, you let me know." We thanked each other for what we had done and would do, and then George left me.

Soon, Rip joined me. We didn't say anything for a while, and then without my asking, without looking at me, Rip said, "I thanked him for supporting me all those years. I couldn't have given my family the life they had without him."

Rip went back several times to see Captain King. After ten days, while I stood outside in Alamo Plaza with Rip and watched as the Negro lamplighters made the plaza glow with gaslight, King died in the Menger Hotel room. The next day, late in the afternoon, after a service in a parlor of the Menger Hotel, a funeral procession followed the hearse to San Antonio's public cemetery and laid Richard King to rest. Captain King didn't need anyone to buy him a memorial; he had already bought his own modest tombstone.

ONE day during the following year, I was awakened early in the morning, before daylight, by fire wagons and screaming men. I put on my clothes and ran from my small house on Flores Street to Main Plaza just in time to see Jack Harris's Vaudeville Theater and Saloon burn itself out and crumple into a heap. By mid-morning, as I was picking through the ash and rubble and sweating in the increased morning heat, I saw Rip watching me. I joined him, and we sat across Soledad and looked at the rubble. Then I heard a bell and looked at San Fernando Cathedral, still standing, still free of the sin around it, sounding a funeral note for a way of life.

In actuality, my life had taken a turn for the better. Billy Sims joined me and Rip, and as he patted me on the back, he gave me a sly wink. Upon Billy's urging, I had taken out more insurance on Jack Harris's Vaudeville Theater and Saloon. Now with the chief competition burned down and me paid off, Billy could hope to get even richer at his saloon, the White Elephant, and I could become leisurely rich. Of course, even as the suspicion sank into my mind, I knew better than to investigate. So did Rip.

So I took my part of the insurance money. I had equity on the property, and we sold it for a tidy sum. Suddenly, I had interest and investments. I still had contacts between cattlemen and cowboys and girls about town. Gambling flourished. The Mexicans had cockfights in Military and Main Plazas, and the remaining saloons thrived. I had bettered my gambling skills and could always be counted on to deal faro, monte, or keno. Of course, I was no Joe Foster.

Flush with insurance money, I put money down to buy the house that I had rented. I became a man of leisure and pleasure and devoted myself to helping Rip. Some afternoons, I'd accompany Rip, Addie, and Lily to San Pedro Springs, where we would have a picnic or rent two rowboats and explore the lagoons and nap in the shade of river willows. Other times, if I woke early enough, we'd all shop for fresh vegetables or meat from the vendors gathered in Main or Military Plazas. And for lunch we might eat from the portable tables that the chili queens set up in the plazas.

In the fall of that year, Rip and I rented a hack for a drive out to Fort Sam Houston, near the city's reservoir, and drove out to see old Geronimo and Natchez. We saw John Sullivan fight, and we saw Quanah Parker stutter through a speech in front of the new Southern Hotel. After the speech, squinting, hesitant, hands dangling at his side, Rip Ford made his way to Quanah and introduced himself. Quanah crouched, ready to attack if need be, but he took hold of the old Ranger's offered hand and shook it.

In 1887, Rip and I watched as workmen armed with mallets, picks, and shovels attacked the old Bat Cave to tear it down to make way for the newly planned and designed City Hall. With the Bat Cave gone, I feared that we would forget Jack Harris and the men he had made, including the present and longtime mayor, Bryan Callaghan. Rip became as interested as I in progress. He was more wary of it than I. He wanted to see it, but he missed what it inevitably erased. So we wrote more and faster.

To match the fashions of the time, I shaved off all my whiskers and cut what hair I had even shorter so that, with my bald pate, I looked like an oblong cue ball. Rip's only concession was to trim his white beard even shorter. In 1889, we watched as workers embedded mesquite blocks around Alamo Plaza to make paved streets.

In 1890, just as night filled the city, together with several of the old Negro lamplighters, Rip and I watched a row of newly installed electric lights hiss themselves on, and a snake of light lit Commerce Street west from Alamo Plaza. The new light was not as soft as the old gaslight—garish maybe, too much light, but I wished that a surviving Jack Harris, the first subscriber to the San Antonio Electric Company with plans to turn his saloon and theater totally electric, could have seen the city lit up. A surviving Jack Harris would never have let his theater and saloon burn down. He would have seen it lit with electric lights.

As the lamplighters turned away from their future to light their past, Rip looked over his shoulder at them and said, "If I still carried a Colt, I'd shoot one or two of them out." A lamplighter held up his hand as a salute to old Rip.

Later that year, we gathered in the middle of Alamo Street with all the German children, next to the streetcar tracks, and watched as a rumbling electric streetcar began its initial run toward San Pedro Springs. And Rip and I bent over with a German boy to peer at the flattened penny he had laid on the track.

In 1891, Rip and I watched the dedication of the shining white limestone City Hall, which had just sprouted out of the ground, and the laying of the cornerstone for what was to become the Texas granite and red sandstone Bexar County Courthouse. After the morning ceremonies for the laying of the cornerstone, Rip and I pulled ourselves onto one of the new electric streetcars bound for Alamo Plaza. As I sat beside him and we bounced down Houston Street, I stared at the utility and telephone poles that seemed to have sprouted like weeds. I stared at the tips of my shoes and said, "Rip, I got a letter a day or two ago. My mother, Elizabeth, your sister, died."

Rip turned from the window and watched the blossoming San Antonio buildings. "Elizabeth," he rolled the name around in his mouth.

"My father died several years ago. I hardly took note. Now my mother."

"In old Tennessee, the pine forest," Rip muttered.

"It's almost like I forgot all of that, my past, the South, my growing up. It's so distant and far away. I've lost it. And try as I might, with all the wonders of transportation, I just can't get to the funeral."

Rip looked ahead, "I guess we both 'gone to Texas.' And once you're in Texas, you can't go back. I don't remember my life before coming here either."

We both got caught up in our sadness and a sudden awareness of a fact that we had lost sight of. We were kin. And in my absence from my family and place of birth, and in his family of women, Rip and I were like father and son. "Maybe you and I ought to go see her grave," Rip said. I simply nodded. "Damn, you're making me remember. Time's going by too fast. Neither one of us realized that we're losing family."

Rip went into some kind of a trance that seemed as though he were just watching growing San Antonio. He turned to look at me. "You know, the male of every species just has this great propensity toward violence and rage." He turned to face me. "You too, Andrew." He turned away from me. "And even those of us carrying this great violence and rage are called upon to protect the rest of the species from it, to protect them from enemies, from harm, even while it consumes us."

I held up a hand, grabbed his shoulder, and shook it. "Are you all right, Rip?"

He looked at me and said, "Yes." Then he muttered, "Yeah, yeah, yeah, I'll do it," to himself. Then he turned to me and gave me an order, "You and I need to board a train and go see Juan Cortina."

SO we two old men got on the train bound for Laredo and from there went on a maze of trains until we arrived at a hotel in Mexico City, and after a night of good sleep, we went to a small, modest house in the suburbs of Mexico City. A servant let us in, and we sat on a couch until a little man walked stiffly in and sat in a chair across from us. I noticed then that he had a smear of red sauce on his chin. Then he slowly smiled, got up, and Rip too stood, and the two old warriors exchanged the Mexican abrazo. Then Juan Cortina saw me and hugged me too.

When Cortina sat back down, a finely dressed, young, chubby woman with a face that looked like it had been flattened came into the room. She looked at Cortina, saw the smear of sauce on his chin, and dabbed at it with her handkerchief. Cortina pushed her away, then with the back of his hand motioned for her to leave so the "hombres, caballeros viejos" could have a talk. As she left, he beamed to us and motioned with his hand after her, proud of his latest young mistress. Remembering Catalina and his confrontation with his mother, I thought that he had lost both his taste and his money to have chosen this particular girl to end his life with.

We stared at each other for several moments, then Rip spoke. "I can hardly remember Spanish. It's been so long."

Cortina looked at me. I tried to translate. "Neither can I," I said. Cortina tried a little English, but got his tongue tied. We stared some more; then Rip and I clumsily started to purr the Spanish and border words, and Cortina stumbled through some English. The three of us came up with some sort of a conversation.

Cortina had been under virtual house arrest for twenty-three years. He never left the city. This is what his wild life had cost him. He said the sounds and smells of Mexico City that came into his house from outside were enticing, but that he missed Brownsville and Matamoros. He said that he didn't think he would live much longer, but Rip and I both assured him that he had a full life ahead. Of course, we both lied to the old man with the sallow skin and drooping cheeks.

He grew pensive, as though lost in memories, and his eyes darted around his room and from Rip to me. "How could I have misunder-stood Mexicans so greatly?"

"You weathered a lot of upheavals," Rip said.

Cortina shook his head and held up his fingers, "Rip, Nevin, I should have been a lawyer like my half-brother Sabas. I should have even been a priest." We all laughed.

"No, not one of us here should have been a priest," I said. Rip gave me a stern glance.

"But what I did was just so much, so much fun."

"So what would you have done if you were a priest?" I asked. Rip again gave me a stern glance, but I gave him another to tell him to go to hell. I was having fun with an old friend.

"You could never have been a priest," Rip said. "So much killing."

Cortina shrugged. "It was a rough world. In Mexico we are older than the United States. We are wiser. And somehow more accustomed to life, so we are more accustomed to death. I fear that there will be a lot more killing in Mexico."

Rip nodded his agreement. He cleared his throat to say, "I have a lot to thank you for."

Cortina held up his hands to stop him. "And I you."

"Your helping Addie. Your leaving those few cows I owned alone," Rip said.

"Seeing to my mother's safety," Cortina said. Cortina looked at the two of us and gestured to Rip, himself, and then me. "It was so hard to see ahead then, but look, we are now three generations of old men."

Rip smiled. "We define old. Pictures of aging in its different stages."

I was a bit insulted because I did not yet want to see myself as old. "Hold on, now. I'm not yet ready to be old."

"Fifty is old," Rip said.

"At fifty, a man should be getting visits from his grandchildren and having a good woman make him tortillas," Cortina said.

"Hell, at fifty you were trying to start a revolution in Mexico," Rip said.

Cortina laughed. "And you. Weren't you fifty when you joined that worthless old Carbajal and tried to rescue Mexico from itself?"

Rip smiled. "No, at fifty, I was winning the last battle of the Civil War. At fifty-one I was trying to rescue Mexico from itself."

"We are lucky to have escaped from our pasts," Cortina said. "Who would have thought we wouldn't have been shot or died from wounds?" Then he pointed at me, "Even you, Andrew."

"I've always tried to lead a civilized life."

"That was a hell of hard thing to do in Texas," Rip said.

A smile crept into Rip's face, then a laugh came out of him, and for a few minutes, Cortina and Rip and I became our old selves. "Let's be glad that we all got better than we deserved," I said.

Cortina held up his hand in acknowledgment. "Now at least we have the luxury of being old men. We survived. We endured. So now they won't shoot us anymore."

Rip started laughing too. "So you see, Andrew, it isn't your new-found civilization protecting you, but it's the luxury of age."

Then the flat-faced girl came in and pulled Cortina up. It was time for the old man's siesta. "Is there anything you need now?" Rip asked.

"My mother is dead. I am disowned, disavowed. No relatives speak to me. I need a lot." Then he smiled. "But no one can give me what I need. That's gone." Then he looked at his new mistress, "Except this fine young lady." They smiled at each other. And his latest mistress, the flat-faced girl, the one with whom he would die, led him away.

WHEN Rip and I returned to San Antonio, he lost interest in writing, and not I nor Lily nor Addie could persuade him to return to it. It was as though he was in a forgetting mood instead of a remembering mood. So I left him to his moods and indulged my pleasures and extravagances. I dusted off the pages of my history of McNelly and scratched in notes and revised sentences. But a man cannot work all day, and writing is intense work, so I gambled, drank, and whored, and thus noticed my own aging. So along with the elderly and the consumptives, I took a streetcar south of town to Hot Wells sulphur baths and dipped my body into the hot, healing, smelly water. I was still a hydropath. My romance with water had lasted longer than any romance with a woman.

As for women, as always, I had the alternative to what most men sought. I had Addie and the young girls on the west side. Addie would go for a rowboat ride with me at San Pedro Springs, or we would take walks through the King William area and imagine all of us wealthy enough to live there. The society people of King William may very well have talked about Addie and me, but only in private. For no one dared question the wife of a hero like Rip Ford.

Historians from the new University of Texas up at Austin, that loathsome town that was too scared to dispose of its own waste, Ben Thompson, and so let him kill our very prominent Jack Harris, came to call on us. We were far enough away from Rip's history and the

Civil War for historians to be interested in both, so they came to Rip for his stories and his notes. He delighted in them. Then we all learned that Juan N. Cortina, the Red Robber Baron of the Rio Grande, died on October 30, 1894. Rip called Lily and me to him, and the writing recommenced.

The red granite courthouse bulged up in 1896, and Rip got a visit from Frederic Remington, who was on assignment from *Harper's New Monthly Magazine*. Though I was bored with the historians and their questions, I wanted to hear and meet Remington. We were in one of the parlors of the Menger Hotel for two days as Rip pontificated to Remington. As he talked, he seemed to lose years, seemed to grow more excited with preserving the memories and the dramas in his head. And he didn't just talk about himself, but recalled Jack Hays, Ben McCullough, Santos Benavides, Edward Burleson, Thomas J. Rusk, Sabas Cavazos, and even Juan Cortina. Even I got excited.

Remington had a painting in his mind, and he asked the old Ranger about the terror the Texians felt when they encountered the Mexican lancers. Rip said, "I reckon to be able to hit a man every time with a six-shooter at 125 yards."

"Then you don't think much of a lance as a weapon?" Remington asked.

"No, there is but one weapon. The six-shooter when properly handled is the only weapon—mind you sir, I say properly."

Both Rip and the portly, dandified Remington looked at me when my hand jerked up from my beer, spilling it. "Excuse me," I said and eyed Rip. For flooding into my mind were memories of my son, John William Ford, and I couldn't shut them off. Then my mind imagined John William fingering that converted Dragoon Colt, feeling its smoothly worn wooden handle and the oiled blue metal. I pushed myself up and said "pardon me," not even minding the wet beer in my lap. The Colt would have been too heavy for the boy to lift. I saw him struggle with it. I saw the opened-end barrel of that converted Dragoon Colt in my mind and heard it explode in my ears. My mind went in a different direction, and I saw John William's forehead punctured by the bullet and a spray of blood and a bullet hole on the wall behind him. I found myself in the Menger lobby.

I felt cold and stepped out of the Menger and into the early summer sunshine in Alamo Plaza. The beer in my stomach had turned rancid, and I stumbled to the gazebo that had taken shape and felt as though I would vomit there with the aged, weathered Confederates looking on. "Handled properly," I thought and recalled Lee McNelly in all his glory invading Mexico. Then I thought of the gallant Lieutenant Robinson following McNelly, only to be gunned down by Jesse Mitchell. And I thought of Jack Harris trying to get his shotgun up with his withered left arm while he took the bullet from Ben Thompson, and Ben Thompson himself riddled with bullets, and King Fisher, handsome even in death, and scholarly, kind Joe Foster, who had no business on the business end of a Colt. My mind settled on an image of a woman running out of a bar across cactus and brush and my arm slowly lowering, holding steady, and my finger pulling the trigger. Then my mind returned to John William and his good-bye to me the last time I saw him, in 1877, when I left for San Antonio. I took off my jacket and looked at the old veterans who stared at me.

One old man, I cannot even recall his name, limped up to me, peered at my face, and asked out of honor to Rip Ford, or maybe out of a final acceptance of me, or maybe because he now saw me as one of them, "Is everything all right for you, Mr. Nevin? Should we call someone?" I looked at his face and saw that he was roughly my same age. To the world I could now pass as one of the veteran Colt users.

In December of that year, the interview, along with Remington's drawing, "Juaruta's Lancers' Attack on the Rangers at San Juan Teotihuacán," appeared in *Harper's New Monthly Magazine*.

In February of 1897, the professors, who for years had been trying to start the Texas State Historical Association and had courted Rip Ford for his influence and his memories, asked me to accompany Rip to Austin to draft a constitution for the upstart new organization. Rip's frame was bent a little, but he fought against it and finally came to depend on his cane. It was a delightful train ride to Austin, and Rip probably would have made it himself, but everyone thought that it might be safer for him to have a traveling companion. Rip resented my presence.

One of the professors gave Rip and me a tour of the muddy campus of the University of Texas with pigs and chickens roaming by. Austin refused to grow up as much as San Antonio had done. We entered a building and sat in a very big classroom. I sat with Rip as a procession of speakers extolled the state and Rip Ford, and the old man beamed. The constitution was read. It was open to all members, even women. Rip pounded his cane on the floor, stood, and shouted, "You mean to tell me you will sacrifice posterity for what will be this failed attempt at female sovereignty?"

A professor and I both found ourselves tugging at the old man's sleeve. "Why not let anyone join?" we both asked.

From the classroom a figure stood. It was a woman, dressed quite smartly for the day. "Sir, I am a professor also. I am a trained historian. Do you mean to imply that my credentials should count any less?"

Ford pounded his cane on the floor again. "I can also see that you are a woman."

The speaker said, "Mr. Ford, we can hardly exclude female colleagues."

"Then this organization can just go to hell."

Rip, with his cane tap followed by two quick pads of his feet, walked out of the classroom while all the eyes, most behind spectacles, watched him leave. When he exited, all the spectacled eyes were on me. I put on my own spectacles to meet the glares. The professors asked me what to do, while the eyes of the two women members scolded me instead of Rip. I suggested that they let me talk to Rip, let him cool off overnight, then ask him to give his blessing to the organization the next day.

It was a cold, drizzly day, and my glasses spotted with the drizzle and fogged from my breath as I walked from the muddy campus to the ugly capitol buildings, then down Congress to Sixth Street, then on to Brazos to the Driskill Hotel. I couldn't find a hack and no one had called one for me. I found Rip stewing in his room in the Driskill Hotel. I cautiously approached him as though he might have had a Colt and been ready to properly handle it. He sat at the writing desk and had turned the furnace up full blast, sealing himself into the room. I pulled the only other chair in the room up to him and stared out the fogged window with him. "Times change," I finally said.

"I know, but I don't have to agree with the changes." Rip wouldn't look at me, as though he were embarrassed.

"There are women on the faculty here."

"I know. But that's not the point." He pulled his head up to look at me. "This is important to the whole state, Andrew."

"Give your support."

"It's important to the whole country." Rip wasn't talking to me now. "We have to preserve all that went on. We have to remember. Otherwise we don't deserve what we have. If the world is better, it is so because of our dead."

"Women helped too," I said.

Rip shook his head. "I never said they didn't. But because we need to remember, this state needs this group. It needs an official sanction for all that happened."

"So don't disappoint those people."

Rip held up his hand to shut me up. "There's groups better than this or at least with a better reputation in the East, at Harvard or Yale. And Michigan and California have prime universities that are going to be as good as the Eastern ones. And look at what we've got." I shrugged. "Baylor University and that muddy tract of lean-tos we were just at. This state," and he lifted his arm to point, "and that ugly university and this organization with this important mission need all the prestige they can get."

I found myself nodding and saying, "Yes, so?"

"So we can't look as though we can't do any better than to get a bunch of goddamn suffragettes to do our work for us."

I suppressed a smile. "Don't you think Addie could just as well run this organization as some Harvard Yankee historian?" Rip had to smile and nod. "So why not agree to it for Addie's sake. For Addie's, for your daughters' sake. Hell, Rip, you're surrounded by women." Rip started to laugh. "Hell, Rip, there's your future, there's your heritage, your memory. It's all women. Who else do you have?"

Rip looked at me, hesitated, and said, "For forty years, curse the luck." He forced a smile. "And you, I got you, Andrew."

"So for my sake?"

The next day the professors came into the room and he gave his approval, his support, and his membership. Rip and I did not go back to campus, but enjoyed a walk in the bright winter sunshine that a fierce Texas norther leaves behind it. We took a hack to the train station and went home to San Antonio.

Rip fought his body and his health for the rest of that year, and he furiously dictated to Lily, and I typed, and because I knew what was coming, I made carbons and kept the carbon paper itself—away from Lily. By September, he had all but given up. By the first of October, he had a stroke. His left side, eye, mouth, and arm twitched and wrinkled. The indignity, I think, rather than the stroke itself sent him into a coma. He'd come out of it for a while and try to talk. But he could only sputter or groan. His left eye was useless, but his right eye darted all over. Then he would go back into the coma.

It was all too much for Addie, so Lula, who was now Mrs. Joseph Maddox, took him into her house. We all knew that he would die in that house. Little Addie, who had married Samuel Delgado de Cordova in Corpus Christi, left her family in a relative's care and came to watch her father die.

One night, he seemed to break through the coma and tried to speak to us, but he could not make words. Only his right eye and hand seemed to communicate. His hand and eye went from Addie the daughter, to Lula, to Lily, and then to Addie his wife. Both sight and hand tried to touch them all, to give them some blessing. Then, because I was standing at the foot of his bed, his eye and hand drifted to me. He reached, and with his right eye, he said that I had as good as become his rightful son. I looked deeply into that eye, and with that eye Rip told me that he had known the truth about John William all these years. Then he went back into a coma. When he lost his last bit of consciousness, it occurred to me that maybe the great fortune of my life was that I got to choose and help make my father.

He died two hours after dark on November 3, 1897. The Masonic brotherhood paid for his funeral, and a Presbyterian minister gave the service. We buried him in the city's cemetery for Confederate veterans. He had never mentioned me in his memoirs.

CHAPTER 21

Memoirs

On the evening of Nov. 3, John S. "Rip" Ford left our midst. With him an era has gone. While his times were full of heroes and warriors like himself, they were lawless times, but they paved the way for our age of progress. We should mourn Rip Ford not only for the loss to our great state and nation, but for our own sakes. For Rip Ford made our comfortable ways possible.

ANDREW NEVIN,
guest writer, San Antonio Express, *November 1897*

FOR several years before he died, with the support of various heroes and historians, the old man tried to get contracts to finish his memoirs. He sent out prospectuses to New York, but to no avail. At the time of his death, they were not published, and in fact, they were probably unpublishable.

Rip Ford's memoirs reached eight hundred pages, and they only got as far as the Civil War and a little of the Reconstruction. He had recalled everything vividly, but one incident would send him off to the next. And neither Lily nor I could always keep up. The old newspaperman's mind was sharp, but he had lost his sense of arrangement, especially with his own life. I, of course, couldn't blame him, for who can organize and make sense of his own life and not skip, jump, and wish?

Sometimes, Rip insisted on referring to himself in the third person—almost as though he were ashamed or had forgotten, or as though that figure that he was discussing was not at all related to the elderly man talking to his nephew and adopted daughter. At times he cussed, at times he gave damaging facts. Sometimes he dictated and editorialized.

Lily, claiming that the family had a primary right to the manuscript, began "cleaning it up" and omitting certain sections, mostly his life prior to coming to Texas and his first and second wives. I argued with her. I demanded the manuscript. She refused. I asked her what literary or journalistic training or experience gave her the insight into her editing. "My family gives me the right. Propriety gives me the right. Posterity gives me the right."

"Texas deserves a true account," I said.

"Taste demands an edited account," she replied. So Rip's daughter and I stopped speaking to each other.

Luckily, I had my carbons and my carbon paper. So I cut down on my nightlife (and my association with Rip's family, even Addie) and began to retype Rip's manuscript. And then I revised my own account of McNelly's escapades. Pidge would have been proud of me.

Eventually, Lily gave her edited memoirs, what were to become the "official" ones, to the Texas State Historical Association. That association didn't have the means to publish them, but they kept them and cataloged them as part of the organization's holdings.

While I wrote, submitted, and revised, Teddy Roosevelt and his Rough Riders came to town to recruit more rough-riding men. Mostly they drank in the Menger's bar, and because I was Rip Ford's nephew and full of stories about earlier rough riders, I joined them and let them buy me drinks.

After a year of rejections, it seemed that no one was interested. I sent the memoirs and my account of McNelly's adventures to William Dean Howells himself. Mr. Howells, I had read, could see that important American books were published. He had power in the publishing industry; he knew everyone, critiqued widely. He was the John S. Ford of American literature. With a clear mission, I followed my manuscripts to New York.

I bought a respectable suit, took the train to Galveston, then watched out the windows as trains took me to New York. In New York, Howells successfully avoided me. After checking into my hotel, I walked the short distance to his building and spent a day waiting in his office, staring at his secretary in his stiff white cuffs and him staring back over his half-framed glasses at me. When it became obvious that I intended to wait, the secretary slipped off his coat and sat in his shirt sleeves, shuffling papers. He could wait as well as I. I followed a client out of Mr. Howells's office and asked about Mr. Howells; I found that he was off work, but that he could be found at Delmonico's.

I walked through the streets of New York with its masses of olive-skinned people, including many olive-skinned women. I thought that I had smelled humans before, either on the trail or in the cities of Brownsville or San Antonio. But the human smell of New York was overpowering. There was no fresh air to compare it too. The air was saturated with human sweat, waste, effort, toil. Mixed with the human smell was the smell of human produce: cooking, spilled beer, and smoke. It was a rank stench, but yet, within an hour, the smell became not only tolerable but nearly sweet.

The town was alive with voices. If I listened closely, I could distinguish German, Italian, Chinese, Syrian, and so on. The voices, like the smells, blended into one overpowering cacophony. I knew that in the alleys and side streets of this city there would be sporting houses where a gentleman could get close to the sources of the smells, right up against her so to speak. I did not go on a search for the dim-lit rooms of olive-skinned women, but stayed true to my course. I did debate, though, whether I ought not to desert San Antonio and move to this city. Had I not been pushing sixty, had Addie, in a certain sense, still not depended upon me . . .

I took a seat in Delmonico's and ordered a sandwich. The restaurant was filled with polished wood and cigar smoke, and the color, the air in the place, was golden. I tried to guess at the vocations of patrons. Under the bowlers, in back of the newspapers, were men who ran dynamos, invested stocks, managed businesses, owned industries, and probably never had seen their steak on the hoof or ridden for three days without a change of clothes. In one corner, in a table to themselves, were a short, round man and a taller man with a mane of wild white hair and a drooping white mustache. Between them was a mangled rack of lamb and a pitcher of beer.

I got up from my sandwich, left it, and made my way to the table. I stood for a while, looking at the two men, who glanced at me then just as quickly shifted their eyes away. "Mr. Howells," I said and stuck out my hand. Howells wiped at his mouth with his napkin, then wiped his hand with his napkin and rose slightly, looking off-balance, as if he would roll forward and on across the room. "I'm Andrew Nevin," I said. And Howells's face puckered. "I sent you a manuscript by John S. 'Rip' Ford . . . and my own."

Howells's face skewered as he tried to place me. When he could not, he motioned to his companion, "Mr. Nevin," he said in a squeaky voice, "this is Mr. Sam Clemens."

The white-haired man nodded then rested his shaggy white head on his palm. His eyes looked foggy. I stuck out my hand to Mark Twain, but he only lifted his eyes. He was sleepy after a big lunch, and he was a little drunk. I turned my attention to Howells. "The reminiscences about Texas."

"Oh, oh," Howells said, and turned to Clemens, "Sam, have you heard of John . . . ," he looked at me.

"Ford," I said.

"John Ford?" Howells repeated.

"A Shakespearean actor, wasn't he?" Clemens's voice was also high, but gravelly, as though it couldn't hold a sound for too long.

"A Texas Ranger," Howells said. "This is his nephew. All the way from Texas."

Clemens tilted his head to see me. "Ask Mr. Nevin if they still eat children in Texas."

"Not for years, now. Mostly we eat frijoles and bacon," I said. Clemens smiled.

"I've never eaten a child myself," Clemens said. "Have you?"

"A small Comanche once."

Twain looked at Howells, who scolded him with his eyes. Twain asked, "Why don't you help us drink this beer?" and motioned toward his half-empty pitcher of beer. "And tell us about life in Texas, where they eat Comanche children."

I looked at Howells, who motioned with his head. And as I sat down, Clemens poured me a beer. "Billy boy," Clemens said to Howells, "how many memories does this gentleman have?"

"It's right around eight hundred pages," Howells said.

"I can't imagine a man would have that much to remember, or that he'd want to remember." Both men giggled in high-toned voices, like old women.

"The man who is remembering was once an important man," I said and sipped my beer.

"What did he do?" Clemens looked between me and Howells.

"Killed Mexicans, Comanches, and Yankees," I said.

"He must not be all bad," Clemens said.

Howells bent to see me, and Clemens pounded the table with his fist, "Then, by God, Mr. Howells, publish that book. The public needs to know all it can about killing Indians, Mexicans, and Yankees." Clemens put an elbow on his chair and leaned toward me. "Did he kill any Negroes? Or, in memory of the Maine, did he kill any Cubans, or Spaniards, or whoever it is we killed in Cuba?" He straightened up, laughing.

Howells gently wiped at his mouth and sipped his beer. He looked straight across at Clemens, then at me, "Mr. Nevin, mine is just one opinion, but I cannot see anyone interested in this very long book of memoirs."

"I think you're wrong," I said. Clemens's eyebrows arched. I leaned across him toward Howells. "Read again. This man deserves to be remembered as another Grant or Lee. He was in virtually every important battle in Texas for forty years. After Sam Houston, he is Texas. This is not fiction but history. History needs John Ford."

"Yes, but I just can't enthusiastically back it." Howells dropped his head. "I'm not a historian. I write fiction."

"Hell, I'll buy two copies," Clemens said and slapped the table. He reached for the pitcher.

"If you would just give it another glance. You'll see that his style is consistent. He interprets events from the inside. We have a record of Cheno Cortina, Iron Jacket, Sam Houston. . . ."

Howells held out his hand, palm open. "I just don't believe that the non-Texas public is interested."

Before I could say anything, Clemens said, "What makes a man think anybody ought to remember him? What gives him the right to think he matters any more than some bug?" He turned to look at me as though daring me to answer.

I started to grow a bit angry. "Mr. Clemens, bugs, as far as I know, don't have consciences or memories."

"Blessed it is, then, to be a bug," Clemens said.

Howells rescued me, "Mr. Nevin. I really don't have much interest in the memoirs. But the shorter manuscript about this McNelly raid, I assume that is yours."

I squinted and stared. "It is mine."

"With a revision, a few deletions, it might attract some attention. It would have to be a Texas publisher."

"They have publishers in Texas?" Clemens asked.

"Not enough people who can read," I said and smiled.

Clemens smiled back and said, "I heard there's three people in Texas who can read."

"I don't know if a national audience would be interested in your story," Howells interrupted his friend.

"Are you a memorable man too, Mr. Nevin?" Clemens asked me. I looked at him and at Howells. If I could have left Brownsville and Rip or San Antonio to make it here, maybe I could have been sitting at an adjoining table with the editorial staff of the *New York Herald*. I could have spent my evenings amongst the pungent smells of Irish, Italian, Greek, Negro women in their dark chambers. I could have been visiting the gentlemen's sporting clubs. I should have lived my life here—along with Pidge Robinson. I looked at Clemens. "No," I stuttered. "I'm not a memorable man. I didn't make history. I ran away from it."

"Well said there, Nevin. I did some running myself." Clemens sipped his beer and gazed at me. "If it's the past, if it's history, it's not going to change." A lock of white hair hung over his forehead. "The rest of us have the unlucky responsibility to deal with change."

I said to Howells, "Maybe I could revise."

"Maybe you could drink some more beer," Clemens said.

With their smiling approval, we all changed the conversation to other topics, and I finished another pitcher with them and forgot about why I had come. The Civil War, fate, my destiny, sent me to Texas rather than east to Boston or New York. I wished it had been my fate to be sitting at this table with these men or men like them, growing slowly drunk as we talked about books rather than cattle prices or Mexican raids.

THE completion of the new City Hall and the Bexar County Courthouse brought more businesses and respectable people to Main and Market Plazas. Though the saloons still thrived, particularly Billy Sims's White Elephant, the vendors were not as welcomed. They interfered with more official commerce and county or city business. The city sent out meat and vegetable inspectors and began fining some of the vendors. In turn, the vendors shifted their attention west toward the area dominated by Greek and Italian merchants and began to congregate more and more around Haymarket Plaza and Giles Market House.

Not just the vendors' location, but the appearance of San Antonio's plazas was changing. San Pedro Creek used to run just west of Military Plaza, right behind the old Spanish Governor's Palace, but by the time I got to San Antonio, except after heavy rains, it was mostly a dried ditch with several footbridges across it. The Spaniards had built San Pedro acequia running in between San Pedro Creek and the San Antonio River, and it passed down the west side of Main Plaza, right in front of San Fernando Cathedral, right down from Commerce and Acequia Streets, the fatal corner. By the turn of the century, the city had drained most of the acequias and all of San Pedro Creek and had laid pipe in them or beside them. For only a while longer would I have the acequia adjacent to my house. Soon, running water from the city's reservoir and pumping plant would be available to most of the city, not just the richer residents. Eventually, we would all have electric lights and city water in our twentieth-century homes. So it was appropriate for the city to change the name of Acequia Street to "Main."

Queen Victoria, who gave her name to the last century, had died two months before. The Spindletop discovery, over near Beaumont, promised enough oil to fuel the entire century. So San Antonio was intent on modernization, on becoming not just the largest of Texas cities, but its jewel—greater, prettier, wealthier than Galveston had ever been. Even God had favored San Antonio, for he had all but destroyed Galveston with the 1900 hurricane. Survivors said you could hear God's voice in the howling wind. In San Antonio, in old Main Plaza, we had God's eyes in San Fernando Cathedral's windows and doors and his voice in San Fernando Cathedral's bells.

So at the dawn of the twentieth century, before sunrise, as the chili queens started their fires and the vendors walked past Main and Military Plazas to their new stands around Haymarket Square, having stayed up most of the night reading what no one wanted, I shoved my edited version of Rip's memoirs and my account of McNelly's campaign under my left arm, held them in place with my right hand, and stood in the morning darkness around Main Plaza. Not only were pipes being laid, but the streets were being widened and paved. Workmen had left their shovels and picks and even their large, ugly mechanical steam shovels beside the dried remains of San Pedro Creek and the ditches, soon to become the buried homes of water pipes. As I walked along the plaza, the city's lights suddenly hissed out, and I was in an eerie half-darkness.

I stood in the alley between San Fernando Cathedral and what had been Frost's Mercantile and was now Frost's Bank Building. In front of me was the ditch that had been San Pedro Acequia. The Bat Cave was already gone. The lynching oak was dying. The property that Jack Harris's saloon and theater had occupied, property that I once had title to, was now home to a furniture dealer. Soon, I knew, the White Elephant would be gone because the space it occupied was too valuable to house a saloon. This century's new businessmen, disciples of Horatio Alger, had grander schemes and buildings in mind than the last century's entrepreneur saloon owners. Only San Fernando Cathedral had survived. Only it was what the new century wanted to remember about the past. And it demanded retribution for sins against godliness and public change and good. It demanded my retribution. What I wanted to tell the truth about, what I wanted to reveal were stories that no one in the new century wanted to know. As much as I detested those violent, wild times and clung to my civilized nature, I was now a part of those times. Just as the country had forgotten Rip and McNelly, just as the state was forgetting them to rush into modernity, so I was already, at sixty, a forgotten man.

I let go of the manuscripts with my right hand, loosened my left arm, and watched as the sheaves of paper fell out from me and into the ditch. My history of my uncle and my history of McNelly were spread across a sticky mixture of mud and dirt at the bottom of the ditch. I bent, grabbed a shovel, and jumped into the ditch. I stabbed at the pages with the blade of the shovel, then I scooped up dirt and put a layer of historic Texas soil over the eight hundred combined pages of Texas history, Rip's history, McNelly's history, and my history.

Sweating, breathing heavily, aware of how soft I had become, I looked up to see one of the chili queens staring at me as though I were crazy. "That's not for you to do. That's for the working men," she said.

"And so it is," I said. I tried to pull myself out but only managed to groan. She offered me a hand. I was afraid that I'd pull her in instead of her pulling me out, so I grunted, strained, and twisted until I got myself out of the ditch. The sun was just coming up over the eastern part of town, over the Alamo.

Then, as the sun rose and its light spread through the downtown streets, I turned south to walk back to my house. The new town rising around me was still a bit strange, but not as threatening because I had let the past go. I told myself to move on, to forget. Forget the Alamo. Forget history. Quit observing. Quit writing. Become a part of the new world. I didn't have to be a witness. I had years yet to live. And on that walk, I felt relieved and forgiven—for several years afterwards.

CHAPTER 22

The Majestic Theater

I had been a pimp, a nancy, a coward, a spy, and a whoremonger, but in the year approaching my seventieth birthday I learned to drive an automobile and helped install plumbing and a telephone in my house. Ninety-six thousand souls made their homes in San Antonio. And ah! what a time and place it was.

Locomotion, faster and more obedient than a horse, freer than a train, under our own control, made us even more mobile and individualistic. Henry Ford had made us Americans. San Antonians could go into their houses and turn a valve, and fresh water, pumped from San Pedro Springs to an aquifer a few feet higher than the rest of the city, gushed into our sinks or bathtubs. We could even heat the water if we wanted. We could pull a chain or a lever, and a swirl of this clean water took our wastes away, leaving us and our homes sanitized and gloriously clean. We had telephones right in our houses. With our telephones, we could talk to friends or neighbors without leaving our sofas. The buildings seemed to be sprouting out of the ground. Streets leading to Alamo Plaza were coated with a new type of pavement, asphalt. And at Fort Sam Houston, men were flying. Pictures were beginning to move. It was the civilized world that I, in particular, had hoped for. It demanded that I forget old manuscripts and past times.

That year when I gained locomotion and plumbing, I read all the obituaries I could find about Sam Clemens's death and wished that I could have attended his funeral. Neither the trains nor my car were fast enough to get me to Connecticut. Though I had met him just once, I began to think of him and William Dean Howells as distant friends and contemporaries.

My money had grown scarce, but as with Rip, suddenly a King Ranch benefactor appeared. George Durham had done well for himself and the King Ranch, and now because he considered me a Little McNelly, because he was inspired by Captain King, besides writing me, still with indecipherable spelling and grammar, he paid my house note. My time then was spent as a part-time bartender, on trips to the public library, or on an occasional game of dominos with the brothers at the Sons of Hermann Lodge. I had bought some of their insurance, talked to them, remembered as far back as a few of them, so some of the older Germans had forgiven me of my debauched and Confederate past and had invited me into the order. Right down from my house, the Sons of Hermann laid the cornerstone for a marvelous new building that would rise with the rest of San Antonio's wondrous buildings.

The price we paid for all of the wonders of the twentieth century was our river. It was now just a trickle. City ordinances forbade bathing in it. The acequias were almost all filled in, and once in a while the city flooded. Sometimes I missed the river, but then I'd go into my house and draw a hot bath.

I should have married Addie. But at that time some older people still remembered. So it would have been unseemly for the wife of the late Rip Ford to have married a known pimp, whoremonger, gambler, and coward. I had too many arguments with Lily, so I left her as the sole guardian of her adopted father's memoirs and memory. Lula stopped inviting me by, and Addie the daughter still lived in Corpus Christi. But I kept in touch with Addie. We took long walks along Houston or Commerce Street. I drove us to the hot baths and Hot Wells resort, where we both soaked in the hot sulphuric water, and to the park at San Pedro Springs or the new Brackenridge Park. We went to the nickelodeons and then the theaters to watch moving pictures, and both of us felt as though we had passed through some portal into a new magical world that was somehow an offbeat but more attractive version of our own world. We sat in front of the Menger in Alamo Plaza and watched as the number of ex-Rangers and ex-Confederates diminished until we were all but alone.

In 1915, while Europe was gutting itself and I was suddenly an aged man, I got a long-distance telephone call from Kingsville, Texas, and through the telephone's magic, I heard George's voice crack. He sobbed as he told me that his Caroline had died. In this age of locomotion, I was determined not to miss her funeral. I was determined that my Buick touring car would make it over whatever roads were available from San Antonio to the new town of Kingsville. What few friends I had told me that I was too old. But a really true friend, a fellow survivor, a younger contemporary, had suffered a loss, and I wanted to show him that I still honored the old days, even if I had joined the modern era and was using its comforts to get to the grave. Addie agreed to go with me.

For our journey, Addie dressed in the freer women's fashion of the time. No more bustles or whalebones for the new modern woman, but sleeker, more streamlined fashions, allowing the lady more locomotion herself. She wore a skirt, blouse, and jacket, just as a man wore a suit. She brought two suitcases with her. As we drove, she tied her hat to her head with a sheer scarf, and I wore a driving cap and goggles. One fine, dry, spring day, we made our own wind to mix with the cool breeze as we sped and bounced and kicked up dust. To feel the air whipping all around us, we drove with the top lowered, but when the dust settled on us and the fine leather seats, I stretched the canvas top of the automobile over us. When we tired of our cocoon, I'd lower the top again. At times, Addie looked over at me with a shock as though asking me if we weren't really two crazy old folks. Other travelers in autos and buggies looked at us to confirm her suspicion.

The roads were haphazard but better than any roads from the old days. Both of us looked out from the windshield at the landscape. It was rougher. The great coastal prairie, with its rich grasses that had made a cattle industry for three countries for over a hundred and fifty years, was filled with cacti, mesquite, chaparral, and brush that I didn't even recognize. Short hackberry trees grew haphazardly. It was just like us to destroy what made us. The ranchers between San Antonio and Corpus Christi were fighting the landscape with modern technology—bulldozers, gas torches, and new strains of grass—but even in doing so they were destroying the last remnants of what they wanted.

But we sped right on by, on to Corpus Christi Bay and a night overlooking the bay in one of the city's finer hotels, where we both inhaled and felt the Gulf breeze take us back to a tropical time in Brownsville. Accustomed and dedicated to San Antonio and its climate that was a mixture of Gulf prairie meeting the drier weather rolling off the plateaus and hills, I had forgotten the joy of salt in the breeze. I remembered a salt-filled breeze, limbs creaking in that breeze, frogs croaking from long ago, a forgotten age, when Addie, Catalina Taracón, Juan Cortina, and I had picnicked on the Mexican side of the Rio Grande while two wars raged around us. I studied the old Addie and saw some of the young Addie. I wished that, as at that picnic, I could turn to my other side and see the other example of feminine beauty, the young and old Catalina.

Then we spent the night in separate rooms. The next day, early in the morning, dressed in our bathing suits, we took a dip in the bay. We drove on to the further legacy of Captain King: that pleasant town, Kingsville.

In Kingsville, we gorged on King Ranch beef and Mexican fried potatoes and cactus. We had wine. We walked down the streets hand in hand. When I walked Addie to her room, she kissed me. That night, as I climbed into my bed, I heard a knock at my door. I opened it to see Addie in her nightgown standing in my doorway. She furtively looked around to see if anyone had seen her, just as she had done years before back in Brownsville, during the war. And I dropped my head to look at myself in my nightgown. "Come in," I was able to say.

She stepped in. And I politely left the door open. She closed it. "It is a new time," Addie said and dropped her aged head. Long strands of gray hair that had loosened from her bun dropped on either side of her face. "Perhaps John William was just in an accident. Perhaps God does not mean to punish us. Perhaps we were just young . . . and foolish."

I said, "Not foolish."

She looked up and held my gaze with her eyes, and she raised one hand and put it in back of my head and brought it forward to rub the top of my slick dome of a head; then she dropped her hand to rub the side of my face. "You've no hair, and you've gotten all wrinkled." We laughed. "Oh dear, I can imagine what I must look like now."

"You look beautiful." We pulled and tugged until we were in the bed together. And made our attempt at septuagenarian love. It was mostly holding and touching and stroking wrinkles we had hardly noticed were there. But it was love, and in the hours that we spent just feeling, we went back to our youth and consummated it.

We woke at daylight to find our mingled breaths in our faces. We were shocked, then we smiled. Addie wanted to get back to her room, but I urged her to stay. I said that it was a new age, a new world with new morals. So she curled up under my arm as we soaked up the spring sunshine. "I still have people in the valley. I think that I'd prefer to be buried with my mother and father in Brownsville."

I was shocked—for Rip's sake. "Your place should be with Rip."

"After our deception and its result, after last night, I don't believe that I deserve to be buried next to him."

I stared at her.

She added, "Maybe God doesn't mind, but Rip would be disappointed."

"Don't be silly. You deserve better than Rip. Carrie McNelly deserved better than Leander. Etta deserved better than Richard King. Pidge Robinson deserved better than Pidgie Mitchell." And then I let myself say something mean. "Caroline deserved better than George."

"Oh, no," Addie said.

"No, no, you are right. Let's not talk about what we deserve."

"Andrew, I wish you had gotten your own family, your own just deserts."

"I've spent my life trying to dodge my just deserts." She kissed me. "Addie, we've both been left out of history. I'm not sure that I would have wanted it otherwise. People like us don't make history. But I want to thank you for helping me make it 'through' history." She kissed me again, but this time I could taste her tears.

The next day, we drove to the King Ranch, which had a fleet of automobiles. Caroline's funeral was in the stately reception room of the newly built King Ranch house. The old one in my memory, with its fortifications and tower, had burned down. George sat in the front in between his mostly grown children—three girls and a boy—and sobbed bitterly. When the oration was over, George stood, still ramrod straight, snorted, and rubbed his nose with his fingers, then pulled a handkerchief out of his pocket to wipe his fingers. He swung a big cowboy hat on his head and led us out to the front of the mansion. Addie and I got in line with a good number of that fleet of automobiles and drove to a gravesite on a hill just above Santa Gertrudis Creek, maybe the very spot where the notion of a giant ranch first formed in Captain King's head. We gathered under a canopy as Caroline was lowered into the King Ranch property. And we took our turns to console a weeping George, who hugged both me and the great widow.

Throughout the service, Addie would gingerly hold my hand and then let go. George and Caroline had over thirty years together. Addie and I had one more night together—at the Kingsville Hotel. Then we drove back to San Antonio.

Later that year, Addie told me, Lula, and Lily that she intended to take a trip to Brownsville to see her sisters and brother. We wished her good-bye and waved as the train left. She never returned. She lived another year. She caught the flu, and it turned into pneumonia. Instead of going to her funeral, I put flowers on Rip's grave. I heard that Addie was buried beside John William in her family's plot. I could never muster the courage to go see the graves. I used the excuse that I was too old for the trip.

In truth, I wished that I had somehow shown Addie how to live with her past. I wished Rip had lived longer so I could have shown him some of the wonders of the twentieth century. I wished I could have made Addie watch more closely so that she could have seen some of the wonders of the twentieth century.

I ARRIVED at the point where I had outlived all the old people from my time; I had nothing to do but watch San Antonio reconstruct itself around me and drink and play dominos in the old bars or with the old Germans at the Sons of Hermann Lodge. Mexico finally went to war with itself, but though we tried to get involved with another filibuster and though some Texas Rangers began shooting Mexicans and displaying their bodies, we wisely—finally—left Mexico's great problems alone. Instead, we got involved in a war in Europe. San Antonio became the center of U.S. military aviation. The *movies* became longer. Eventually, the air filled with radio broadcasts. The river was a polluted, dying wreck.

After our "great war," the one that would end all wars, the puritanical forces that accounted for most that is wrong in this country got together and essentially ended San Antonio's connection with its past. The Ladies' Temperance Union, the descendants of the Know-Nothings, and the truly unmanly men voted in Prohibition. The night Prohibition went into effect, several bars bordering downtown just opened their doors. Drink it all, the owners declared, for they could no longer sell it. An Irish bar owner and man-about-town, who claimed to whomever would listen to him that he'd never live to see Prohibition, fulfilled his prophecy. Together with his best customers, he drank up his stock until he died of a stroke minutes before Prohibition went into effect. I was much luckier; with some help from some younger older men, I caught a streetcar home.

William Dean Howells died, but no one seemed to remember him or care about the writing he left behind. He was out of literary fashion. McNelly and Rip were out of historical fashion. I was out of social fashion, a relic who belonged with the unremembered.

A year later, I survived the awful flood of 1921, but stood elbow deep in water as I watched my possessions floating around me. Several policemen had to rescue me by humiliating me and carrying me out of my house. After my escape from the flood, the police convinced me that I truly was an old man. They said that I ought to seek out a home for older people, or at the very least, they suggested that I hire someone to watch over me. When the land dried up, the police again appeared at my house and insisted that I be tested for a "driver's license." The state licensing people claimed I could not drive well enough to own a car. The audacity of those little people! My world became smaller, a circle within walking or streetcar distance. I turned my attention to dominos with the old Germans and bought myself a radio.

Buildings went up that were so tall that they'd seem to tumble if a strong wind blew. There were no unpaved streets, no chickens in the city. There was water, plumbing, toilets. And best of all, in darkened, grand buildings that made the approaching modern world seem magical, were "movies." Some of these moving pictures were "Westerns." I bless the day I limped through downtown on my cane and happened into a movie theater. With alcohol outlawed, the movie theaters replaced Jack Harris's Vaudeville Theater and Saloon and Billy Sims's White Elephant as the grandest, gaudiest buildings in town. The Aztec and the Texas opened in 1926, and then later still the grandest of all—the Majestic. I could take the streetcar or one of the new gasoline-powered motor buses from my house to downtown and watch magic flicker in front of my eyes.

From the movies, I could go to the library and read the meager collection of books about moving pictures. I looked at the fan magazines. I studied criticism just translated into English from Russian and German. And early in 1930, a new public library with a glazed, marble-like exterior, two painted, stone elephants guarding its entrance, and brass inside, became an air-conditioned haven for me and my cinematic research. Had I been born forty or fifty years later, instead of escaping from the Civil War, instead of running to Brownsville, I would have escaped the Great War by running to Los Angeles and joining the cinema industry. In my old man's dreams, the ones that dismiss time and make it malleable so that we have our lives to live over, I decided that I would have become a motion picture director. In one particular picture, *The Iron Horse,* as I read about the actors and assistants, I saw the words *directed by John Ford.*

My mind wouldn't let me concentrate on the feature, for it recalled my John Ford, old Rip. And when I forced my attention to the new John Ford's work, I noted that his West, his Westerners, his railroads—while similar to my West, Westerners, and railroads—were not mine. A couple of years later, I saw another feature directed by this John Ford, *Three Bad Men.* I went back three times to this movie to study it and its world so I could compare it to the world in my memory. I had a sudden urge to let "mine" be known. This John Ford, who was what I would have wanted to be were I fifty years younger, was stealing from me. I wanted to steal back from him. So began my adversarial relation with the makers of these "Westerns."

On my trips to the library, I began to read not just forward, about the movies, but backward—about my past. I read an obituary for Ruth Maddox, who died in 1927. Lula was buried next to her father. I found, to my astonishment, delight, and horror, accounts of the Texas Rangers as written by a scholar who was now a member of Rip's State Historical Association. Some were boring scholarly papers that no one would want to read, others were adventure stories in popular magazines, and still others were outright fiction. This Professor Webb from that muddy University of Texas in Austin had articles about modern Rangers, the six-shooter, or Mexican bandits. One cited several interviews with an aging, nearly blind ex-Ranger, William Callicott, living somewhere in Austin County outside of Houston. I felt sorry for McNelly and Rip and then for Howells and even Clemens. History had forgotten them or twisted them up into something they wouldn't want to be, movie material. And then I felt sorry for me. McNelly had left me off his rolls. Rip never mentioned me in his memoirs. I had no documentation. It was as though I never existed.

But still the wonder created by that flickering light in front of me excused the corruption of the wishes and desires of dead men. For that wonder promised a future, a new and better world. I should have been a part of that world, not the world that this movie maker and this scholar reminded me of, my old world, full of violence, death, hardship, and yet delight and its own lost wonder.

My doctor said that I was very lucky that some venereal disease hadn't killed me. He warned me that I may yet lose some toes because of my diabetes. He told me to take care of myself. I told him that, at my age, what else could I do? So to take better care of myself I hired high school girls, mostly olive-skinned ones from the west side of town, to come over to my house after school to take care of me, to prepare my dinners, to clean my house. But mostly I wanted some company in the afternoon, and I enjoyed watching them as they cooked or cleaned.

THE magic was in the coolness. As you walked in, your blood, which had bubbled and roiled in the summer Texas sun, simmered then cooled and spread like a cold bath inside you to your toes and fingers, as in the old days, when swimming in the spring-fed waters of the San Antonio River. Curled and hunched as I was, I stopped and tried to straighten to feel my blood cool my extremities as George tried to fold me into an aisle seat. George was in town for the Texas Stockmen's Association meeting.

"Feel, feel it, George," I said. And George sniffed the air like a horse anticipating trouble. I had brought him to a Western, *The Big Trail*.

I pulled my neck up and pushed my head back so that it lay on my shoulders, and I cussed this frame of mine that decided to twist and curl me. Even my toes in my soft leather shoes hurt because they twisted around each other like old, coarse grapevines.

I leaned and then rolled, like a turtle in its curved shell, to feel the softness of the cushioned chair and to look up at the domed ceiling to see pinpricks of light, like tiny holes punched into the ceiling to let you know about the harsh summer light outside and your cool dark womb inside. They were really tiny lights, but I could still pretend.

And then it started, and shades of light in degrees of gray spread over a giant rectangle, one that grew and grew, past any that I had ever seen before, until I could barely take it all in. And the gray made people and landscapes and horses and cattle and wagons. My eyes darted from corner to corner, and my head, swiveling a beat or two behind, tried to keep up with my eyes.

"It's a hell of a lot to look at," George said to me, too loudly.

Music swelled, names appeared on the rectangular screen. Then a wagon, on the screen, rolled over us. Then the giant people on the screen didn't gesture like the characters in the silents, instead, they *talked!* The cows bellowed, wind whistled through pines. I could listen to everything. Sometimes, during a talkie, I'd close my eyes just to hear the sounds. "Wish they'd shut up for a while," George said too loudly. "I can't watch and listen all at once."

It was majesty in the appropriately named Majestic Theater. The movie was so grand, so complete in itself that I could forget that it was merely *about* something that I remembered. Actually, the images were closer to what Rip would have remembered. He would have been one hundred and fifteen years old, and I wished that old man would have been with me. George was good company, but I think that Rip could have seen the majesty. He chased the Comanches and Mexicans out of Texas. Rip and I would have enjoyed watching lies about his time in the new age of wonder.

I had two radios in my house on South Flores. I had light with the flick of a switch. I turned a knob, struck a match, and my oven burners warmed my meals. Electric fans kept a breeze flowing through my house, and if I got really hot, I could open the door to my icebox and let the steam from a large block of ice, delivered to my box, cool me. This was my century, a civilized one, the one I had wanted, but I wouldn't live too much further into it. I looked over at George. "Wonder," I said.

Old too, but not yet my ancient age, he munched his popcorn and grunted, "I like real horses."

"But, George, these horses, the ones that rear up on command, like no cowboy's horse ever did, are going to take the place of real horses."

"I like real horses. And why do they make it so cold in here?"

"Air-conditioning, George. Think of it, think, Texas cooled!"

Someone *sshhed* us. "Who the hell does he think he's talking to?" George said and turned to look for the person who had *sshhed* us.

"George, watch the movie. Let the others watch the movie. Let me watch the movie."

So George fidgeted and shifted in his chair and munched his popcorn and got up several times to buy a drink or go to the men's room. *The Big Trail* was directed by Raoul Walsh. I'd never seen a rocky mountain, and I couldn't imagine how a Conestoga wagon got into the Rockies, same as I could never figure how cattle could get into mountains or even hills. So I agreed with how Walsh made it look. But I didn't like the story—too simple. I wanted to go to the library and read something about the crossing of the Rockies in Conestoga wagons and see if what I could conjure up would look like what Walsh made it look like.

When the movie was over, George uncurled me from my seat, straightened me up, and helped me up the aisle. Once we got outside in the awful afternoon July sunshine, intensified by the man-made concrete canyons lining Houston Street, higher than any real mountain in Texas, sweat beaded up on our necks and stained our collars and dripped out from under our hats and down our faces. George had on a light suit and a tie, but he still wore his old, sweat-stained cowboy hat from the King Ranch. We walked to Soledad, and I said, "Here is where we wait."

It was a bus stop, exactly one short block north of the site of Jack Harris's Vaudeville Theater and Saloon. Soon, the gasoline-powered motor buses would replace all the old electric streetcars. I lived right on a bus line. I could get from my house on South Flores to the Sons of Hermann Hall to the Majestic, Aztec, or Texas Theater and to the library building with its guardian lion and elephant.

We stepped back under the awning of a building to get into some shade. "Why do we have to wait in this heat?" George said, then thought. "I like it better than that artificial cool in that theater." He was growing crankier than I was at his age.

"You ought to see it at night, George. It all lights up. Electricity. They've got neon lights now, too. The street glows brighter than the sun. You stare up into the sun at noon you get blinded. You can't stare half as long at the lights on Houston and Commerce Street."

"Aren't the stars good enough?"

"It's a wonder, George. There are colors. Great gaudy colors: red, purple, green. And they make shapes—a saddle, a horse, a figure supposed to look like Davy Crockett. It's not at all like the old soft glow of gaslights. It's a wonder. Think what the future will be like."

George took off his wide cowboy hat and wiped at his face with the flat of his hand. "We're too old to be worrying about a future. We're out to pasture now. We ought to enjoy it."

"God, I want to see what's coming."

"I never seen an old man like you. You ought to be worrying about the past. Hell, that's all they want to know about."

I lifted my straw hat to let the sweat pour down my face, and tried to slip out of my jacket. George helped me get my jacket off and then slipped out of his own jacket. "You need to be somewhere cooler."

"Like back in the theater," I said. People milled around us. Some listened. There were even greater crowds in downtown San Antonio than the days of Jack Harris's Vaudeville Theater and Saloon.

"They keep talking to me, you know."

"Who?" I asked as I leaned into my cane, took my handkerchief out of my pocket, and wiped at the sweat on my face.

"Some historians, and now this newspaper man from here in town. They want me to tell all I know about the Captain."

"That's good," I said. "And what do you tell them? How do you put it?"

"I don't like 'em. They think I'm the only one left." He looked down at me. "Isn't it a might hot for you to be out at this time of day?"

"Yes," I said. "The last one?"

He smiled and then said, "Hell, ol' Bill Callicott talked to this historian from the University of Texas, this Webb fella, and I'll bet ol' Bill colored it up considerable. Him leading a charge and mowing down Mexicans. And that professor probably just lapped it all up."

"I've seen some of that Webb guy's articles." I looked down Soledad toward Commerce, the site of Jack Harris's old saloon. "If it weren't for Prohibition, we could have a drink." A lady in back of me looked down her nose at me.

"I don't drink, anyway," George said. He was becoming more like Rip. If I hadn't sold the property where Jack Harris's saloon stood, instead of a large new bank stretching up several floors above me, I might have had a speakeasy to give me a drink.

"Look, Andrew," George said and stared at the tips of his boots, the newer, currently fashionable kind with pointed toes and long, slanted heels, unlike any I saw on any of the Little McNellys. "You don't have to worry. I'm leaving you out."

"What? Out of what?"

"My story to that reporter. Eventually, I'll have to talk to him."

"Leave me out?" I muttered more to myself than to George, just like McNelly had.

"And I know, as addled and blind as he was, ol' Bill Callicott left you out of his story. You won't be embarrassed. And we're going to set the record straight on that lying N. A. Jennings, who wasn't even there and had all these great things to say about himself."

"Has anyone ever looked at Pidge Robinson's reports?"

"What's those?"

"Anyone found Juan Cortina's pronunciamientos?"

"What's those?"

"Is Commander Kells still alive? Did anyone ever talk to him?"

"Calm down, calm down, Andrew. Step into the shade. Let me buy you one of them cool soda waters or something." I shook my head. George peered into my face, said, "You don't look too good," and left me. I looked up at the tall building hiding the sun from me but letting its heat cook me. I heard voices. They were the voices of Juan Cortina, Lee H. McNelly, and Rip Ford floating around me whispering to me to tell the story. They were stern voices. Then the disembodied voices of Catalina Taracón and Addie Ford and even John William whispered to me to tell the story. But what story? Whose story? How to make it make sense? What to put in? Who to leave out? And in leaving out, in deciding, we no longer make it true; it becomes just as false as cattle in the Rocky Mountains.

I leaned against a plateglass window and felt some of its coolness against my back. And I saw George with a long-legged gait running across Soledad, disrupting traffic, with an orange soda water bottle in his hand. Wonder is in the future or now. The past may have gotten us here, but it is no longer of any consequence. I crumpled, my legs gave out, and I felt my head hit the sidewalk.

When I woke, George was holding the cool orange soda water bottle against the side of my face, and a cop was pushing people back from me and saying, "Give him air. Give him air." I heard a bell, San Fernando Cathedral. It and God had survived all these years. And apparently I had survived my fall.

George and the cop helped me until I was standing and looking into the plateglass window and listening to the second toll of San Fernando Cathedral's bell. What I saw was a new Underwood typewriter. "Are you all right?" the cop asked.

"He's just old," George said to the cop and the onlookers. "He's almost ninety."

Like a child pointing toward the Christmas toy he wanted, I extended my finger toward the typewriter. "George, can I borrow some money?"

"Hell, you can have some money," George said and began digging in his billfold.

"Buy me that," I said, pointing to the typewriter.

GEORGE rested the typewriter on his lap for our bus ride home, and I rested my new ream of typing paper and carbons on my lap. We headed south and passed San Fernando Cathedral. I raised one hand as though to salute it. "So I guess you gone completely senile," George said.

"George, tell the truth to that reporter. Tell him everything."

George shook his head, "What's got into you?"

"The movies," I said.

Back at my house, George and I drank iced tea from my new icebox, sat at my kitchen table, and caught up with who was doing what, who had died, and what property was changing hands while I fiddled with my new typewriter. Because my hands sometimes shook, George helped me load the ribbon. After a while, I began pecking at the keys. "What good is all this new shit?" George asked.

"What good is the old?" I asked.

"At least, at least, we had a, a, a goal."

"To invade Mexico," I said. "The wonder," I continued, "is in remembering the past, keeping it alive no matter how bad it hurts. Take it with you, for it is you. Without it, you see no wonder, just light flickering on a screen." I looked at the letters I had made on a blank piece of paper. "Just letters on paper. Just an old church bell. Just some more property for your ranch, for Texas, for the U.S. You look at those things, you hear those things, you visit those areas, and you see just what is there—no future, no past, just what is there."

"Andrew, look, you start seeing ghosts and visions, they lock you up," George said. "Andrew, you want me to call a doctor?" I shook my head. "You going to be all right?" I nodded.

"You got to feel the past to have a sense of wonder in the future."

"I just like to know what is," George said and frowned.

George left me and went back to his hotel room for the Southwestern and Texas Cattle Growers Association's annual meeting. Whenever business brought him to town, he visited me. He also sent money, and he wrote. His writing was improving, which was my point.

I pounded on my typewriter, getting used to it, before I actually started to write anything. It was awful. And my fingers just didn't work right. I held up my hands to look at my fingers. They were as crooked as my toes. The knuckles were twisted and swollen, so not only did the tips of my fingers point in the wrong directions, but my joints hurt. I steadied my hands above the keys and looked at my misaligned fingers.

Just before dark, Carmen walked in. She no longer knocked, and I no longer expected her to. For a year I had hired her as my young cook and cleaner. She was my latest high school helper.

Gloriously young, with curly black hair that collected on her brown shoulders, slender, rounded calves that stuck out from under her skirt, she kicked off her shoes and made her way into my kitchen. She worked around me, pulling things from my icebox, pulling other things from a new brown paper grocery bag, slicing until she had my dinner. That night, I had thinly cut Mexican-style steak, a few hashed potatoes, and some grilled onions. She ate silently with me but stared at me.

After dinner, she cleaned up while I typed and tried to find a place to start my story. After the dishes were washed, she stepped in front of the table directly in front of me, and I raised my head to see her. She smiled, undid the first button of her blouse, spread it across her shoulders, then wriggled until one bare shoulder was out of her blouse. With my misaligned fingers poised approximately where they belonged on the keys to my typewriter, I said, "Not tonight, Carmen. No, not tonight," and returned my eyes to the blank page.

I heard her rustling, but I heard no footsteps. So I returned my eyes to her. She had a frown. I made myself smile. So she smiled, and slipped her shoulder out from under her blouse. I nodded, and then she slipped her other shoulder out from under her blouse.

I paid Carmen for this service, too. I was ninety. There was not much I could do. Her striptease was for my memory. I watched. I remembered the smiles and the calls of the young girls like Carmen who lived in the jacales just outside of town in Brownsville and San Antonio. I remembered Catalina's arms wrapped around me while she looked up into my face as though I were her only and best lover. I remember Addie's hurried kisses while we were so alone and scared during the war. I remembered Addie's last real kiss, the last I was to receive as a lover, in that Kingsville hotel. Those memories were me, and though I wouldn't live much longer, I was alive for one more night because of Carmen.

With her clothes in a lump around her ankles, her arms trying to hide some of her nakedness, her smile beaming, I appreciated the great kindness and humanity Carmen had just shown me. Her smile was a wonder. And it brought me home. I remembered Juan Cortina's gracious manner that hid his barbarity. I remembered Rip Ford standing straight up and squinting down a tame San Antonio street as though waiting for a Comanche or Mexican attack. I remembered the words "directed by John Ford" that made me laugh out loud, disturbing the other viewers. Maybe old man Rip never died and found some new way to make us listen to him.

Or maybe it was now up to me, too, to make the world listen to Rip. I remembered that long ago when I left my home state for Ohio and Yankee territory, just knowing things seemed to be enough. But then the Civil War interrupted my thinking, and my survival pushed aside my desire to know. Now, not knowing, but something akin to it, like understanding or telling, seemed more important than my fated, inevitable, short-term survival. It occurred to me that the last fifty years of my life I had spent watching old people die, until there was just one more old man left to die: me. But because of this wonder-filled, civilized new age, I felt alive. And because of all those people who were dead, but still talked to me through memory and imagination, I didn't want to die. The only solution, it seemed to me, was to talk for Rip and all the rest. Fifty-five years before, I didn't know enough to get it right. Thirty years before, when I buried the manuscripts in front of San Fernando Cathedral, I hadn't yet listened or learned enough. Now I knew. I knew what I realized when Rip died, but had forgotten when I took his and my manuscripts to Howells and Twain. With history we can choose our own fathers—and sons, and lovers, and families.

Rip patted me on the back and said it was about time that I came to my senses. Cortina asked me not to call him the "Red Robber Baron of the Rio Grande." George said I was crazy. Pidge said to get started. Addie scolded me with her eyes and said that I should be careful and that I should be ashamed of myself for what I paid Carmen to do. Catalina told me that I knew what I must do. Then, with her smile lighting her face, Catalina told me to include her, but to be sure to make her attractive and to defend her reputation. Jack Harris reminded me of his last words to me: that I was a reporter, that I should follow my talents and write down what other people did instead of risking my life in useless gunfights about pride. Then McNelly, sick and dying, his bare feet sticking out of his gown, gave me my order: "Write it down. Write it down."

I looked at Carmen and felt tears on my cheeks. "Thank you, Carmen," I said, and she gathered up her clothes and put them back on in a corner out of my sight.

Then I felt a hand on my shoulder. It was Rip Ford's. He nodded and said, "Write it down, Andrew." Oh, how I missed that old man.

With her clothes on, Carmen stepped closer to me and craned her neck as my keys slapped the paper. "Look," I said and pointed at what I had typed: *In the stultifying, late afternoon Brownsville heat, which made even the flies fat and lazy and promised an even hotter, marrow-shriveling summer, I waited in my favorite whorehouse, the Bivouac, to buy a goat for my nephew.*

She bent over the paper and read. After a moment of thought, she straightened and asked, "What, what's this 'whores' and 'goats'? You're an evil old man. You'll give me el ojo."

"Can you type?"

"I'm learning. At Main High, they teach me." Main High was on Main Avenue, old Acequia, just north of Main Plaza.

"Do you want to help?"

"How much more money do I get?"

"No more. You just get to help."

She straightened. "You must be putting a curse on me. Why would I help?"

"A long time ago I helped my uncle write his book because . . . because I thought it was a good book. His adopted daughter helped. Now I'm listening to them all. And I want to write my book. But look at my fingers." I held up my hands.

"You hear people? You crazy old man. You will put a curse on me."

I nodded. "Yes, maybe I can make you hear them, too."

She raised her hand to her head, as though to make herself or help herself think. "Will it be a good book? Not full of bad things?"

"I don't know. But you can type. And you can help."

"Will I still have to, to . . . to take my clothes off?"

I smiled and she smiled back at me. "Maybe sometimes, if you'd like, as a favor, for free, same as typing this book."

"So what do I get?"

"You get to help me write history, and you get to remind me of my history when you take off your clothes."

"I don't know if that's enough." She smiled, no, she beamed at me. "But I'll help. You pay me like you do, same amount. And I help write your book . . . and take off my clothes sometimes."

So I cut down on the movies that I went to, and I didn't go to the library or the Sons of Hermann Lodge as often, but Carmen came to my house as early as she could, right after her high school class, and together we began to write this down. Once in a while, I'd look up from my memory or the voices I was hearing and catch Carmen's eyes, and we'd both smile at each other. I had outlived or lost everyone I knew. The person whom I now knew, whom I saw, was Carmen. She was my only family. And thus as I followed my orders and Carmen hers and wrote it down, I made Carmen my beneficiary. But more important, I entrusted this manuscript to Carmen's care—and to the capriciousness of fate, fashion, and time.

ANDREW JOHN NEVIN born Dec. 10, 1840, died May 5, 1931

Yesterday evening, long time San Antonio resident and raconteur Andrew Nevin was found dead in his south side cottage. Confidant of famed Texas Ranger John S. "Rip" Ford, former reporter and critic for this paper, and part owner of the infamous Jack Harris's Vaudeville Theater and Saloon, he leaves no known relatives or heirs. A young maid who cleaned his house found his body and reported his death to police. George Durham of the King Ranch will claim his ashes and spread them over the King Ranch property. He died of natural causes.

—San Antonio Express, *May 7, 1931*